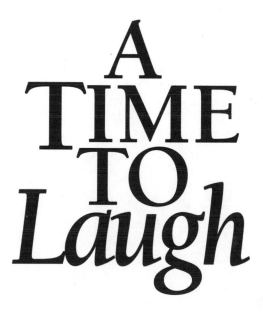

# A TIME TO Laugh

# A TIME TO Laugh

B.J. Oropeza

HENDRICKSON
PUBLISHERS

Copyright © 1995 by Hendrickson Publishers, Inc.
P. O. Box 3473
Peabody, Massachusetts 01961–3473
All rights reserved
Printed in the United States of America

ISBN 1–56563–183–8

First Printing—November 1995


**Library of Congress Cataloging-in-Publication Data**


Oropeza, B. J., 1961–
    A time to laugh: the holy laughter phenomenon
examined  /  B. J. Oropeza.
    Includes bibliographical references and index.
    ISBN 1–56563–183–8 (paper)
    1. Toronto Airport Vineyard (Church)  2. Gifts,
Spiritual—Case studies.  3. Revivals—Ontario—Toronto—
History—20th century.  4. Laughter—Religious aspects—
Pentecostal churches.  5. Toronto (Ont.)—Church history—
20th century.  6. Church renewal—Vineyard Christian
Fellowship.  7. Vineyard Christian Fellowship—Doctrines.
8. Pentecostal churches—Doctrines.  I. Title.
BX8785.Z7T676   1996
289.9'4'0971354—dc20                                    95–41398
                                                            CIP

# TABLE OF CONTENTS

91887

# PART 1

# THE HOLY LAUGHTER PHENOMENON

# 1

# THE LAUGH HEARD AROUND THE WORLD

January 6, 1995: It was supposed to be just another morning radio interview on WSCF, an FM station from Vero Beach, Florida. The guest was Randy Clark, one of the most prominent leaders of the "Toronto Blessing" renewal. In the midst of the interview, announcer Greg Phillips started weeping and fell to the floor in a futile attempt to leave the studio control room. Then station manager Jon Hamilton also began to weep. Then another employee (who was not a charismatic) fell to the floor. In a kind of chain reaction, other staff members reacted in similar ways. Hamilton invited the listening audience to drop by the studio at the Central Assembly of God church. While listening to the program some listeners felt a deep conviction, and others pulled off the road weeping as they heard the broadcast.

As people from around the area poured into the church and studio area they too wept and fell to the floor. Pastors from various denominations started arriving and concurred that what was happening was a genuine move of God. Small children were "slain in the Spirit," lying on the floor up to two hours. Some reported visions and healings. Since that unusual Friday morning, the average attendance at the Central Assembly of God church, pastored by William "Buddy" Tipton, has jumped from 600 to as much as 1,300.[1]

---

[1]J. Lee Grady, " 'Toronto Blessing' Spreads in U.S.," *Charisma* (Mar. 1995) 56–57.

One report of the incident says, "Hypocrites and back-sliders have been responding to God's invitation to repent by the hundreds. Things are different in our city. Over 36 pastors have united across denominational lines in support of this spectacular turn of events. Revival is here, and church is fun again."[2]

Revival? Here's a second picture of the current phenomenon. A woman erupts in laughter in the third aisle at a weeknight Vineyard church fellowship. A young man in the first aisle convulses uncontrollably while the woman next to him whips her long hair in a frenzy before falling to the ground in ecstatic bliss. The sound of a lion's roar echoes through the sanctuary as the congregation breaks forth with crying, giggles, moaning, roaring, and prophesying. The cacophony reaches a crescendo resembling a Halloween carnival. "This is normal Christianity!" cries the preacher, "We are experiencing a refreshing touch from the Spirit of God."

Both these portrayals depict the new phenomenon sweeping Canada, Great Britain, the United States, and elsewhere: the Holy Laughter renewal, or the "Toronto Blessing" as some call it. When we read the two accounts side by side, we see the difficulty inherent in evaluating this movement. Few would dispute that the first account sounds like a genuine move of the Spirit. Then again, few would find nothing disturbing about the second account. Is the Holy Laughter phenomenon a genuine revival? Here are some observations.

## HOLY LAUGHTER HAS TRANSCENDED DENOMINATIONAL BARRIERS

Perhaps the most prominent person associated with Holy Laughter is South African evangelist Rodney Howard-Browne. During his meetings he typically asks the audience (sometimes the entire audience) to stand and say what church they attend. A large proportion of the typical audience come from independent charismatic churches. Also represented at these meetings are the Methodists, Mennonites, Presbyteri-

[2]J. Duhwigg, "Melbourne Revival" in "Breaking News folder" (Christianity Online), 16 Jan. 1995.

ans, Pentecostals, Nazarenes, Anglicans, United Church of Canada, and other denominations, all seeking to be touched by Holy Laughter. The gamut of those who have experienced the phenomenon ranges from dispensationalists to Roman Catholics.[3]

In September 1994 a Salvation Army conference in Derby, United Kingdom, hit by Holy Laughter "was likened to 'an absolute battlefield,' with uniformed Salvationists falling to the floor."[4] At St. Luke's Episcopal Church in Akron, Ohio, people have been falling to the floor during holy communion ever since members from the church visited the Airport Vineyard in Toronto. "Some people laugh hysterically, while others 'dissolve in tears of joy,' " explained the once-skeptical rector of the congregation, Chuck Irish.[5] Pastor Gene Preston of Union Church in Hong Kong reports:

> The ecumenical spirit of my congregation . . . and my own eclectic approach to spirituality prompted my pilgrimage to Toronto last August. Union Church, the oldest church in Hong Kong (founded in 1844), is nondenominational, attentive to the scriptures in the Reformed tradition, evangelical, but not charismatic. Yet when I returned to Hong Kong, I found that "the blessing" from Toronto was bursting forth among key leaders in the Hong Kong congregation.[6]

Holy Laughter also touched the normally reserved author Mona Johnian, who serves with her husband Paul at the Christian Teaching and Worship Center near Boston: "On several occasions I broke out in the joy of the Lord and laughed unashamedly. We leaped and shouted when the Spirit 'moved' upon us. We lost all fear of man and what others might think of us. . . . Boldly we made it clear that we were going 'all the way' with this awakening!"[7]

Johnian now shares the message of this "anointing" with other churches. When she spoke at the First Baptist Church in

---

[3]Joe Maxwell, "Is Laughing for the Lord Holy?" *Christianity Today*, 24 Oct. 1994, 78.

[4]Mick Brown, "Unzipper Heaven, Lord," *Telegraph Magazine*, 3 Dec. 1994, 27–28.

[5]Grady, "Toronto Blessing," 54.

[6]Gene Preston, "The Toronto Wave," *Christian Century*, 16 Nov. 1994, 1068.

[7]Mona Johnian, *The Fresh Anointing* (South Plainfield, N.J.: Bridge, 1994) xii–xiii.

New England, "At least sixty percent of the congregation fell to
the floor under the power of the Holy Spirit where they lay in
communion with God in tears, laughter or peaceful silence.
This was certainly not 'order' as usual for this dear church.
Some might even call it disorderly."[8]

John Arnott, pastor of the Airport Vineyard in Toronto, •
writes that the renewal ". . . is so life-giving that denominational differences have melted into obscurity, as a fresh love
for Jesus has become pre-eminent; leaders of every denominational persuasion have come and drunk deeply of this fresh
outpouring. The Holy Spirit is the only true unifier!"[9]

## HOLY LAUGHTER HAS TRANSCENDED NATIONAL BARRIERS

Over thirty countries have witnessed the new movement.
In the Toronto Vineyard, author Guy Chevreau writes, "Over
400 local pastors have come, at least to investigate; over 4,000
pastors, spouses and leaders from all over continental North
America, and as far away as Britain, Chile, Argentina, Switzer-
land, France, Germany, Scandinavia, South Africa, Nigeria,
Kenya, Japan, New Zealand, and Australia have come to receive the outpouring."[10] In October 1994 Kansas City Metro
Vineyard pastor Mike Bickle said that between 300 and 400
churches in England alone have experienced this renewal.[11]
By May 1995 Stephen Strang, publisher of *Charisma* magazine, estimated the number of churches in England impacted
by the "blessing" at 4,000.[12] Other countries affected include
Mexico, Holland, Belgium, Albania, and Siberia.

Although Holy Laughter has primarily affected the Western world, other parts of the world have also reported the
phenomenon. After receiving an "anointing" from Rodney
Howard-Browne, Ken and Nancy Curtis—who serve as mis-

---

[8]Ibid., 59.

[9]John Arnott, preface to Guy Chevreau, *Catch the Fire: The Toronto Blessing* (HarperPerennial; Toronto: HarperCollins, 1994) viii.

[10]Chevreau, *Catch the Fire*, 18.

[11]Mike Bickle, "Toronto Report," 16 Oct. 1994 (Grandview, Mo.: Metro Vineyard Fellowship of Kansas City), audio tape.

[12]Stephen Strang, "More, Lord!" *Charisma*, May 1995, 102.

sionaries from the Carpenter's Home Church in Lakeland, Florida—have taken the message of Holy Laughter "around the world." They report that the Spirit's joy has reached Russia, the Philippines, Singapore, Uganda, and Kenya.[13]

In Yamato, Japan, Tsugumichi Ohkawa, president of Calvary Bible Seminary, claims that the renewal has so impacted his country that Pentecostals and evangelicals have sought to work together in closer unity.[14] But not all the reports have been positive. In the Netherlands, for example, the Dutch magazine *Opwekking* reported Warren Lancaster, director of the Netherlands Youth With A Mission (YWAM) as claiming that the renewal has brought to their churches a potential for much confusion.[15]

## HOLY LAUGHTER HAS INFLUENCED GREAT NUMBERS OF PEOPLE

It would be difficult to calculate how many people have experienced or witnessed this phenomenon. In Toronto alone, an estimated 200,000 people from various countries and denominations stepped through the doors of the Airport Vineyard church in just one year (1994).[16] Since the renewal first came on 20 January 1994 the church has opened its doors for services six days a week. Church membership, however, has failed to grow. The number of faithful members wavers between 250 and 350. Many consider the Toronto Airport Vineyard as the renewal center for Holy Laughter.

Mona Johnian reports, "We have ministered to a minimum of 60,000 people by holding three weekly services of three to four hours each. At least 20,000 people have been visitors from various states and countries."[17] In North America, Holy Laughter has hit over 7,000 churches. According to Mike Bickle,

[13]Ken and Nancy Curtis, "The Laugh Heard 'Round the World," 1994 (Lakeland, Fla.: Spiritual Warfare Ministries), video tape.

[14]Daina Doucet, "What is God doing in Toronto?" *Charisma*, Feb. 1995, 22.

[15]Anton Hein, "YWAM Apologizes," America Online, 22 Feb. 1995.

[16]Steve Long, "The Airport Vineyard: An Insider's Story," *Christian Week*, 9 May 1995, 10.

[17]Mona Johnian, "Flowing with Revival," *Charisma*, Feb. 1995, 14.

before this phenomenon broke out several years ago in Argentina, the country's biggest churches averaged 3,000 to 4,000 members. Now close to a dozen churches reportedly number around 100,000 members![18]

The renewal is also no respecter of age. Both adults and children have experienced the movement. In his book *Catch the Fire*, Guy Chevreau dedicates an entire chapter entitled "An Embarrassment of Riches" to personal testimonies of those who have been touched by the renewal. Four of the testimonies belong to children between the ages of 11 and 13. Chevreau writes that a child named Heather was healed of dyslexia and got so excited that she began praying for other classmates.[19] Eleanor Mumford, wife of Pastor John Mumford of the Southwest London Vineyard, reports:

> I went to a Christian school in Clapham the other day and talked to them about the Lord, and I prayed for them. The Lord fell upon those five-year-olds and they were laughing and weeping and crying out to the Lord. The teachers were affected, the parents were rolling around. I thought, "God, this is a glorious thing you are doing. This is fantastic."[20]

When healing evangelists Charles and Frances Hunter, known as the "Happy Hunters," prayed for a five-year-old girl, she reportedly got so "drunk in the Spirit" that her parents had to carry her from the church service to the car. The Hunters ask, "We might all wonder and say, 'What is the purpose of a five-year old getting drunk on the power of the Holy Ghost?'" And they reply, "I can guarantee you this: that little girl's life will never be the same. She has had a touch from God that many children never receive and her life will be affected because of this until Jesus comes back."[21]

Prominent Christians who have endorsed or participated in the movement include Pat Roberston of the 700 Club, British author Michael Green, Canadian broadcaster David Mainse, televangelist Marilyn Hickey, Stephen Strang, of *Charisma* magazine, Paul and Jan Crouch of Trinity Broadcasting Network, Ralph Wilkerson of Melodyland, and Oral Roberts

---

[18]Bickle, "Toronto Report," 16 Oct. 1994.

[19]Chevreau, *Catch the Fire*, 171–72.

[20]Eleanor Mumford, "Spreading Like Wildfire," *Renewal*, July 1994, 13.

[21]Charles and Frances Hunter, *Holy Laughter* (Kingwood, Tex.: Hunter Books, 1994) 109.

and his son Richard, who canceled classes for two days at Oral Roberts University so that the students could experience the moving of the Spirit through Rodney Howard-Browne. Although he has not experienced the Toronto Blessing himself, George Carey, archbishop of Canterbury, does not condemn it. He personally knows two people who claim "it was a very refreshing event."[22] Right before Holy Laughter burst forth at his Rhema Bible church, Word Faith teacher Kenneth Hagin had prophesied:

> If you stand still, you do not well. Reach out; reach into the realm of the Spirit by the hand of faith. Take that which belongs to you and that which the Father desires to give you. He cannot give it to you unless you receive it. So take it tonight. Receive! Deliverance is ours. Victory is yours. Whatever you may need, reach out and receive. And your spirit will be glad, and you'll laugh. . . . And the blessing of the Lord will be yours![23]

Jack Hayford, author and pastor of the Church on the Way in Van Nuys, California, writes that the Toronto Blessing is a "God thing": "I say 'God thing' because whatever anyone feels about the events at the Toronto Airport Vineyard, there seems to be evidence of a work of Almightiness—however attended it may be with signs of human frailty or imperfectness."[24]

## HOLY LAUGHTER IS CHARGED WITH ENTHUSIASM

Whatever one may think of Holy Laughter, one thing is certain: the bodily "exercises" at these meetings are sure attention-getters. One reporter at the three-day Catch the Fire conference in Toronto describes it this way:

> The man sitting beside me, Dwayne from California, roared like a wounded lion. The woman beside Dwayne started jerking so badly her hand struck her face. People fell like dominoes,

---

[22]Kenneth L. Wood with Jeanne Gordon, Carol Hall and Barry Brown, "The Giggles Are for God," *Newsweek*, 20 Feb. 1995, 54; cf. Brown, "Unzipper Heaven," 30.

[23]"Winter Bible Seminar '95: Holy Ghost Power and Glory!" *The Word of Faith*, May 1995, 9.

[24]Jack Hayford, "Stanced Before Almightiness: Addressing the questions, 'How do I respond to remarks and talk of the "Toronto Blessing"?' " (Van Nuys, Calif.: Living Way Ministries, 1995), tract.

collapsing chairs as they plunged to the carpeting. They howled like wolves, brayed like donkeys and—in the case of a young man standing near the sound board—started clucking like a feral chicken. And the tears! Never have I seen people weep so hysterically, as though every hurt they'd encountered had risen to the surface and popped like an overheated tar bubble. This was eerie . . . people were screaming, their bodies jerking unnaturally, their faces contorted with tics. Yet the most unsettling were the laughers, those helpless devils who were now rolling around on the floor, holding their stomachs, their minds obviously gripped by some transformative, incomprehensible power. As I looked around, petrified that this weird phenomenon might take command of *my* sense, it occurred to me that the people in that room hardly appeared to be basking in the glory of God's great beneficence. Instead, they looked like they were in agony.[25]

## HOLY LAUGHTER IS CONTROVERSIAL

The wild ecstatic phenomena accompanying this renewal are perhaps the main reason why it is so controversial. *Some say it's a revival.* They refer to similar phenomena occurring in other revivals such as the eighteenth-century Great Awakening under Jonathan Edwards or the Azusa Street revival at the beginning of the twentieth century.

Randy Clark affirms, "This is the most powerful revival that has hit this country since Azusa Street. . . . It will be the greatest revival we've ever seen before it's all over. It won't surprise me if it lasts 20 years."[26] Others such as John Arnott call Holy Laughter the "nameless, faceless revival" because those through whom God is primarily demonstrating his power are not superstar evangelists or pastors. In fact God often works through laypersons or the pastors' wives such as Eleanor Mumford and Carol Arnott. Arnott believes "this will lead to major, major revival in the Western world nations, I believe it's going to come between the year 2000 and 2005. This is a time of restoration in the body of Christ similar to the time of John the Baptist's ministry prior to the coming of the Messiah."[27]

---

[25] Robert Hough, "God is Alive and Well and Saving Souls on Dixon Road," *Toronto Life*, Feb. 1995, 2.

[26] Grady, "Toronto Blessing," 56.

[27] Dave Roberts, "Airport Pastor Speaks Out," *Alpha*, Sept. 1994, 4. Rodney Howard-Browne also says the best is yet to come: "This is the beginning. I believe the day is soon approaching when the presence of

Convinced this is a move of God, Arnott proclaims, "It's about time the church had more faith in God's ability to bless us than Satan's ability to deceive us."[28] Steve Long, associate pastor of the Toronto Vineyard, proclaims, "We are experiencing renewal of the church, with limited revival. Five thousand new followers of Christ is no small potatoes, especially when you take into account the outreach of other renewal centres."[29]

*Some say it's a refreshing.* In an article subtitled "What many people in our churches are experiencing is NOT revival. But it is the only thing that becomes revival," John Wimber, senior pastor of the Association of Vineyard Churches, admits that this is "not yet" a revival. "True revival is marked by widespread repentance both within the church, and among unbelievers. Although as many as four thousand have been converted to date (in various Vineyard churches) we've not yet seen the dynamic of thousands and thousands of people coming to Christ rapidly."[30] He encourages Vineyard pastors to use "renewal" or "refreshing" to describe the current movement.

*Some say it's a false revival or an end-time deception of Satan by which many could be led astray.* Larry Thomas, former Bible college professor for Jimmy Swaggart Ministries and now president of Amazing Grace Ministries, calls Holy Laughter a "false revival" detrimental to the Christian faith. He says that it bears no real resemblance to past revivals, it lacks the preaching of repentance and righteousness, and it can lead to a false Christ and false gospel: "Paul wrote to the Galatians that anyone who preaches another gospel (and that includes adding anything to the gospel he preached) was accursed. This current fad has promoters who have already added to the requirements for salvation."[31]

---

God will fall on a whole congregation and every single sinner in the house will be saved" (*Rumors of Renewal Study Guide*, Word Publishing, Nelson Word Ltd., 1995).

[28] Gail Reid, "After the Laughter," *Faith Today* Mar./Apr. 1995, 18–23. Summary reprinted in "Blessing and Confusion out of Toronto," *Current Thoughts and Trends*, June 1995, 26.

[29] Long, "An Insider's Story," 10.

[30] John Wimber, "Season of New Beginnings," *Vineyard Reflections: John Wimber's Leadership Letter*, May/June 1994, 1; "Visitation of the Spirit," *Ministries Today*, Sept./Oct. 1994, 8; "John Wimber Claims Source of 'Toronto Blessing,' " *Evangelical Times*, Nov. 1994, 9.

[31] Larry Thomas, *No Laughing Matter: A Biblical Analysis of the "Laughing" Revival* (Excelsior Springs, Mo.: Double Crown, 1995) 33; cf. 34–39.

One person wrote to *Charisma* magazine, "I have friends who have experienced this 'blessing' and who now have a crazed look in their eyes and twitch uncontrollably. I do not find this behavior edifying the body of Christ."[32]

But those who themselves experience the phenomenon believe they are being renewed in their walk with the Lord. "I was renewed tremendously. I have a deeper passion and love for Jesus, and a greater hunger for the presence of God in my life. Going to Toronto was one of the best things that has ever happened to me,"[33] said Debi Jeong, Fuller Theological Seminary student from Pasadena, California. Her response exemplifies that of many who have personally experienced Holy Laughter.

Although this book takes a hard look at the phenomenon of Holy Laughter, we will refer to it with the term most often encouraged by its supporters—"renewal." Some say "let's wait and see." Many remain undecided. They want to wait and watch for either positive or negative results. Against this view Mona Johnian writes, "I'm concerned that many are in danger of creating a false comfort zone for themselves. By the position they're taking, they are saying: 'I'm not sure about this present move. I'm just going to wait and see what happens.' But Jesus said, 'He who is not with Me is against Me' (Matt 12:30, NKJV)."[34]

Johnian's careless and divisive approach should not intimidate those who are still on the fence. Simply because certain people feel they are getting blessed does not mean everybody is. We should never base our judgment of such a pervasive movement solely on our own experiences. Not all experiences are the same. Let us hear the entire counsel of Scripture and discernment on the matter. Could you imagine the apostle Paul giving a reckless "thumbs up" to the demon-possessed girl at Philippi when she first proclaimed "These men are servants of the Most High God, who are telling you the way to be saved" (Acts 16:16–18)? Scripture encourages us to "test all things" *including* alleged manifestations of the Spirit (1 Thess 5:19–21). After hearing Paul preach, the Bereans

---

[32] Mark Myers, letter in *Charisma,* April 1995, 11.
[33] "The Toronto What?" *The Semi: A Publication for the Fuller Theological Seminary Community,* 30 Jan.–3 Feb. 1995, 3.
[34] Johnian, "Flowing with Revival," 14.

were not chided but commended for putting his teaching to the test of Scripture (Acts 17:11).

On the other hand, some have condemned Holy Laughter without reflection, ignoring all the positive reports outside their often limited perspective. Advocates on both sides of the issue use Scripture to support their position. Does Scripture *clearly* condemn Holy Laughter? Does it *clearly* endorse it? If it is absent from Scripture, what does that mean? Does it mean Scripture forbids it or permits it, or does it mean something else?

As you may have noticed, there are no easy answers. Holy Laughter is not monolithic. There seem to be both negative and positive elements in the movement. Nevertheless, a "wait and see" approach does seem a bit too passive. What about those who are struggling right now with this issue because Holy Laughter has invaded their church? What about the young man who has just found out his fiancee is following the movement after she was "slain in the Spirit" at a Rodney Howard-Browne meeting? What about the church member who is constantly asked whether or not he agrees with Holy Laughter? Or what about the pastor who is losing some of his church members over this? A "wait and see" approach does not resolve such tensions.

In this book we will attempt to discern the wheat from the chaff, true spirituality from fleshly counterfeits. In a no-nonsense manner, we will take an honest look at Holy Laughter and critique it where it needs to be critiqued, defend it where it has been wrongly criticized, and impart guidelines for discernment regarding its phenomena. Like those who lead the Holy Laughter movement, I myself am a charismatic. Namely, I believe in the gifts of the Holy Spirit as outlined in 1 Cor 12 and related passages, and I operate in some of them myself. I have experienced the miraculous. Moreover, I have faithfully attended a Spirit-filled Pentecostal church for the past fifteen years. I say all this to establish that I am not an outsider when it comes to the moving of the Spirit. I am critiquing this phenomenon as one who has personally experienced the power of the Holy Spirit.

Chapter 2 will present a brief history of the movement and profile some of its chief players. Chapter 3 will examine Rodney Howard-Browne and his connection with the Word Faith movement. Chapter 4 will cover the teachings of the Vineyard;

it will also address the prophetic aspect of the movement in relation to the Kansas City Prophets, the Third Wave, and the Kingdom Now or Latter Rain movements. In chapter 5 we will take a closer look at the renewal phenomena, with a view to determining their sources. What do we make of the laughing, roaring, weeping, trembling, and similar phenomena? Chapter 6 will address these phenomena in the light of Scripture. We will suggest how one should understand biblical data that appears to support being "slain in the Spirit" and other unusual phenomena. Chapter 7 will discuss propriety in worship; here we will get a better focus on what Paul meant in 1 Cor 14 when he charged that all things be done in a decent, and orderly, manner. In chapters 8 and 9 we will compare Holy Laughter to the phenomena of past revivals. In conclusion, chapter 10 will give some final guidelines for discernment on Holy Laughter.

*2*

# TRACKING DOWN THE MOVEMENTS OF THE MOVEMENT

"**W**ell, Jesus, bless Frances!" were the last words Frances Hunter heard the minister say before she fell to the ground. She felt stuck to the floor, as though someone had drenched it with Elmer's Glue. Then it happened. Like "divine alka seltzer," a "bubbling" carbonated at the core of her being. Slowly it bubbled from her stomach upwards until "it abruptly came out of my mouth in the form of the loudest laugh I have ever heard. I had put my hand over my mouth in an effort to stifle what I knew was going to be laughter, but even though I had gotten my head off of the floor by this time, no pressure on my mouth could keep the laughing back. I laughed, laughed, laughed and laughed."[1]

This event did not take place at Toronto or a Rodney Howard-Browne meeting, but in the early 1970s, at a Houston banquet held by the Full Gospel Businessmen's Fellowship. After thirty minutes of non-stop laughing, Hunter stood up "released" from the "Holy Ghost glue." Then at one of their healing services, the Hunters reported that a lady fell to the ground and began to laugh. When she got up she started pounding her fists on another woman! Alarmed, the Hunters raced to do damage control, but the woman she was beating said, "Don't worry, she's all right. . . . She's a nurse who has had

---

[1]C. and F. Hunter, *Holy Laughter*, 22–23.

Guillain-Barre syndrome for over four years and has been unable to lift her arms. . . . while she was laughing, the power of God came all over her and she was healed."[2]

The Hunters also reported that everyone who had been "slain by the Spirit" that night was laughing. Outbreaks of laughter filled the meeting; then the Hunters themselves joined the fun. Another lady ran "down the aisle screaming and said, 'I had a mastectomy last year and had my left breast removed, and while we were all laughing, God grew a new breast back on!'"[3]

After this episode the Hunters, concerned to maintain order in their services, consulted their friend Reverend Lester Sumrall about the phenomena. He said "What you experienced in your service is holy laughter. . . . Anything that is of God is holy and anything that is holy has power connected to it."[4] Since those early days of their charismatic endeavors the Hunters claim they have seen the laughing phenomenon break forth occasionally at their meetings. But it wasn't until Rodney Howard-Browne laid hands on them at a winter camp meeting in Lakeland, Florida, 1993, that the Hunters saw Holy Laughter break forth abundantly in their ministry.

The "Happy Hunters" might be among the oldest veterans of Holy Laughter, but it did not start with them. Long before the charismatic movement of the '60s and '70s, people involved in historic revivals experienced the laughing phenomenon.[5] Thus, tracing it back to its origin is extremely difficult. We will venture into tracing only some of the most significant movements which have experienced these phenomena.

## THE BEGINNINGS: CLAUDIO FREIDZON AND OTHER FORERUNNERS

The Happy Hunters aside, one of the other forerunners to the current movement was A. L. Gill, a missionary from California. He claims to have seen Holy Laughter in his meetings since 1983. But it wasn't until the summer of 1993 that the

---

[2]Ibid., 25–26.
[3]Ibid., 27.
[4]Ibid.
[5]See chapters 8–9 for examples.

phenomenon reached its climax at a seminar in Vision Christian Center in Lawrenceville, Georgia. The move of the Holy Spirit was so intense that locals dubbed it the Chestnut Street Revival (after the location of the church). Other ministers experiencing the phenomenon since 1986 include Tony and Marj Arbam, from Arkansas, and John Lipton, currently in Dover, England.[6]

Murray Robertson, senior pastor of Spraydon Baptist Church, Christ Church, New Zealand, remembers laughter breaking out at an Auckland "Signs, Wonders and Church Growth" conference in August, 1986, after John Wimber preached. Robertson laughed and rolled around on the floor for four and one-half hours. Since that meeting he claims God has specially endowed him with healing power and renewed evangelism.[7]

Perhaps the most widely recognized precursor is Claudio Freidzon, an Assemblies of God pastor and evangelist from Argentina. In a 1994 sermon Mike Bickle reported that the laughter had started seven years before, with Freidzon. At that time the largest churches in Argentina couldn't claim a membership of over 4,000. Now, according to Bickle, close to a dozen churches command a membership roster of about 100,000.[8] Bickle attributes the success to the current renewal. Another report claims that the revivals in Argentina started in 1984 in the city of La Plata, when Evangelist Carlos Annacondia held a crusade in the Church of the Diagonal, which is pastored by Alberto Scataaglini. Other reputed catalysts of the Argentine revival include Edgardo Silvoso, Omar Cabrera, and Hector Gimenez. Reportedly, extraordinary miracles occurred, such as the raising of the dead, the creation of previously removed bodily organs, and even the restoration of tooth fillings.[9]

By spring 1992, in four years Freidzon's King of Kings church had grown to 2,000. But thinking something was

---

[6]Richard Riss, "History of the Revival of 1993–1995," unpublished paper (7th ed., Jan. 17, 1995) 2.

[7]Murray Robertson, "A Power Encounter Worth Laughing About," in *Power Encounters among Christians in the Western World*, Kevin Springer, ed. (San Francisco: Harper and Row, 1988) 149–57.

[8]Bickle, "Toronto Report," 16 Oct. 1994.

[9]Doris Wagner, "Learning From the Argentine Revival," *Equipping the Saints* (Winter 1991) 28–30.

missing in his ministry, he visited healing televangelist Benny
Hinn at the Orlando Christian Center. After being prophesied
over by Hinn, Freidzon went back to Argentina and saw his
church immediately double in size. The Holy Laughter phenomenon prevailed more strongly than ever at his meetings,
attracting enough attention for Freidzon to launch a crusade
in a stadium seating 65,000. As the crusade progressed, Freidzon had to add extra services in order to minister to all
the crowds.

## RODNEY HOWARD-BROWNE

In April 1993, Assemblies of God pastor Karl Strader, of the
Carpenter's Home Church in Lakeland, Florida, invited the
South African evangelist Rodney Howard-Browne to preach at
his 10,000–seat church. Strader used both television and radio
to record the event. In four weeks church attendance soared
from 1,500 to 8,000. A total of about 100,000 people attended
the event, with some services lasting to 2:00 AM. When all was
said and done 2,260 new converts were baptized.[10]
Many look to these meetings as the starting point of prominent recognition for the renewal. Since the meetings at Lakeland, Rodney Howard-Browne has become a household name
among charismatics, and even among many non-charismatic
evangelicals. He has appeared on Paul and Jan Crouch's Trinity
Broadcasting Network and the cover of *Charisma* magazine.
And he continues today to minister around the globe, conducting an average of 550 meetings a year.[11] Although some
would consider this a "nameless, faceless revival," Rodney
Howard-Browne currently stands out as the most significant
evangelist of the movement. He is sometimes called the "Holy
Ghost bartender" or the Rodney Dangerfield of Christianity.
Who is this man from South Africa?

---

[10]Dave Roberts, *The "Toronto" Blessing* (Eastbourne, UK: Kingsway, 1994) 88.
[11]Rodney Howard-Browne, *The Touch of God: A Practical Workbook on the Anointing* (Louisville, Ky.: R.H.B.E.A., 1994), "About the
Author," n.p.

## THE WONDER YEARS

June 12, 1961 marks the birth of Rodney Morgan Howard-Browne in Port Elizabeth, South Africa. "I was raised in a Pentecostal church. . . . As a 5-year-old boy, I'd go up to give my life to Jesus every week,"[12] remembers Howard-Browne. He claims it was at this age that he was born again. At the age of eight he was filled with the Holy Spirit. He attributes his early conversion to the influence of his parents. He recalls that his father would sometimes prophesy at the dinner table.[13] Both his parents were extraordinary Christians:

> I remember my parents praying until all hours of the morning . . . I remember the time my mother fell and broke her arm in three places. The preacher came out to the house and prayed for her, and only four days after they put the cast on her, she cut it off. I was standing outside the bathroom door, pleading, "Oh, Mom, please don't cut it off!" I thought if something was broken, it would fall off! She had her hand in the tub and was praying in the Spirit as she cut the cast off. She *knew* God had healed her.[14]

Young Rodney hungered for his own personal touch from God. Then at a prayer meeting in July 1979 he cried, "God, tonight is my night! Lord, either you come down here and touch me, or I'm going to die and come up there and touch You."[15] After shouting for twenty minutes he felt the touch of God:

> It felt like liquid fire—like someone had poured gasoline over me and set me on fire. My whole body was tingling. The best way I can describe it is that it was as shocking as if I had unscrewed a light bulb from a lamp and put my finger in the socket. I *knew* it was God. When it hit me in my belly, I began to laugh uncontrollably. . . . Your head says, "What are you laughing at?" Your head says, "Shut up!" It bubbles. It was so overwhelming, I couldn't stop it, and I didn't want to stop it. It was joy unspeakable and full of glory. . . . The next minute, I was weeping for no reason. I got drunk in the Spirit, like the people on the Day of Pentecost. I was walking around laughing at nothing, weeping at nothing, and speaking in other tongues, first one and then the other. . . . I thought the experience would only last about an hour. One day, two days, three days went by. By the fourth day, I was getting

---

[12] Rodney Howard-Browne, *Manifesting the Holy Ghost* (Louisville, Ky.: R.H.B.E.A, 1992) 5.

[13] Ibid., 10.

[14] Ibid.

[15] Ibid., 13–14.

worried! Now I wasn't praying, "Send the fire" anymore; I was
begging, "Lord, please lift it! I can't bear it anymore!"[16]

## THE CALL TO MINISTRY

The next year he entered the ministry at age eighteen. He
claims God told him, "I want you to pray for the fire that fell on
you in 1979 to fall on other people—the same fire, the same
drunkenness, the same infilling."[17] In October 1981 he married his wife Adonica. They now have three children. Gordon
Kelmeyer, staff member at Rhema Bible Church in Johannesburg, reported that Rodney first started ministering for Youth
For Christ. He then enrolled at the Rhema Bible Training
Center before pastoring a Full Gospel Church of God in Mol-
teno.[18] According to Peter Riggall, administrator of the Rhema
Bible Church, Rodney Howard-Browne was also an assistant
pastor at the Rhema Bible Church.[19]

He apparently pastored this church until 1985. Then in
December, 1987, Rodney and his family moved to Orlando,
Florida, "to fulfill what the Lord had told Rodney. As America
has sown missionaries over the last 200 years, the Lord said that
He was going to raise up people from other nations to come to
the U.S.A., and that He was sending a mighty revival to America."[20] As he stepped on American soil, Howard-Browne had
only $300 in his pocket and a few speaking engagements set
for the next month.

"We began studying about past revivals in America. The
cry in our hearts was that God would shake America," but
the first two years were "spiritually dry."[21] Then in April 1989
things began to turn around for Rodney. When he preached in
Albany, New York, the audience started falling out of their
seats, some laughing, some crying. The noise forced him to
stop his sermon. "Lord, You're ruining my meeting," com-
plained Rodney. The Lord reportedly responded, "The way

---

[16]Ibid., 16–17.

[17]Ibid., 18.

[18]Perucci Ferraiuolo, "Questions of Credibility," *Christian Research
Journal*, Winter 1995, 45.

[19]James A. Beverley, *Holy Laughter and the Toronto Blessing: An
Investigative Report* (Grand Rapids: Zondervan, 1995) 63–64.

[20]Rodney Howard-Browne, *The Coming Revival* (Louisville, Ky.:
R.H.B.E.A, 1991), inside dust jacket.

[21]Julia Duin, "Pass the New Wine," *Charisma*, Aug. 1994, 23.

your meetings have been going lately, they deserve to be ruined. I will move all the time if you will allow Me to move."[22]

For the next four years, Rodney Howard-Browne eked his way through ministry, gaining more prominence in Pentecostal circles due to the signs and wonders at his meetings. It was during this time also that he enrolled in a correspondence course with the School of Bible Theology in San Jacinto, California. There he earned a "doctorate of ministry" degree. According to one state Department of Education employee, the Pentecostal-oriented school has no faculty, and is akin to a "diploma mill."[23] Then in April 1993 Howard-Browne preached at Karl Strader's church, and the rest is history.

## BLESSINGS FROM TORONTO

John Arnott is far from being a flamboyant revivalist. He's just an ordinary guy, fiftyish, with a deep calm in his voice and easygoing manner. But as the senior pastor of the Toronto Airport Vineyard, he is the leading figure of the Toronto Blessing.

### THE ORIGIN OF THE AIRPORT VINEYARD

After attending Ontario Bible College (1966–68), Arnott spent the next decade running a travel agency and trading real estate. He married Carol in 1979. In 1981 they helped establish a ministry in Stratford, Ontario, after God spoke to John about ministering in the Canadian city. In 1986 the church connected with the booming Vineyard ministries. Again the Lord spoke to Arnott in 1987 to start a Vineyard church in Toronto. In 1990 he rented space by the Toronto airport by the intersection of Derry and Dixon roads.[24]

Having witnessed healers like Kathryn Kuhlman and Benny Hinn, Arnott felt he needed more of the supernatural in his church. He sought a spiritual impartation from Hinn and Rodney Howard-Browne, but his most significant touch of God came through Claudio Freidzon. In November 1993 the Arnotts

---

[22] Ibid.
[23] Ferraiuolo, "Questions of Credibility," 45.
[24] Hough, "God is Alive and Well," 3; Roberts, *"Toronto" Blessing*, 62–63.

attended a conference in Argentina conducted by Ed Silvoso, Luis Palau's brother-in-law, where Freidzon prayed for Arnott and asked him to "take" the empowerment. Arnott felt the Lord say to him, "For goodness sake will you take this?"[25] Arnott took it and reported significant healing and restoration.

## THE RANDY CLARK CONNECTION

After Argentina, at a Vineyard board meeting in Palm Springs, Arnott learned from another Vineyard minister, Happy Leman, about a powerful renewal taking place through St. Louis Vineyard pastor Randy Clark. Arnott invited the soft-spoken Clark to preach at his church beginning January 20, 1994. This date marks the beginning of the Toronto Blessing. "It was a Thursday night," Arnott recalls, "and—boom—80 percent of our church were laughing and on the floor. It looked like the Battle of Atlanta."[26] About twenty-five people came to Christ during the first few meetings; then the meetings were extended for a few more weeks; then they became the six-day-a-week services which have continued ever since, attracting over 200,000 visitors.

Clark himself had not been uncritical of the movement when he first came into contact with Rodney Howard-Browne. He reports that in August 1993 he had nearly suffered a nervous breakdown before attending a Howard-Browne meeting at Kenneth Hagin's Rhema Bible Church in Tulsa, Oklahoma. Skeptical about the Word Faith environment, Clark wrote off a lady who was experiencing the laughing phenomenon as being "in the flesh." Then a blind three-year-old girl fell under the power of God, and Clark concluded that she could not have been imitating the adults. Something was really happening there.

When Clark fell under Howard-Browne's prayer, he was still skeptical until he found himself "stuck" to the ground when he attempted to get up. Then the laughter hit him. Clark said, "I could feel this power in my hands—like they got ice cold . . . I never had that happen before. And Rodney Howard-Browne came up and said, 'This is the fire of God in your hand—go home and pray for everybody in your church.' And when I prayed in my church in St. Louis, 95 per cent of the people fell."[27]

---

[25] Roberts, *"Toronto" Blessing*, 65.
[26] Brown, "Unzipper Heaven," 28.
[27] Riss, "History of the Revival," 20–23.

## FROM TORONTO TO ANAHEIM

Arnott believes the Toronto Blessing will make the great revivals of the past "look like specks of dust on the windshield of history."[28] He believes that God is on "phase one" right now. He desires Christian unity and love. Once this happens "phase two" will see a greater outpouring of signs and wonders—an outpouring so powerful that a great harvest of souls will commit themselves to Christ. "I expect thousands and millions to come in. The stuff that goes on in our meetings? It's nothing. You haven't seen anything yet," says Arnott.[29] Why Toronto? Toronto associate pastor Marc Dupont says, "Toronto is, according to the United Nations, the most ethnically diverse city in the world. It's a great city for something to be birthed in because it can be a sending out place."[30]

Since those early days in Toronto, the "blessing" has spread to most of the 500 Vineyard churches, with the exception of a few defectors. In the summer of 1994 the Anaheim Vineyard, led by John Wimber, experienced the phenomena connected with Holy Laughter in a significant way at a Vineyard conference called "Let the Fire Fall." Now the Anaheim Vineyard reserves certain nights for the renewal experience.

The renewal has stirred up controversy in the Vineyard churches; especially concerning the "roaring as a lion" and other animal phenomena. The Association of Vineyard Churches board meeting in early fall 1994 responded to the phenomena with a paper entitled "Summary Report on the Current Renewal and the Phenomena Surrounding It," and an insert entitled "John Wimber Responds to Phenomena." The papers attempt to formulate a balanced approach toward assessing the Toronto Blessing.

## INFLUENCE ON GREAT BRITAIN

On May 24, 1994, four months after the renewal's inception in Toronto, Eleanor Mumford returned from the Toronto Airport Vineyard to her husband's Vineyard church in Putney,

---

[28] Hough, "God is Alive and Well," 3.
[29] Ibid.
[30] Roberts, *"Toronto" Blessing,* 62.

southwest London. Shortly after she enthusiastically explained to the congregation what was happening in Toronto, Holy Laughter hit her church.

That same month Nicky Gumbel, curate of London's largest Anglican church, Holy Trinity Church in Brompton Road, attended a Mumford prayer meeting. He took the phenomena back with him. The Anglican parish "began to shake, laugh, cry, and fall to the floor."[31] His church has also reported the lion "roaring" (a phenomenon described as usually happening to men).[32] Since that time, news of Holy Laughter has appeared almost daily in the British secular media, and the church is attended by such celebrity converts as former topless model and singer Samantha Fox.[33]

Terry Virgo, British head of the New Frontiers charismatic churches, first encountered the Holy Laughter renewal in Columbia, Missouri, after Rodney Howard-Browne had come to the area. In May 1994, Holy Laughter broke forth as well at his church, Church of Christ the King in Brighton, England.[34] More recently, he felt the Lord speaking to him, "I have attended many of your meetings, now I am inviting you to attend one of mine!"[35] Gerald Coates, director of Pioneer People, an independent non-denominational group comprising over 100 churches, has also embraced the Holy Laughter. At London Bible College Coates spoke for twenty minutes, and the Spirit touched students with laughing and cries of repentance. One student who was touched by God and fell to the ground had written a 10,000-word thesis against the charismatic movement.[36]

At the Queens Road Baptist Church in Wimbledon, south London, Holy Laughter struck in early September 1994, with church members rolling down the aisles, weeping and laughing. Other phenomena that have broken out in Great Britain

---

[31] Brown, "Unzipper Heaven," 30.

[32] Clive Price, "Holy Laughter Hits British Churches," *Charisma,* Oct. 1994, 84.

[33] Martin Wroe, "British Masses are Moved by the Spirit," *Marietta Daily Journal,* 10 Sept. 1994, D1.

[34] Price, "Holy Laughter Hits British Churches," 82–83.

[35] Terry Virgo, "Fresh Outpourings of the Holy Spirit" in *The Impact of 'Toronto,'* Wallace Boulton, ed. (Crowborough, UK: Monarch, 1995) 28.

[36] Gerald Coates, "On the Crest of the Spirit's Wave," *Renewal,* Feb. 1995, 20.

include barking, crowing, mooing, and pawing.[37] David Pytches, Anglican vicar of St. Andrews, Chorleywood, Herts, is a prominent advocate of the renewal. He himself has experienced "roaring in the Spirit" for long periods of time.[38]

The British churches are as a rule not casting aside discernment, even as many of them embrace the renewal. Of the tens of thousands in Great Britain who have experienced it, most claim they have been genuinely touched by God, with positive results following.[39] Bryn Jones, leader of the Covenant Ministries (another church network) embraces the renewal but does not print miraculous testimonies unless he can verify the miracle. He states that he will not allow the hype and the excessive "manifestations focus" of some of those involved to color his views. On the other hand, even such a "watchdog" as Doug Harris, director of the counter-cult ministry Reachout Trust, cautiously claims the renewal is from God.[40]

Holy Laughter has spread like wildfire throughout Great Britain, transcending denominational barriers: Baptists, Pentecostals, Anglicans, and Catholics are experiencing it.

## OBSERVATIONS

### THE "BLESSING" IS TO SOME EXTENT TRANSFERABLE

From Claudio Freidzon to John Arnott, from Rodney Howard-Browne to Randy Clark, from Clark to Toronto, Toronto to Eleanor Mumford, and Mumford to Great Britain, the Holy Laughter "anointing" is to some extent transferable. On the other hand, some have called it the "nameless, faceless" revival, because one does not need to receive the laying on of hands from certain "anointed" ministers to get Holy Laughter. It can be received from anyone. To call this a "nameless" revival, however, is not entirely appropriate. John Wimber and Rodney Howard-Browne are not exactly "nobodies."

[37]Wroe, "British Masses," D1.
[38]Patrick Dixon, *Signs of Revival* (Eastbourne, UK: Kingsway, 1994) 29.
[39]Wroe, "British Masses," D1.
[40]Clive Price, "British Cautiously Embrace Renewal," *Charisma*, April 1995, 58–59.

At any rate, we should avoid the error of reductionism. Not every instance of Holy Laughter can be traced back to Claudio Freidzon, Rodney Howard-Browne, or Toronto. As noted at the beginning of this chapter, there have been others independent of these men who have been touched by the phenomenon. Keith Saunders, pastor of Christian Outreach Centre in Barnstaple, Devon, England, claims the renewal phenomena touched his church, along with churches in Swinden, Brighton, and Scotland in the spring of 1993—independently of anything happening in Toronto or with Rodney Howard-Browne.[41] Patrick Dixon writes:

> Whatever is going on has been transmitted by hundreds or thousands of individuals from place to place, carrying their own personal experience of the power of God. While perhaps 1,500 British church leaders had been to Toronto from Britain by September 1994 . . . it is also true that what is happening has been thoroughly anglicized as it has spread around the UK. Things were already happening in the UK on a smaller scale long before anyone had heard of a church at Toronto Airport . . . For example, falling, shaking and laughter in 1987 at the Waltes Bible Week (Bryn Jones), but more immediately, in October 1993, when a number of people in Kensington Temple were affected by "holy laughter," including one woman who was almost unable to make the bus journey home, embarrassing her friend because she looked so drunk.[42]

## WE SHOULD NOT UNQUESTIONABLY ACCEPT EVERY ACCOUNT OF THE RENEWAL AS AUTHENTIC

Can the renewal accounts be trusted? Investigating every claim of those who are for the most part advocates of the renewal would amount to a multivolumed series. Not every story we hear is true. Some accounts have been embellished, some exaggerated, and some are based on hearsay. I find the Happy Hunters' stories to be less credible than others; and although Rodney Howard-Browne's stories sometimes seem questionable, he claims they are true.[43]

In the final analysis, it would be foolish to hold that all positive accounts of Holy Laughter are false. The vast majority

---

[41] Keith Saunders, letter, *Charisma*, April 1995, 11.
[42] Dixon, *Signs of Revival*, 17–18.
[43] See his interview with Jim Beverley in Beverley's book, *Holy Laughter*, 53–65.

of those experiencing, conducting, and relaying these events are Christians who have some sense of integrity. One of the strongest cases against atheism is the argument from experience. If millions of people claim to have a personal relationship with God, then it is reasonable to assume that at least some of them really do. In a similar way, if we hear hundreds of accounts in connection with Holy Laughter that lead to positive or even miraculous results, it is reasonable to assume that at least some of them are true. We must avoid the temptation of making overarching condemnations based on generalizations and selectively cited negative evidence, while sweeping all the positive evidence under the rug.

Part of this tendency to deny a supernatural work of the Holy Spirit arises from the untenable assertion that the supernatural gifts of the Spirit ceased in the first century.[44] Such a view almost forces one to rule out a priori any contemporary miracles worked in the name of Christ, or to attribute them to Satan. The unmistakable impression many Christians get regarding the supernatural is that, in our age, Satan is more powerful than God! Supernatural outpourings of the Spirit may be mistakenly explained away as precursors to the final deceptive apostasy of the Antichrist.

## MANY REPORTS ARE POSITIVE

I have read report after report, testimony after testimony about those who have witnessed or experienced the phenomena. The majority of accounts are positive. And many of those who testify of its positive nature are not leaders but lay persons, with little to gain personally by reporting what they have experienced. This is one of my strongest reasons for believing that it is wrong to denounce or condemn this movement out of hand.

---

[44]For some refutations of the cessationist view of spiritual gifts consult Wayne Grudem, *Systematic Theology* (Grand Rapids: Zondervan/Leicester, UK: InterVarsity Press, 1994) 1016–38; Jon Ruthven, "On the Cessation of the Charismata: The Protestant Polemic of Benjamin B. Warfield," *Pneuma* vol. 12 no. 1 (Spring 1990), 14–31; Jack Deere, *Surprised by the Power of the Spirit* (Grand Rapids: Zondervan, 1993); Stanley M. Burgess, *The Holy Spirit: Ancient Christian Traditions* (Peabody: Hendrickson, 1984); Gary D. Kinnaman, *And Signs Shall Follow* (Tonbridge, UK; Sovereign World, 1992); C. Peter Wagner, ed., *Signs and Wonders Today* (Altamonte Springs, Fla.: Creation House, 1987).

Even the most adamant skeptic has trouble explaining away an account like the Florida radio incident with Randy Clark, mentioned in chapter 1. Gerald Coates's experience at the London Bible College is another example of a report that is hard to explain away. Given their accuracy (and there is no a priori reason to deny this), the most unbiased conclusion one could come to is that God sovereignly visited these people.

## SOME REPORTS ARE NEGATIVE

Not all reports have been positive, however. Since many of the reports do come from advocates of the renewal, there may be a tendency—perhaps unintentional—to omit some of the negative incidents. But some do experience the "down side" of the renewal, and decide against it on that basis. Guy Chevreau admits, "There are always some who come, take a look, and conclude that the noise and the exuberance they witness are more fitting at a football game than a worship service; they shake their heads, and leave, mumbling in essence, 'I don't believe that's God, and I don't want it.' "[45]

Jim Beverley, professor of theology and ethics at the Ontario Theological Seminary, interviewed representatives from several denominations "and was variously told that a beneficent God would never choose to have us bray like a lovesick donkey, that the Vineyard model promotes a quick-fix approach to spirituality, that the manifestations are actually satanic in nature."[46] One of Beverley's colleagues attended the Airport Vineyard and was pushed down when he failed to be "slain in the Spirit."

The renewal is definitely causing some people to leave their churches, and congregations split between those who do and those who do not support the phenomena. One such church was Heron Park Baptist Church in Scarborough, where Deacon Chris Cole reports having found herself growing arrogant and judgmental against the lack of enthusiasm in others.

Sometimes people are touched at a renewal meeting, but no fruit follows. One couple left their church, frustrated that biblical teaching had been sacrificed in order to allow more time for the phenomena. This couple claims that one of the

---

[45] Chevreau, *Catch the Fire*, 27.
[46] Hough, "God is Alive and Well," 3–4.

ministers tried to exorcise a demon from their teenage daughter. "The girl was in fact suffering from a severe asthma attack and almost died. She is now in counseling trying to adjust to this incident."[47]

Ironically, most of the secular reports have not been negative. The secular press has in fact taken a notably irenic approach.[48] One suspects that laughing churches seem appealing to people who are unhappy, depressed, or dissatisfied with their current circumstances. On the other hand, there are those who think the strange phenomena indicate mass hysteria.[49] There are problems—unmistakable incidents of division, disorder, pride, alienation, and quackery—just as there seem to be undeniably positive aspects.

What then do we make of the mixed reports? I suppose we could investigate and document every claim—good or bad—and submit each healing account to the scrutiny of medical professionals in order to arrive at a feasible conclusion. An investigation of this magnitude, however, would take much too long—doubtless longer than this renewal will last. There is an easier way. We can examine the general results or "fruit" the renewal produces; we can look into Scripture; and we can examine the teachings of those who promote the renewal. Let's begin exploring these avenues.

---

[47] Reid, "After the Laughter," 22.
[48] Dave Roberts, "Revival Call," *Alpha,* Aug. 1994, 15; Johnian, "Flowing with Revival," 14.
[49] Beverley, *Holy Laughter,* 73.

# 3

# UNCOVERING THE TEACHINGS OF RODNEY HOWARD-BROWNE

In the preliminary days of the current renewal Rodney Howard-Browne prophesied that God would do a new supernatural work through the "new wine" of the Spirit. Word Faith teacher Kenneth Copeland then spoke in tongues to Rodney, and Rodney returned the favor. Both men laughed as they spoke in tongues to one another. Later that evening Rodney fell to the floor when Copeland laid hands on him. Copeland prophesied:

> The greater realm that you've been seeing all evening long is the stage set before you that I've called you to walk in, and this is only the beginning. It is only the start of the outpouring that has already begun of the former and latter rain. Keep yourself prepared. . . . The spirit that has been sent of the devil to hinder and to hurt and to hold you back has been broken and he will not hinder you any more.[1]

One of the most controversial aspects of the ministry of Rodney Howard-Browne (RHB hereafter) centers upon his association with Word Faith teachers. As noted earlier, he is a graduate from the Rhema Bible Training Center in Johannesburg, which is closely affiliated with Kenneth Hagin's ministry. RHB also refers favorably to older faith healers such as Smith Wigglesworth, who suffered from kidney stones a number of

---

[1]Citation from Riss, "History of the Revival," 6–8.

years but refused to get medical help; A. A. Allen, who had a drinking problem and died of liver disease; and William Branham, who taught that the Trinity was of the devil.[2] But we should be careful not to automatically write RHB off as a Word Faith teacher because of his early background or associations. We must avoid the fallacy of guilt by association. What does RHB himself teach?

## WORD FAITH CRITERIA

Let us first ask ourselves, what is the Word Faith movement, commonly known as "name it and claim it theology," or "the health, wealth and prosperity gospel," or "positive confession"?

> This doctrine is accompanied by a basic presupposition: that all Christians are to be physically healthy and materially rich. The presupposition controls the confession. Thus, if one is in need of physical healing one must find a verse concerning healing . . . then audibly quote this verse in the face of all physical circumstances to the contrary. By believing in one's heart and speaking with one's mouth this verse, the healing will eventually be manifested by faith. The result is always to be positive, hence, "positive" confession.[3]

Word Faith teaching emphasizes positive confession to the extent that faith in one's confession actually becomes the driving force; Word Faith teaching asserts that confession will sovereignly get you whatever you want. Hence, even God is subject to a Word of Faith practitioner's confession. As long as an alleged biblical promise is claimed, God is thus blackmailed to perform his word. D. R. McConnell traces the origin

---

[2] See Stanley H. Frodsham, *Smith Wigglesworth: Apostle of Faith* (Springfield: Gospel Publishing House, 1948); Scott Shemeth, "Allen, Asa Alonso" in *Dictionary of Pentecostal and Charismatic Movements,* Stanley M. Burgess and Gary B. McGee, eds. (Regency Reference Library; Grand Rapids: Zondervan, 1988) 7–8; William Branham, "Revelation Chapter Four #3" (Jeffersonville, Ind.: Voice of Good Recordings, 1961), audio tape. In an interview with Jim Beverley, RHB clarifies that Branham was originally a man of God, but he went astray doctrinally in later years. See James Beverley, *Holy Laughter,* 57.

[3] H. Terris Neuman, "Cultic Origins of Word-Faith Theology Within the Charismatic Movement," *Pneuma* Vol. 12 no. 1 (Spring 1990) 32.

of the Word Faith movement to E. W. Kenyon and the heretical New Thought sect.[4] Beyond positive confession, guaranteed healing and unlimited prosperity, Word Faith theology teaches that Christians are little gods. Also, some Word Faith adherents believe that Christ's atonement was not completed on the cross; instead, he literally became sin for us and suffered in the flames of hell under Satan between his death and resurrection. It was in hell that Jesus became born again.[5] These are perhaps the major tenets of Word Faith theology.

What then makes someone a Word Faith teacher? Does a teacher belong in the Word Faith camp when he or she teaches *any one of the tenets,* or *some of the tenets,* or *all of the tenets* listed above? Here's where the issue gets a little muddy. We may wish to offer a simplistic clarification, by distinguishing between Word Faith theology and its teachers. However, although a minister is Word Faith if he or she teaches all Word Faith tenets, what about someone who teaches guaranteed healing alone and rejects or even denounces all other Word Faith tenets? In the 1970s and 1980s, for instance, Hobart Freeman taught guaranteed healing, but he was not a Word Faith teacher. R. W. Shambach borders on guaranteed healing by promoting A. A. Allen's book *God's Guarantee To Heal You,* but it would be unfair to label him as a full-blown Word Faith teacher based on that fact alone.

What if a teacher held to the "little gods" doctrine and the "born-again Jesus," without positive confession or health, wealth, and prosperity? What if someone confessed divine healing and prosperity but recognized that God, according to his sovereign will, may not say yes to his or her prayer? Are such people Word Faith? I think it is best to say that one must at least hold to positive confession, guaranteed healing, and unlimited prosperity in order to be called a Word Faith teacher.

There are also *degrees* or *levels* of Word Faith teaching. A preacher who teaches Word Faith about twice a year is not on the same level as those who do so almost every time they speak. The Word Faith elements in Marilyn Hickey's teaching,

---

[4]See D. R. McConnell, *A Different Gospel: A Historical and Biblical Analysis of the Modern Faith Movement* (2d rev. ed.; Peabody: Hendrickson, 1994).

[5]For documentation consult Hank Hanegraaff, *Christianity in Crisis* (Eugene: Harvest House, 1993).

for instance, are far less prominent than those in the teaching of Kenneth Copeland. In all fairness I cannot categorize the two as equally aberrant. Copeland clearly holds to all the tenets of Word Faith including the "little gods" and "born-again Jesus"—other Word Faith teachers do not.

Then there are problems with *definition and popular jargon*. Preachers love to mimic their favorite preachers by using the same anecdotes, lines and gestures as their "heroes." Many Pentecostal and charismatic ministers have this mentality, and they are sometimes wrongly classed as being in the Word Faith camp because of the jargon they use. A classic example of an abused piece of jargon is the phrase "by his stripes we are healed" from Isaiah 53:5. Pentecostal ministers often quote this phrase when praying for the sick. Unlike Word Faith teachers, however, they do not believe that this verse guarantees divine healing in the present age. Remember, believing in divine healing is not wrong. Every Pentecostal, charismatic, and third waver believes this. They believe God can heal anyone of physical disease, but he is not obligated to do so in this present age. Likewise, God may prosper individuals, but this doesn't mean he *must* do so. When we go beyond this balanced view to hold that divine healing and prosperity are *guaranteed* for every believer in this present age, we have stepped over the line of orthodoxy into false doctrine. Such a belief makes our faith sovereign instead of God.

And so faithful charismatic and Pentecostal ministers are sometimes wrongly classified as Word Faith because of the phrases and jargon they use. Many naive preachers unwittingly adopt popular jargon used by popular televangelists without understanding the full ramifications of the teachings behind it. Their problem is not heresy, but a lack of discernment and doctrinal clarity. And that seems to be a continual problem with many conservative American Christians in general and with Pentecostals in particular. Anti-intellectualism, Christian superstardom, and a lack of originality in evangelical circles all share the blame.

We must therefore avoid categorizing preachers as Word Faith teachers simply on the basis of the jargons and phrases they may share in common with Word Faith teachers. Some Word Faith critics fail to pursue the question: What does the preacher *mean* by what he is saying? How frequently is he saying it? What Word Faith tenets does this preacher *clearly* hold? If I'm not sure, shouldn't I make an honest attempt to contact the preacher and ask him what he means?

Why am I making these qualifications? I want to establish that we should examine teachers on their own terms instead of carelessly placing them in our preconceived categories. I have seen too many Christians, especially from nonPentecostal backgrounds, make the mistake of assuming that the preaching of Pentecostal or charismatic teachers amounts to a procrustean bed. Again, just because a teacher uses common Pentecostal jargon, this does not necessarily mean that person teaches Word Faith. Just because a teacher believes in divine healing and prosperity, this does not automatically place him or her in the Word Faith camp. And just because a teacher teaches a single Word Faith tenet, this does not mean he or she teaches them all. Rodney Howard-Browne is one of these preachers whom some of his critics have, in this manner, wrongly classified as a Word Faith advocate.[6]

## RODNEY HOWARD-BROWNE ON PROSPERITY AND DIVINE HEALING

Having read RHB's writings on financial stewardship and prosperity, I have concluded that he does not believe in a prosperity that promotes greed, materialism, or using God as a means to get rich. He denounces ministers who fleece the church through clever gimmicks: "Don't be trapped by the pressure used by some who manipulate the Body of Christ. Don't allow gimmicks to force you into giving. . . . If you feel any pressure to give, just wave the bucket good-bye when it

---

[6]This study covers only RHB's printed materials. A thorough assessment of his messages on tape is beyond the scope of this book. A word of caution to anyone planning to embark on such a project: Preachers are far more likely to "mess up" or say things that can easily be misunderstood over the pulpit than in a book. Even some of the most orthodox preachers could be made to appear to contradict themselves if someone were to string together careless statements they have made over the span of many years. We should never isolate and exploit unclear or bizarre statements made by a preacher. Remember, not only does God hate heresy, he also hates slander.

passes you."[7] RHB believes that ministers who are motivated by money instead of ministry have lost the anointing.[8] By the same token, Christians should never identify success with materialism;[9] a Christian who prospers should bless others by meeting their needs in every area.[10] For RHB, selfishness should not be a motivation for desiring God to bless us; money and materialism should not be our priorities.

Nevertheless, RHB definitely believes in prosperity:

> People say, "Well we've seen the excesses." Does that mean that because somebody drives a car under the influence of alcohol, we will never drive again? . . . No, you are going to go and drive properly. Just because there are a few dingbats that go overboard in the area of finances and into excess, doesn't mean that we are never going to seek the blessings of God.[11]

RHB also declares that poverty is a curse, but he does not seem to believe someone is cursed if they are poor; but rather that it is the *mentality* of poverty which brings a curse. Poverty can "rob Christians of their joy, it will break up marriages, it will cause sickness. People lie awake at night trying to figure out how they are going to pay their bills."[12]

He sometimes uses passages that are wrongly understood as supporting prosperity, such as 3 John 2 ("Beloved, I wish above all things that you may prosper and be in health even as your soul prospers") and Galatians 3:13 ("Christ redeemed us from the curse of the Law being made a curse for us.").[13] The first passage simply describes a personal greeting that John the apostle sent to a Christian friend named Gaius. The apostle never intended this passage to be understood as a promise for anyone who wishes to claim prosperity or divine healing. Galatians 3:13 is not a promise that God will keep us from all the curses outlined in Deuteronomy 28. The "curse of the law"

---

[7]Rodney Howard-Browne, *Thoughts on Stewardship: Volume 1* (Louisville, Ky.: R.H.B.E.A., 1993) 53 cf. 13, 28, 37.

[8]Rodney Howard-Browne, *The Touch of God: A Practical Workbook*, 90.

[9]Rodney Howard-Browne, *Walking in the Perfect Will of God* (Louisville, Ky.: R.H.B.E.A., 1991) 13–14.

[10]Howard-Browne, *Thoughts on Stewardship: Volume 1*, 73; idem, *Thoughts on Stewardship: Volume 2* (Tampa: R.M.I., 1995) 19.

[11]Howard-Browne, *Volume 2*, 11.

[12]Ibid.; cf. *Volume 1*, 18–19; *The Touch of God: A Practical Workbook*, 93.

[13]Howard-Browne, *Volume 1*, 7; *Volume 2*, 55.

most likely refers to the human inability to keep the Law of Moses faithfully; hence, to avoid sinning. We are thus subject to sin and in need of Christ as Savior.

Many would argue that Christ provides us not only with salvation through the cross, but with other blessings too, including divine healing and prosperity. Since Christ reversed the curse of Adam on the cross—and our redemption will ultimately lead to our obtaining glorified bodies that will never get sick or die after Christ returns—we can affirm that physical blessings in this present age are *possible* (but not guaranteed). Consequently, God sometimes heals and blesses us in this present age even though he is not "bound by his Word" to do so. Word Faith, on the other hand, teaches that God *must* heal you. If he doesn't, it is because you either lack faith or harbor unconfessed sin.

But RHB doesn't make this careful distinction between the blessings of this present age and our perfected future blessings. He simply writes: "When Jesus Christ died on the cross, He redeemed us from the curse of the law—poverty, sickness and spiritual death. For spiritual death, Jesus gave us eternal life, for sickness, divine healing and health, and for poverty, wealth."[14]

Worse than this, one is left with the impression that prosperity and divine healing are an absolute guarantee when he states, "In the same way that you would reject sin, you should reject the temptation to sin, to get sick or to live in poverty,"[15] and, "what they don't realize is that their salvation entitles them to soundness, wholeness, healing, preservation, deliverance, and God's blessings. The good news of the Gospel is that everything is wrapped up in salvation."[16] Once we appropriate the promises of God, the implication seems clear: the "devil of poverty" will flee and God will bless the Christian financially. In another place he writes, "Whenever the Word of God is spoken in faith from the lips of a believer, then God's healing power is activated. Jesus often spoke the word and many were healed."[17]

---

[14] Howard-Browne, *Volume 2*, 55; cf. *Walking in the Perfect Will of God*, 5; idem, *What it Means to Be Born Again* (Louisville, Ky.: R.H.B.E.A., 1992) 26–27.

[15] Howard-Browne, *Volume 2*, 56.

[16] Ibid., 38; cf. 39.

[17] Howard-Browne, *The Touch of God*, 37.

If taken to their logical inclusion, these statements on prosperity and healing would seem to write off Christians who live in poverty or have not been healed as either being in sin or lacking faith. Such a view is unmistakably Word Faith theology. The writings of RHB have not addressed the question about those Christians who trust God and serve him faithfully but do not get healed or do not prosper financially. Does RHB believe that we are guaranteed these things—now, in this present era—through Christ's atoning death, or does he admit that God in his sovereignty does not always heal and financially prosper all believers? He needs to clarify this issue.

## THE BIBLE ON PROSPERITY AND DIVINE HEALING

We currently live in an enigmatic age of "now and not yet." We are sometimes allowed a "taste" of the blessings and powers marking the fully realized kingdom of God. But the full benefits of our future glory still await us at Christ's second coming (cf. Heb 6:5). Thus we can experience the redemption of our souls, but the redemption of our mortal bodies does not occur until the second coming (Eph 1:7; Rom 8:19–23). Our faith must always submit to God's sovereign will (1 John 5:14–15; James 4:13–17; Matt 26:39, 42; Rom 15:31–32). And according to God's sovereign purposes it is sometimes his will to deny our requests and permit sickness and poverty to strike us just as they did Paul, Timothy, Trophimus and the church of Smyrna (2 Cor 11:23–29; 12:7–9; 1 Tim 5:23; 2 Tim 4:20; Rev 2:9).

The prosperity message works well in countries like the U.S., but what about in third world countries? How well will financial prosperity go over among Christians in India, Ethiopia, or Somalia? Would RHB's message that "poverty is curse" condemn the early Christians, who worshipped in the catacombs to avoid persecution? A mentality of financial prosperity might not get very far under a government that severely oppresses Christians. Yet such oppressed Christians are entirely precious in God's eyes, and their faith often shames that of any prosperity preacher. I think God is more pleased by our faithfulness to him in the face of trials, sicknesses, and persecutions than by our faith to receive health, wealth, and prosperity. We obtain joy through sufferings, perhaps more so than through blessings.

The Bible does not always depict poverty as a curse or prosperity as a blessing. Many times the wicked also prosper. The central theme of the book of Habakkuk is the prophet's question to God: Why does he permit the wicked to prosper? God often assists and defends the poor and the oppressed (Luke 4:18; James 2:1–7; 5:1–5; Rev 2:9–11). They are not a cursed people. On the contrary, Jesus considered them blessed (Luke 6:20–26; 16:19–25).

To his credit RHB has distanced himself from Word Faith teachers, and even pokes fun at the "Word of Faith or Teaching Movement" that refuses to make negative confessions. In his opinion, such teachers avoid listening to people's problems, and thus there is "something wrong" with what they believe.[18] He writes:

> I've gone to some churches in the States where the speaker got up and said, "Today I want to talk about twenty ways to become prosperous and get a new car." I thought, "God, have mercy!" We're through with all that junk. . . . People get so hung up about the way you live, how you dress, and what you drive. They're missing the whole importance of why we're here on earth. Who cares where you live? . . . We become hung up on material things that are non-essential to eternal life. When you get to heaven, is God going to say, "Well done, thou good and *successful* servant. Bring the fancy wristwatch here. I've always wanted one myself, to be honest with you." No! He's going to say, "Well done, thou good and *faithful* servant."[19]

I have not seen sufficient evidence that RHB definitely holds to other Word Faith tenets such as positive confession, "little gods," or the "born-again Jesus." His teachings on healing and prosperity are certainly confusing, and much too close to Word Faith ideas for comfort, but without further evidence I think it would be unfair to place him in the Word Faith camp, especially when he himself categorically denies that he is a Word Faith teacher.[20]

But several issues surrounding his view of healing and prosperity still need to be hammered out. In what sense does he understand prosperity as part of the atonement? Is divine healing a *benefit* or a *guarantee* of the atonement in this present age? Christian leaders need to dialogue with him, and he

---

[18] Howard-Browne, *The Coming Revival,* 16–19.
[19] Ibid., 20.
[20] Roberts, *"Toronto" Blessing,* 97.

must be willing to set aside some time from his busy schedule to meet with them.

## OTHER TEACHINGS OF RODNEY HOWARD-BROWNE

### THE ANOINTING

Like many Pentecostal and charismatic teachers, RHB proclaims a teaching called "the anointing." According to RHB the anointing is "the power of God manifested. We could say that the anointing is the manifested presence of God. . . . The anointing is tangible—it can be felt. Just as electricity is tangible, so the anointing is tangible."[21] This anointing is also transferable through the laying on of hands. RHB recalls one time when he was about to pray for a sick woman at a Methodist church:

> I got my hand halfway to her head, almost like a gunslinger would draw a gun out of a holster and point it at his opponent. Suddenly, unexpectedly, it felt like my finger tips came off. I felt a full volume of the anointing flow out of my hand. The only way I can explain it is to liken it to a fireman holding a fire hose with a full volume of water flowing out of it. The anointing went right into her. It looked like someone had hit her in the head with an invisible baseball bat and she fell to the floor.[22]

He believes the anointing can flow through various means such as blowing, touching an anointed handkerchief, and so forth. The means are not important—what really matters is that there is a "point of contact in which someone can release their faith."[23] The anointing, however, bounces off unbelievers; "it is like laying hands on a refrigerator."[24]

Nevertheless, RHB assures us the anointing is not hype that people conjure up through physical "hoopla" such as the stirring up of emotions, shouting, singing, dancing, or even preaching. He admits that many times he has failed to preach with the anointing. Such preaching, in his view, amounts to

---

[21] Rodney Howard-Browne, *The Anointing* (Louisville, Ky.: R.H.B.E.A., 1992) 3–4.
[22] Howard-Browne, *The Touch of God*, 63.
[23] Ibid., 67, 109.
[24] Ibid., 107.

mere teaching.[25] He continues, "The anointing is not people falling under the power, yet many times the anointing can overcome people and the phenomenon of them falling under the power will be witnessed. These are the results of the anointing."[26] The phenomena of Holy Laughter, such as being "drunk in the Spirit" or "slain in the Spirit," are some physical results of God's manifested presence.

But RHB has more than one understanding of the term "anointing." He states that when someone is born again they are "anointed." As we saw earlier he affirms that regular teaching is not anointed; yet paradoxically, it is one of the fivefold gifts of the Spirit mentioned in Eph 4:11–13. Such gifts are a supernatural endowment not imparted by humans but recognized through "the call and the anointing on an individual's life."[27]

RHB has even taught that when Jesus lived on earth, he had to depend on the anointing, for "nothing Jesus did was because He was Jesus the Son of God. The Bible says that He laid aside His royal robes of deity."[28] But if Jesus stripped himself of deity when he was on earth then he could not truly be God, for God never changes his divine nature (Heb 1:9–12; 13:8; James 1:17). Although his incarnation veiled his divine glory, there could never be a time when Jesus was not God (Heb 13:8). The Bible clearly teaches that Christ has always been God, even while living as a man here on earth (John 5:18; 10:30; 14:7–10; 20:28).

In an interview with Jim Beverley, RHB clarified his viewpoint by affirming that Christ was the God-man on earth and that his miracles derived from both his deity and humanity.[29] Rodney's clarification vindicates him from the charge of heresy, but it clearly contradicts the wording of his earlier claim that "nothing Jesus did was because He was Jesus the Son of God."

When the Spirit is emphasized by using impersonal terms such as the "anointing," "electricity," "power," and "bubbles," we should make sure we balance out these metaphors by stressing the person of the Holy Spirit. To his credit RHB

---

[25] Howard-Browne, *The Anointing*, 6–7, 12.
[26] Ibid., 13.
[27] Ibid., 21, 28; cf. 12.
[28] Ibid., 15.
[29] Beverley, *Holy Laughter*, 58–59.

teaches that the Holy Spirit is God, Third Person of the Trinity, and that he cannot be manipulated by humans. He gets extremely bothered by those who equate the Spirit with laughter or tongues![30] But after seeing RHB in action, one can mistakenly think the Spirit is an invisible bolt of lightning that randomly strikes people in the congregation whenever RHB points their way or lays hands on them. Perhaps he should practice more what he preaches: discerning the *person* of the Holy Spirit.

## THE SALVATION EXPERIENCE

RHB claims that foundational truths are important to safeguard against doctrinal deception and falling away.[31] Among these truths are the message of salvation and of the born-again experience. A complete turning away from sin ought to take place in the lives of those who are truly born again. Moreover, if sinners come to a church week after week without getting saved, then something is wrong with that church, "They should sense the presence of God and they should be convicted—not condemned—and should want to repent."[32] At the end of his booklet entitled *What it Means to Be Born Again* Rodney prints a "sinner's prayer" based on Rom 10:9–10, and rightly includes "I repent of all my sins."[33]

Moreover, RHB does not flinch from talking about hell.[34] But he remembers a strange incident: "One night I was preaching on hell. . . . and [laughter] just hit the whole place. The more I told people what hell was like, the more they laughed. When I gave an altar call, they came forward by the hundreds to be saved."[35] He also recalls a childhood incident in which he cried for over two hours for lost souls who were going to hell.[36]

Whatever one makes of these events, RHB appears to have compassion for the lost. He promotes evangelism and people

---

[30] Rodney Howard-Browne, *The Reality of the Person of the Holy Spirit*, 4, 7, 17.

[31] Howard-Browne, *What It Means to Be Born Again*, 1.

[32] Ibid., 28–29; cf. 5.

[33] Ibid., 33.

[34] Ibid., 15–20.

[35] Duin, "Pass the New Wine," 24.

[36] Howard-Browne, *What it Means to Be Born Again*, 8.

do get saved at his meetings. Of course we may wish to investigate the genuineness of these conversions. Certainly, his teachings in themselves, confusing as they may be, would not prevent a true conversion experience. But I doubt that if one hundred people verbally accepted Christ at one of his meetings, all the conversions would be genuine. Unstable Christians, backsliders, and people who have wrong motives respond to altar calls all the time. Then again, I find it even more difficult to believe that *none* of the people who respond to altar calls at RHB's meetings are truly converted. RHB's teaching and ministry does not amount to a mere "bless me" club. He *does* preach against sin, encourage repentance, and promote evangelism.

Unfortunately, the born-again experience presented by RHB is skewed by his disturbing view that blessings are provided in the atonement: "But when Jesus comes inside, He cleans the house out. Your lifestyle will be affected. You start loving people. Your marriage gets turned around. Your finances get healed. Your sick bodies get healed. That's what the new birth does."[37]

## THE FIVEFOLD MINISTRY

Although RHB denounces self-proclaimed apostles, he nonetheless teaches a fivefold ministry of apostles, prophets, evangelists, pastors, and teachers—as outlined in Eph 4:11.[38] He believes that one who is considered a modern-day apostle or prophet does not—by virtue of that office—gain the right to abuse his or her authority: "some try to lord it over the whole Body of Christ and operate in almost a cult-like manner when they demand respect and take the authority where it's not due them."[39] RHB likens such individuals to "Charismatic gurus."

Unlike those holding Kingdom Now, Latter Rain, or Dominion theologies,[40] he apparently understands the modern-day apostle as a missionary, not as one who receives new revelation or rules over the entire church.[41] Further, he holds that the fivefold ministry gifts "cannot be imparted by man.

[37]Ibid., 26–27.
[38]Howard-Browne, *The Touch of God: A Practical Workbook,* 12, 17, 19.
[39]Ibid., 24.
[40]See chapter 4 for a better understanding of these terms.
[41]Howard-Browne, *The Anointing,* 16, 27–28.

We can only recognize the call and the anointing on an individual's life. There are no fivefold callings among the laity."[42]

## RODNEY HOWARD-BROWNE AND MANIPULATIVE TECHNIQUES

Marjoe Gortner was a young southern Pentecostal preacher in the early 1970s who would lay hands on people and see them fall "under the power." People attending his meetings were charged with enthusiasm. Only one catch: Marjoe was not a Christian! He simply put on a good act, in order to get parish members to give of their finances. The 1972 documentary *Marjoe* shows people who were seeking spiritual experiences being easily fooled by this "ministry." Gullible Christians in Marjoe's audience could even get "healed" by convincing themselves that there was a man of God behind the pulpit. Meanwhile Marjoe went through all the theatrics of an assertive charismatic faith healer. He knew how to get the crowds excited, how to manipulate them to give liberally to his "ministry." Many a naive Christian attended his meetings in an effort "to feel good and be entertained."[43]

Some have affirmed that RHB employs similar manipulative techniques. If we sit through one of his services, we will often see him ask first-time visitors to raise their hands and stand up. Some people are asked to repeat important phrases with him. He also uses what some call "trigger words" such as "Isn't God great?" and then allows a minute or two to pass before he talks again—in the meantime, some members of the audience begin laughing. Sometimes he gets people in the audience to raise both their hands. Such a posture almost predisposes people to overbalance and fall backward when Rodney lays hands on them or says, "Fill! Fill! Fill!"

One reporter who saw RHB in action says, "It seemed to me that the Holy Spirit was conspicuous by his absence; the people even had to be *told* that he was present."[44] He noted in

---

[42] Ibid., 28

[43] V. Bailey Gillespie, *The Dynamics of Religious Conversion* (Birmingham: Religious Education Press, 1991) 121.

[44] Mike Taylor, "Down and Out at Wembley," *Evangelicals Now*, Feb. 1995, 9.

his report that only those for whom it was expedient to fall fell. RHB did not fall, nor did the camera men. Moreover, his entire message focused on what was to take place—the outward manifestations of the Holy Ghost. By the end of the service the reporter felt angered: "I had gone to the meeting expecting some kind of spiritual atmosphere, but there was nothing at all—it was neither of God nor demonic; it was totally flat. The entire thing was most similar to stage hypnotism."[45]

Despite RHB's claim that it is not him but the Holy Spirit who touches people at his meetings, he seems to help out the Holy Spirit by shouting things like "Fill! . . . Let it bubble out your belly . . . laugh like this . . . Ah ha hah, ah ha ha ha ha. . . . Wooooo! Woohoooo!"[46] He has definitely opened himself up to criticism by indulging in such antics, and his lack of discernment and careless statements only increase the critics' ammunition.

## ON DISCERNMENT: HOLY LAUGHTER STYLE

Some have suggested RHB discourages discernment at his meetings so that no one can figure out the whole thing's a hoax. After noting that the Holy Spirit, the flesh, and the devil will manifest at revival meetings, RHB claims:

> But I'd rather be in a church where the devil and the flesh are manifesting than in a church where nothing is happening because people are too afraid to manifest anything. Every time there is a move of God, a few people will get excited, go overboard, and get in the flesh. The other believers will get upset, saying "That couldn't be God." Don't worry about it. And if a devil manifests, don't worry about that either, Rejoice, because at least *something* is happening![47]

But his statement is not as bad as it may appear. Though that statement is not worded in a tactful way, RHB is attempting to point out that you cannot have a revival without both the flesh and the devil being present. Many leaders from past revivals would agree. When both good and bad manifestations arise in the same church service, these may indicate that the Spirit is at work but the devil is also at work counteracting the

---

[45] Ibid.
[46] Howard-Browne at the Carpenter's Home Church, Lakeland, Florida, 9 Mar. 1993.
[47] Howard-Browne, *The Coming Revival*, 6.

Spirit's move. Nevertheless, RHB does not entirely escape the charge of anti-intellectualism when he writes statements such as: "Don't follow what your head tells you. Don't listen to your head. Your head's gotten you in enough trouble as it is. Follow what God's telling you in your heart."[48] If we are skeptical about Holy Laughter he tells us to apply the Gamaliel principle in Acts 5:38–39: "Refrain from these men, and let them alone: for if this counsel or this work be of men, it will come to naught; but if it be of God, ye cannot overthrow it; lest haply ye be found even to fight against God."

In assessing this principle, however, we must remember that the book of Acts is a descriptive work. It is not meant to be taken in a prescriptive way as are the epistles of Peter or Paul; that is, we should not necessarily follow everything that people say or do in Acts. Should we "cast lots" to determine God's will as the apostles did in Acts 1? Should we wait for tongues of fire to appear over our heads as occurred in Acts 2? Should we argue and go our separate ways as did Paul and Barnabas in Acts 15? In the same way, Gamaliel's statement is not always a good rule to follow when questioning whether something is of God. Time has established the success of many cults and religious groups such as the Jehovah's Witnesses, but contrary to "the Gamaliel principle," this does not mean they are of God.

Against the anti-intellectual counsel to "wait and see," we must affirm that it is godly to use one's ability to discern, even at a church service (cf. Acts 17:11). Yes, Christians should avoid being overly critical, but they should never cast aside discernment in the process. Even RHB admits that devils could manifest themselves at a meeting where God's presence abides. Without discernment, how can we hope to distinguish the false from the genuine?

But let us not overlook the fact that RHB does have convictions about deception. If Christians are overtaken by false doctrine, RHB tells us, they will lose their peace and joy. He teaches against false prophecy, and acknowledges that not all instances of speaking in tongues are of God.[49] He dislikes the spiritual warfare movement which overemphasizes the devil:

[48]Howard-Browne, *Walking in the Perfect Will of God*, 23–24.
[49]Rodney Howard-Browne, *Flowing in the Holy Ghost* (Louisville, Ky.: R.H.B.E.A. Publications, 1991) 17, 27, 37.

"This game of spiritual warfare is nothing more than a spiritual nintendo [sic] game played by baby Christians who have no understanding that Jesus defeated the devil two thousand years ago."[50] He teaches that Christians should not base their beliefs on experiences, but on the Word of God.[51] He admits that sometimes people "get in the flesh" at his meetings: "If someone comes into a meeting, rolls around on the floor, laughs in the Holy Spirit, or does it in the flesh, at least he's not getting drunk or taking dope. We can help him mature in spiritual matters."[52]

## MASTER CHARLATAN OR SIMPLE PENTECOSTAL PREACHER?

Is RHB's motive for discouraging critical observation at his meetings to protect himself from being exposed as a manipulator? I have attended a RHB meeting myself, and I sensed no mass manipulation or mass hypnosis. Frankly, I don't think he is the type to pull off a deception of this magnitude. He is not a dynamic speaker—in fact, I found him rather boring. If RHB were a phony, what would be his motive? He does not habitually beg for money as Marjoe did. We must understand that similarities in style between genuine preachers and some charlatans do not indicate similarities in motive.

Having read page after page of RHB's writings, I have found them riddled with inconsistencies, careless blunders, trite sayings, sloppy doctrine, and misapplied Scriptures. Sloppy? Yes. Shallow? Yes. Masterly deception? No! I'm convinced that RHB is not clever or sophisticated enough to pull off mass hypnotism or mass manipulation. For a parallel, we may consider the argument of the skeptics who, refusing to believe Christ's resurrection, claim that the disciples stole their savior's body. What these skeptics fail to recognize is that these simple fishermen were not psychologically equipped to pull off such a deception. Christ's disciples were not the James Bond type—schooled in the art of deception. Nor is RHB. He is what he claims he is: a simple Pentecostal preacher.

---

[50] Howard-Browne, *The Touch of God: A Practical Workbook*, 41.
[51] Howard-Browne, *Volume 2*, 37.
[52] Howard-Browne, *The Coming Revival*, 8.

What then do we make of his gestures, "trigger words," and other techniques that suggest manipulation? Anyone taking a course in homiletics will find that repeating key words, encouraging audience participation, using hand gestures, and modulating the emotion, pitch, tone, volume, and speed of one's delivery all contribute to persuasive preaching. Are these techniques wrong? If so, why are they taught in virtually all our seminaries? Obviously, few consider them wrong—unless RHB uses them!

I think RHB does realize that some of his gestures, jokes, and words will normally trigger a desired response from the audience. He has preached enough times to know what "works." But how is this any different from a perfectly orthodox preacher who practices his sermon on Saturday night and considers how he will tell a sad story which he anticipates will move his audience tomorrow morning? Despite this small-scale manipulation—if one wishes to call it this—both the orthodox preacher and RHB trust that the Holy Spirit will still move through their message without feeling they have barged in on God's territory.

However, I cannot endorse everything RHB does at his meetings. When he says, "Laugh like this . . . ha ha ha!" or "Fill! Fill! Fill!" as he lays hands on someone, I sometimes feel that he *is* barging in on the Holy Spirit's territory. If God is genuinely visiting his people at such meetings, as RHB believes, then RHB does not need to help him out! Additionally, if the Spirit is really moving, then RHB doesn't need to condition the audience by telling them what is going to happen or how God will touch them. Nevertheless, this error is not as severe as mass deception. Christians wrongly try to help out God all the time.

By all appearances, many people are being touched and saved through RHB's ministry. Whatever one thinks of him, he does not appear to be a mass-hypnotist, a charlatan, or a cultist. Despite his errors and shortcomings, I still consider him my Christian brother, and affirm that his teachings are not so twisted that we could judge the Holy Laughter phenomena as false by virtue of his doctrine.

## THE END-TIME REVIVAL?

A disturbing teaching of RHB that many of his critics overlook centers upon his view of the end times. In his 1991 book

*The Coming Revival* he writes: "In 1980, the Spirit of God said through Rev. Kenneth E. Hagin, a prophet in the United States, that the world is on the verge of a great move and manifestation of the Spirit of God—the greatest hour in the history of the world."[53] RHB believes we are embarking upon the greatest revival the world has ever known. We now are living "in the *last* of the last days."[54] He asserts, "The Last Revival Has Begun! I believe we slipped over the edge into this great outpouring in 1990. . . . The first drops of rain are beginning to fall from the final wave of God's glory!"[55]

RHB calls this revival "the final outpouring of the Holy Spirit," the "final moment," and the "culmination of all other revivals."[56] This revival, he says, will be even greater than that experienced by the apostles on the day of Pentecost.[57] In this "last days revival" the entire body of Christ will be used by God in a special way. The greatest harvest of lost souls will take place; angels will manifest themselves; judgment will come upon the nations; and people who are merely playing church will drop dead like Ananias and Sapphira. Creative miracles will occur in which eyeballs, legs, and arms will form out of nothing.[58]

The children of God will move in the supernatural in an extraordinary way. RHB anticipates, "One of these days a true prophet, anointed of God will be a guest on one of these television talk shows. When they start to mock him, he will simply look at them and say . . . 'you will be blind for three days as a sign to you and this audience.' The talk show host will scream, 'O my God, I can't see! I can't see! I'm blind!' "[59]

This end-time revival prediction is not merely a hopeful speculation of RHB, nor something he believes just because of Kenneth Hagin's prophecy. He himself prophesies of this final outpouring. In his book *The Reality of the Person of the Holy Spirit*, RHB gives two prophecies under two separate "Proph-

[53] Howard-Browne, *The Coming Revival*, 2.

[54] Howard-Browne, *The Reality of the Person of the Holy Spirit*, 25.

[55] Howard-Browne, *The Coming Revival*, back cover.

[56] Ibid., 22, 24; cf. *The Anointing*, 18; *Fresh Oil from Heaven*, (Louisville, Ky.: R.H.B.E.A., 1992) 2, 20–21; *The Touch of God: A Practical Workbook*, 13.

[57] Howard-Browne, *The Reality of the Person of the Holy Spirit*, 11.

[58] Howard-Browne, *The Coming Revival*, 25–27.

[59] Ibid., 27.

ecy" subheadings. A portion of the first one reads, "Drink at the well. For it matters not the things that shall come upon the earth in these last days. It matters not that men's hearts have failed them for the fear of the things that will come in these last days."[60] The second prophecy warns:

> The end of all things is at hand, and the work that must be done must be done quickly. So think not with the natural mind. Do not try to understand and conceive with your natural mind that which I am doing, but allow my Spirit to enter into your heart. . . . You shall rise up in boldness, and you shall be counted among those that shall be used in a powerful way in these last days. Rise up. Lay aside the things of the natural. Lay aside the things of tradition.[61]

RHB also claims: "God once told me, 'There are so many echoes in the world, but I'm going to raise up a voice in this last generation that will not echo the others. They will speak as a voice, as an oracle of God.' "[62] The key word here is the "last generation." God allegedly told Rodney we are living in the final generation. How does RHB understand this in terms of the end times? According to his teaching, the coming revival will be over in about "four or five years," then great persecution will set in and "then Jesus Christ will split the eastern sky" as he returns.[63] If we are now entering into this final revival which will last about five years, and persecution is to follow with the rapture as its end result, then we can expect Christ's return within the next few decades.

Now here's the problem. What scriptural warrant do we have for believing Christ will return in our lifetime? For generations, prophecy buffs have often told their audiences that they were living in the final generation. In his bestseller entitled *Eighty-Eight Reasons Why the Rapture Will Be in 1988,* Edgar Whisenant had many Christians fooled into believing in a 1988 rapture, because that year marked an entire generation (40 years) from 1948—the return of Israel to Palestine.[64]

---

[60]Howard-Browne, *The Reality of the Person of the Holy Spirit,* 21–22.

[61]Ibid., 27–28; cf., idem, *Manifesting the Holy Ghost,* 18–19.

[62]Howard-Browne, *Flowing in the Holy Ghost,* 6.

[63]Howard-Browne, *The Reality of the Person of the Holy Spirit,* 28.

[64]Hal Lindsey also suggested this date in his bestseller *The Late Great Planet Earth* (Grand Rapids: Zondervan, 1970).

Today, many others are still setting or suggesting dates for the second coming. The ominous year 2000 is particularly popular. It is clear, however, that Scripture nowhere teaches that we can know the time of Christ's return. We cannot definitively know he will return in our lifetime.[65] Christ clearly taught that no one knows the time of his return (Matt 24:36; Mark 13:32). We cannot even know the time or season of these events (Acts 1:7). How is it that those who claim we are living in the last generation know what Christ himself did not know?

Anticipating abuses that could arise from this error, RHB writes, "You should live as if Jesus were coming today. Be ready—yet not expect Him for a hundred years. There are too many people saying things like, 'We can't send our children to college because Jesus is coming.' 'We can't get married now because Jesus is coming.' 'We can't buy this house now because Jesus is coming.' "[66] But what makes RHB's prediction unique and—for some—persuasive, is that it is backed up by the claim of prophetic utterance. God himself has allegedly spoken through Rodney that this is the final generation. In other words, RHB's teaching on the proper attitude toward the end times is correct, but this doesn't nullify the fact that, contrary to Scripture, many will think that Christ is returning in another decade or two because of his prophecies.

What if this renewal fizzles out? What if it does become a full-fledged revival, but not the *final* revival before Christ returns? What if severe persecution doesn't follow it? What if severe persecution does come in our life time, but Christ doesn't? I have a feeling many people in this current renewal are headed straight for disappointment and disillusionment. RHB teaches that a person should repent if he or she makes an error regarding an alleged revelation from God.[67] I pray he will do likewise if these predictions don't come to pass.

---

[65] Many date setters try to argue we can know the final generation based on the signs of the end times in Matt 24. I have demonstrated that such signs are perpetual signs given throughout the entire church era. Contrary to certain popular evangelical teachings, earthquakes, famines, pestilences, wars, and so forth are *not* necessarily on the increase. For more information see my book entitled *99 Reasons Why No One Knows When Christ Will Return* (Downers Grove, Ill.: Inter-Varsity Press, 1994).

[66] Howard-Browne, *Fresh Oil from Heaven*, 8.

[67] Howard-Browne, *Flowing in the Holy Ghost*, 17.

# 4

# TAPPING INTO THE ROOTS OF
# THE TORONTO BLESSING

The 1984 vision of Kansas City Fellowship "prophet" Bob Jones goes something like this: The ballroom was full of jubilant company. The festive crowd represented the first "anointing" that would refresh the church. Then civil war broke out. It was the blue coats against the gray. In an October, 1994, service, Toronto Vineyard teacher Wes Campbell added, "James Ryle has had a similar vision. The Lord showed him how the blue coats stand for the revelatory: the revelation, and the gray for gray matter: man's wisdom. And in this context, the north fought the south and the south fought the north, and the south wanted to keep the people enslaved."[1] After the bloody war between these Christians finishes, said Campbell, God will bring in a harvest of one billion souls.

After Wes Campbell discussed this prediction, Stacy Campbell, Wes's wife, prophesied, ". . . but the Lord hates, haaaaates division. . . . But I tell you, nonetheless, that division will come, and it is even now brewing like a leaven in the church. . . . The Lord wants you to purpose in your heart this night, is it God or isn't it, and to stand by your commitment as you are called to stand by your confession of faith."[2]

---

[1]Wes Campbell, 14 Oct. 1994 (Toronto: Airport Vineyard), audio tape.
[2]Ibid.

"The Lord has revealed to many of His prophets that there will soon be a great outpouring of His Spirit. This revival will be greater than all those preceding it,"[3] proclaimed another prophetic voice, from Rick Joyner, in 1988. A great number of prophets and apostles will be raised up with the "spirit of Phineas," who saved God's people from a terrible plague. The fishing net for catching new souls will overflow. Wars will increase in number, and there will even be some limited nuclear exchange among the third world nations. Large mobs of people will destroy everything in their path and extraordinary miracles will mark the day.[4]

These apocalyptic pictures represent predicted events which are reportedly coming to pass through the current renewal. Holy Laughter, say those prophesying, will become the greatest revival that has ever swept the world. The renewal's strange phenomena, such as "roaring as a lion," are considered a prelude to a new dimension of supernatural manifestations. The prophets anticipate a billion new converts, a group of super saints, a "civil war" between Christians who support the revival and those who don't, nuclear war and supernatural powers. To achieve a better understanding of these prophecies we must first step back and explore teachings that have undoubtedly influenced the Toronto Blessing. What are the prophetic roots connected with the Toronto Blessing that nourish and produce these prophetic utterances? The roots include a remnant of teachings from the Kansas City Fellowship, the Manifest Sons of God, the Latter Rain movement, and the Third Wave. Let's uncover these roots.

## KANSAS CITY FELLOWSHIP CONNECTIONS

The 1984 Bob Jones prediction is one of the prophetic cornerstones of the current renewal. Jones held the prominent position of a Kansas City prophet, along with John Paul Jackson and Paul Cain. Under the pastoral leadership of Mike

[3]Lance Lambert, David Minor, Rick Joyner, *He Will Tell You Things to Come* (Fort Lauderdale, Fla.: Derek Prince Ministries International, 1988) 14.
[4]Ibid., 19–21.

Bickle, Kansas City Fellowship (KCF hereafter) flourished in the late 1980s before it submitted to the leadership of John Wimber and transformed into the Metro Vineyard in 1990. Paul Cain is by far the most popular "prophet" from KCF.

## PAUL CAIN: A MODERN DAY PROPHET?

Cain rose to prominence after warning John Wimber to take a more authoritative role regarding holiness in the Vineyard churches. He prophesied that an earthquake would announce his coming to Southern California, and another one would take place when he left. As predicted, an earthquake shook Pasadena on December 3, 1988 when Cain arrived, and a major quake hit Armenia on December 8 when he left.[5]

Who is Paul Cain? At the age of forty-four Cain's pregnant mother, Anna Cain, was dying of tuberculosis when an angel was said to have visited her, telling her she would be healed. She was to name her son "Paul" because his ministry would parallel that of the apostle. The angel said to Anna that the sign of this prophecy would be that she would live to an unusually old age. She died 60 years later at 104.[6]

The 1950s was the decade of the healing movement. Young Cain toured the country when big names such as William Branham, Oral Roberts, Jack Coe, and A. A. Allen dominated that movement. Although Cain was never much of a big name himself, he sometimes substituted for Branham, whom he considered a mighty prophet of God.[7] Before his meetings, Cain would sometimes blindfold himself to avoid distractions as he sought visions and direction from God. His special gift was to employ the "word of knowledge," in which he supernaturally revealed to selected individuals—not knowing them beforehand—their names and problems. When he was engaged to be married, the Lord is said to have told Cain that his fiancee displeased him. Cain made a deal with God—saying

[5]Michael Maudlin, "Seers in the Heartland," *Christianity Today,* 14 Jan. 1991, 21.

[6]David Pytches, *Some Said It Thundered: A Personal Encounter with the Kansas City Prophets* (Nashville: Oliver Nelson/Thomas Nelson, 1991) 19–31; Maudlin, "Seers in the Heartland," 21.

[7]Although Cain considered Branham to be a prophet, he acknowledges that Branham went astray doctrinally in his later years. See "Interview Paul Cain," *Equipping the Saints,* Fall 1990, 9–12.

that if he wanted him celibate, he would have to take away his sexual desire. Cain has been single ever since.

In 1958 Cain became disillusioned with the healing movement "because of the number of ministers who succumbed to pride, competition and immorality."[8] He left the movement and pastored some small churches until he publicly resurfaced again in 1987 when the Lord led him to a "new breed" of Christians—the KCF. God had reportedly told him in 1956 that a new breed of Christians would become a "faceless generation," which would give all glory to God. A unique revival would break forth through them.[9] The "new breed" was also called by Cain "Joel's army." God allegedly declared to Cain, "I am going to take you aside into the desert until a new breed of men is raised up. In the days to come this ministry will be taken forward without superstars."[10]

Cain believes that miracles will continue to increase until the church does "greater works" than that of Jesus (John 14:12). Joel's army will bring Christian unity, purity, and power. Entire hospital wards will be healed and over one billion people will be saved.[11] On November 2, 1992, Cain reports having had a dream that Bill Clinton would win the American presidency. He gave five headlines that would appear on U.S. newspapers before the election. Cain wrote the details in an envelope to Pastor Rick Joyner, post-marked a day before the results. The headlines appeared as written by Cain. Joyner said, "The most amazing and wonderful aspect of this dream was that Paul Cain saw the Lord putting His Spirit upon Bill Clinton and changing him into another man just as he did King Saul in 1 Samuel!"[12]

But Cain has encountered his share of critics who question his prophecies. Post-marked predictions are nothing new even among psychics and scam artists. What would impress people

[8]Paul Thigpen, "How Is God Speaking Today?" *Charisma* Sept. 1989, 52.

[9]Kevin Springer, "Paul Cain: A New Breed of Man," *Equipping the Saints*, Fall 1989, 13; Ras Robinson, "A Modern-Day Prophet: Profile of Paul Cain," *Fullness*, Nov./Dec. 1989, 15.

[10]Pytches, *Some Said it Thundered*, 46, cf. 132.

[11]Maudlin, "Seers in the Heartland," 22.

[12]Paul Cain and Rick Joyner, "The Clinton Administration: Its Meaning and Our Future," *The Morning Star Prophetic Bulletin*, Jan. 1993, 1–2.

more would be if Cain's prediction about Clinton getting filled with the Holy Spirit came to pass—with positive political action resulting. Cain has failed the test of prophetic accuracy on more than one occasion. One such prediction which demonstrably went astray occurred in 1990. An Anaheim Vineyard advertisement for "Revival Fire" (a John Wimber conference in Anaheim beginning January 28–31, 1991) read, "It has been prophesied by Paul Cain that revival will break out in Great Britain in October 1990." John Wimber flew his family to the United Kingdom to await the event. No objective revival took place.[13]

### ERRORS IN KANSAS CITY

According to the Vineyard, modern-day prophecies are not always one hundred percent accurate. Mike Bickle claims that prophecy has three aspects: revelation, interpretation, and application. A person's revelation could be of God, but the person's interpretation or application of that revelation could be wrong. Vineyard advocate Jack Deere gives the example of a prophet who saw a vision of a dark cloud with a dollar sign over a man's head. The prophet wrongly accused the man of financial impropriety, when the Lord was probably trying to reveal that an employee of the man, discovered two weeks after the vision, was extorting finances.[14]

It is pointed out by sympathetic scholars that some aspects of Old Testament teachings, such as the prophetic guidelines found in Deut 18, do not necessarily apply to the New Testament gift of prophecy. Christians today do not live under a theocratic system that stones false prophets. Furthermore, in the New Testament the congregation is exhorted to "judge" prophecies given in the church (1 Cor 14). This may imply that the incidents of false prophecy were high, in contrast to the total accuracy required in Deut 18. Wayne Grudem argues that

---

[13]Nigel Wright, "An Assessment," *Themelios* 17 no. 1 (Oct./Nov. 1991) 20; John Wimber attempted to do damage control by writing that revival comes in stages. The first stage is accompanied by signs and wonders; the second, by unity. Wimber was already claiming that the first stage "was the most prevalent" in 1990—at least three years before the Holy Laughter renewal. See John Wimber, "Revival Fire," *Equipping the Saints,* Winter 1991, 10–13, 21.

[14]Maudlin, "Seers in the Heartland," 19.

the prophet Agabus made a mistake when prophesying about Paul's future captivity under the Romans. Agabus wrongly said it was the Jews, not the Romans, who would bind him (Acts 21:4, 10–11, 33; 22:29).[15] Regardless of the extent to which prophecies must be accurate, no one is willing to claim that modern prophecies are on the same level as inspired Scripture.

One stated value of the Vineyard is "risk taking" that allows trial and error: "so we are willing to be patient with people's weaknesses and failures while they learn."[16] A number of prophecies by modern day "prophets" have not come to pass. Bob Jones is said to have had only a 65% success rate. Other prophets are said to have been only 10% successful, with the most mature reaching only 85% to 95% accuracy.[17] Biblically, when someone claims to be speaking a message from the Lord, if what he or she proclaims does not come to pass then this is considered false prophecy (Deut 18:20–22; Jer 14:14; 28:16–17; 29:23; Zech 13:3). Finally, no matter how one understands New Testament prophecy, false prophecy should not be taken lightly. Those who have been around for any length of time in Pentecostal and charismatic circles have seen enough examples of personal prophecies gone wrong to realize that such erroneous utterances can absolutely devastate the lives of those over whom modern-day "prophets" prophesy.

Clearly, if a prophecy is found in error, the one who spoke it needs to repent. When such a one refuses to repent or tries to justify a false prediction, I have no qualms about calling such an individual a false prophet. Moreover, it is not enough simply to ask forgiveness every time one prophesies amiss. Constant prophetic failure indicates that one does not really have a gift of prophecy. The gift of prophecy was given for

---

[15]Grudem, *Systematic Theology*, 1052–53. The entire incident in Acts 21–22 is difficult to interpret. Grudem's arguments are certainly plausible. Others, however, have pointed out that while it is true that the Romans were the instrumental cause, it was the Jews who were the efficient cause of Paul's binding. They brought about the whole circumstance. Thus, Agabus' prophecy, though imprecise, was nevertheless true.

[16]"Anaheim Vineyard Christian Fellowship," Agenda leaflet for 9 July 1995, n.p.

[17]Rick Joyner, "The Prophetic Ministry," *The Morning Star Prophetic Newsletter*, 3 no. 2, n.d., 4. Cited in Robert Hunter, "The Vineyard Movement's Toronto Blessing: Instrument of Revival or Instrument of Deception?" (Internet hunter44@flexnet.com., n.d.), 7.

edification, exhortation, and comfort (1 Cor 14:2). Also, regardless of the accuracy of an individual's prophetic record, if any person teaches false doctrine, that one is a false prophet (Deut 13; Gal 1:8–9; 2 Cor 11). Also, if someone is immoral or abusive, that person should not be permitted to prophesy (cf. Matt 7:21–23).

Fed up with the false predictions, mysticism, and erroneous teachings of KCF, Ernie Gruen, pastor of Full Faith Church of Love in Kansas City, preached a message to his church entitled "Do We Keep Smiling and Say Nothing?" accusing KCF of false prophecy and misconduct.[18] In a 233-page exposé entitled "Documentation of the Aberrant Practices and Teachings of Kansas City Fellowship," Gruen documented the bizarre visions (normally five to ten per night) of Bob Jones; the "elect seed" and "new order" teaching of Mike Bickle that promoted elitism; and other strange teachings, visions, and prophetic abuses.[19]

Shortly thereafter, in the early summer of 1990, Mike Bickle placed his 3,000 member church under the wing of John Wimber and the Vineyard. Bickle confessed some mistakes in his ministry and Wimber sought to reconcile Gruen and Bickle. A list of fifteen errors were acknowledged by KCF, including a lack of accountability for prophecies that do not come to pass, the establishment of doctrine on revelation without biblical support, the use of prophecy to gain control over others, and an attitude of superiority over others.[20]

Gruen retracted the testimonies he had acquired from disgruntled former KCF members, accusing Paul Cain of false doctrine and occultism, and promoting one undocumented account of a baby dying because the mother refused to put the infant in a hospital due to a personal prophecy she received from the KCF. John Wimber responded to some of the other charges made by Gruen, but he failed to address them all.[21]

---

[18]Lee Grady, "Resolving the Kansas City Prophecy Controversy," *Ministries Today,* Sept./Oct. 1990, 50.

[19]Ernest Gruen, 10, 12–21, 89; Roy Rivenburg, "A Question of Faith," *Los Angeles Times (Orange County ed.)* 28 Jan. 1992, E8.

[20]Clifford Hill, "Kansas City Update," *Prophecy Today* 6 no. 5, n.d., 6.

[21]John Wimber, "A Response," *Equipping the Saints,* Fall 1990, 4–7, 13–14. Jim Beverley argues that Wimber's response was faulty. See Beverley, *Holy Laughter,* 124–26. Kansas City Fellowship was renamed the Metro Vineyard. In 1991 the Vineyard disciplined Bob Jones after he

Mike Bickle did the right thing by making KCF accountable to other Christians. Unfortunately, prophecies about the super-Christian "Joel's army" are still circulating. And we still must ask: What exactly does Paul Cain mean by Joel's army and a "new breed" of Christians apparently coming forth out of the current renewal? What do we do with Bob Jones's last day church consisting of our children that will be called "the bride"?[22] How do such teachings escape charges of elitism? The Vineyard has not entirely weeded out the troublesome roots of KCF. The roots seem to go even deeper when we compare KCF elitism with the Latter Rain movement from Saskatchewan, Canada, in the late 1940s.

## ABERRANT TEACHINGS FROM THE LATTER RAIN MOVEMENT

The first generation of Pentecostals had all but died out by 1947, and frustrated Pentecostals in Canada wanted renewal. In November of that year, a group of 70 students at Sharon Orphanage and Schools in North Battleford, Saskatchewan, fasted and prayed. Three months later, beginning February 12, 1948, the Spirit fell on believers. George and Ern Hawtin, Percy G. Hunt, Herrick Holt, and Milford Kirkpatrick were at the forefront of the new outpouring, in which students fell to the ground "slain in the Spirit," and spiritual gifts were received by those who were prayed over.[23]

The movement which developed out of these events soon became characterized by the doctrine of restorationism or "Latter Rain." Originally popularized during the Holiness and Pentecostal revivals, the Latter Rain teaching centered on the prophecy in the book of Joel (2:23) that predicted a blessing from God in the form of "former" and "latter" rains. They

---

fell into sexual misconduct, and as of May 1993 Gruen and Bickle have reconciled, having "forgiven each other of all offenses" ("Kansas City Feud Declared Dead," *Christianity Today*, 19 July 1993, 51).

[22] See Stephen Cannon, "Old Wine in Old Wineskins: A Look at Kansas City Fellowship," *The Quarterly Journal: Personal Freedom Outreach* 10 no. 4 (Oct-Dec. 1990), p. 9.

[23] Richard M. Riss, *A Survey of Twentieth-Century Revival Movements in North America* (Peabody: Hendrickson, 1988) 112.

interpreted these "rains" as the moving of the Holy Spirit. The first outpouring was taken to have occurred on the day of Pentecost, as recorded in Acts 2. The Saskatchewan or Sharon revival was taken as the second or "latter" rain.

Restorationism involves the belief that the end-time church will emerge as a spotless bride, led by end-time apostles who will prepare the way for Christ's second coming. The restorationists see church history in terms of a circular motion. The church once, in the New Testament era, operated with signs and wonders, but it declined, reaching its low point during the Middle Ages. It is now reemerging through the signs and wonders experienced in the Pentecostal and charismatic movements—making a complete revolution.[24] Restorationists thus expect the apostolic signs and wonders of the first century to reemerge, or to be surpassed by those performed by a group of end-time apostles and prophets. The goal of the Latter Rain movement is to become the bride of Christ. Thomas Holdcroft writes: "In conclusion, it can be said that the New Order's goal of a glorious church without spot and wrinkle is indeed a worthy goal. Though we may not agree that the pathway leads us via North Battleford, we certainly agree on our destination."[25]

Abuses pervaded the new movement, and this prompted the Assemblies of God to expose the errors present at the Sharon "revival." In 1949 the General Council listed six errors:

---

[24]Martin Luther started the upward trend through justification, John Wesley advanced it further through inner assurance, but through the Pentecostal movement the historical circle has now almost reached a complete revolution.

[25]Thomas Holdcroft, "The New Order of the Latter Rain," *Pneuma* 2 no. 2 (Fall 1980) 58. George Warnock's *The Feast of Tabernacles* added more prophetic anticipation to the movement by teaching that although the outpouring of Pentecost was fulfilled in Acts 2, we had yet to see another great outpouring of the Spirit during the Feast of Tabernacles. Current restorationists often believe in postmillennialism—the positive end-time belief that the world will be Christianized before the return of Christ. Hence, the "kingdom now" teachings of Earl Paulk and others are often connected with restorationism and the Latter Rain movement. For a critique of "kingdom now" teachings, consult Robert Bowman with Craig Hawkins and Dan Schlesinger, "The Gospel According to Paulk: A Critique of Kingdom Theology, Part One," *Christian Research Journal* 10 no. 3 (Winter/Spring 1988) 9–14; "Part Two," *Christian Research Journal* 11 no. 1 (Summer 1988) 15–20.

1. The overemphasis on imparting spiritual gifts through the laying on of hands and prophecy.
2. The belief that modern-day apostles and prophets are the foundation of the Church.
3. The "new order" teaching on confession of sin and deliverance to man "which claims prerogatives to human agency which belong only to Christ."
4. The impartation of the gift of languages for missionary service.
5. Imposing personal leadings through prophetic utterances.
6. Distorting the interpretation of Scripture.[26]

Many of these themes are still found in varying degrees in many independent charismatic churches. Certain Holy Laughter leaders, such as Terry Virgo, Bryn Jones, and Gerald Coates, have past ties with Latter Rain teachings.[27]

---

[26]William W. Menzies, *Anointed to Serve: The Story of the Assemblies of God* (Springfield, Mo.: Gospel Publishing House, 1971) 325; Richard M. Riss, *Latter Rain* (Mississauga, Ont./Etobicoke, Ont.: Honeycomb Visual Productions, Ltd. Kingdom Flagships Foundation, 1987) 119.

[27]Nigel Wright, "Restoration and the 'House Church' Movement," *Themelios* 16 no. 2 (Jan./Feb. 1991) 4–8. William Branham also left deep impressions upon the Sharon group in 1947 through his healing ministry in Vancouver, B.C. Many still consider him a prophet even though he denied the Trinity and made false predictions that the millennium would begin in 1977, as well as a "Thus Saith the Lord" prophecy that Los Angeles would sink into the ocean. Branham also taught that the mark of the beast was denominationalism. He thus called people out of the "antichristian" creeds of orthodoxy. He taught, based on Revelation 2–3, that the church has gone through seven church ages, the last ending with Branham as the end-time messenger for the "lukewarm" Laodicean church. The Bridal age began after February 28, 1963, when the sign of a strange cloud ring hovered over the Northern Arizona sky. Branham built a clear case of Christian elitism through his various teachings. He also taught the "serpent seed" doctrine, namely that Eve had sex with the serpent in the garden of Eden, and that the offspring of this perversion was Cain, with the descendants of Cain being the intellectuals and scientists of this day. Branham made a distinction between two types of people—non-intellectuals and intellectuals, non-creedal Christians and creedal Christians. Similarly, some leaders in the Latter Rain movement considered organized churches as "Mystery Babylon," the Whore of Revelation 17–18 that is still under "denominational bondage." More recently, Bill Hamon made a distinction between three classes of Christians: (1) Those who speak in tongues; (2) those who speak in tongues but are still involved in a denomination; and (3) those who don't speak in tongues. For documentation, see Richard M. Riss, "The Latter Rain Movement of 1948," *Pneuma* 4 no. 1 (Spring, 1982) 34; William Branham, *An Exposition of the Seven Church*

Christian elitism blatantly appeared through the doctrine of the "manifest sons of God." This Latter Rain teaching, conceived through a vision during the 1948–49 "revival," taught that only those connected with the Sharon group could become part of this elite last days group.[28] The manifest sons of God teaching holds that at some future point during the final tribulation, but prior to Christ's second coming, the saints will become perfected both spiritually and morally. These "super saints" are often interpreted as the 144,000 in Rev 7 and 14 and the male-child of Rev 12.[29] This new class of Christians will lead the final evangelistic thrust and perform great signs and wonders. One can easily see the similarities between this and Paul Cain's and Metro Vineyard's "Joel's army" or "new breed."[30]

## ELITISM AND THE MANIFEST SONS OF GOD

The idea of an end-time "new breed" of Christians perpetuates elitism by inescapably implying that those who do

---

*Ages* (Jeffersonville, Ind.: Spoken Word Ministry, n.d.) 322; idem, *The Spoken Word: The Rapture* (Jeffersonville, Ind.: Spoken Word Publications, reprint 1985) 39, cited in Michael Moriarty, *The New Charismatics: A Concerned Voice Responds to Dangerous New Trends* (Grand Rapids: Zondervan, 1992) 63; C. Douglas Weaver, *The Healer-Prophet William Marrion Branham* (Macon: Mercer University Press, 1987) 113; David Graham, *The Doctrine of Sonship* (Springfield, Mo.: Bill Britton, n.d.) 4.

[28] Riss, *Latter Rain*, 95–96.

[29] Latter Rain teachers normally argue that the male-child in Rev 12 cannot refer to Christ or the Christian church because every event from Rev 4:1 onward depicts the future, not the past. While this is *generally* true, the prophecies in Rev 4 to 22 do not preclude the past or present. Hence, allusion to Caesar Nero in Rev 13 and depictions of old Babylon and contemporary Rome in Rev 18 are fairly clear. In fact, the three and one-half years in Rev 12 easily fit into the Jewish war with Rome from A.D. 67 to 70. The male-child in Rev 12 would thus represent Christ while the woman would represent the messianic community. Unlike the preterist, however, I am not saying that these past events exhaust the meanings of such passages. I still believe there are future elements to these prophecies, but we will not understand their full meaning until the fulfillment of the end times takes place. Instead of understanding the 144,000 in Rev 7 and 14 as a number symbolically representing the entire church, those who are influenced by the Latter Rain tell us this is an elite Christian group.

[30] However, Paul Cain denies that he teaches the manifest sons of God doctrine. See *Equipping the Saints*, Fall 1990, 9–12.

not participate in the current renewal, or the signs and wonders movement, are second-class Christians—although few in
the renewal would admit this.

Is there any biblical basis for belief in an elite class of
Christians in the end times, be they "manifest sons of God,"
"Joel's army," or a "new breed"? Highly speculative interpretations of passages taken to refer to the manifest sons of
God—such as Rom 8:19–23, Rev 7, and Rev 12:1–5—get us nowhere.[31] At best, such passages demonstrate only that teachers of Christian elitism have built their doctrine on unclear
and speculative scriptures instead of on clear ones. Virtually
every false doctrine finds a hearing this way. If the clear teachings of Scripture don't support your view, go to the unclear
ones and give them esoteric meaning.

More importantly, one must first demonstrate that we are
living in the end-times for these prophecies to pertain to our
time. On what basis can we demonstrate this? Simply believing this is the final generation does not make it so. And how
can one support the veracity of prophetic utterances by declaring that these are the end times, when Christ already
warned that it is not for us to know when the restoration
will take place (Acts 1:6–7; cf. Matt 24:36)? It is certainly possible that a final, end-time revival will take place, but Scripture shows us that it is not possible for us to know that this
current renewal, even if it becomes a great revival, is *that
final revival.*

The "greater works" than Christ that Christians will do in
John 14:12 are only possible because Jesus went "to the Father." If we compare this phrase to John 7:39 and 16:7 the
meaning is evident. It was expedient that Christ depart so that
the Holy Spirit might come to empower the disciples with
greater "works" than Jesus. But these works have little to do
with signs and wonders. The disciples' works were greater
than Christ's because they proclaimed the salvation message
of Christ's atonement and resurrection which was not possible
before Christ's death. Also, we should not overlook the quanti-
tative aspect of Christ's promise. Christ was one, the disciples
were many. With the help of the Holy Spirit, their preaching

---

[31] Romans 8 may actually refute the manifest sons of God doctrine
by indicating that the children of God will not be completely renovated
until the entire creation is renovated.

could reach many more people than Christ ever reached, as the salvation of 3,000 on Pentecost demonstrates (Acts 2).

## JOEL'S LATTER RAIN: FUTURE OR FULFILLED?

Does Joel 2:28–32 or Acts 2:17–23 teach an end-time revival of unprecedented signs and wonders? In Joel 2:1–27, the prophet predicts a future day when a northern enemy would attack Israel. This is called the "great" day of the LORD (2:11). Although the "locusts" of Rev 9 also appear in this passage, the primary intent of Joel 2:1–27 was fulfilled when the northern armies of Assyria and Babylon devastated Israel (most likely c. 587 B.C. [Babylonian invasion]) No invasion like this had ever happened before or would ever happen again (Joel 2:2).[32]

Yet there is a promise in all this. If the Israelites would repent, God would never again let the nations devastate them (Joel 2:15–19). He would prosper them by sending the "early" and "latter" rains. In other words, God would supply them with an abundant harvest of food by sending them "both the autumn and spring rains" (Joel 2:23 NIV). Once we understand the context of this passage, we see the incredible stretch of imagination one must exercise to get this passage to mean a final outpouring of the Spirit upon Christians during the end times.

On the day of Pentecost, Joel 2:28–32 was fulfilled as recorded in Acts 2:17–23. The "last days" Peter mentions are the very days in which the apostles lived, not the end times. The "last days" indicates the entire church era from the ascension of Christ to the present day, not the merely the coming end

---

[32]This great invasion is not referring to the final army in the "great tribulation," nor to a prophetic Christian army. The phrase "none like it before or after" is a Hebrew idiom for *any* great trial or invasion—not literally *the* greatest or worst—as seen by its use when comparing Joel 2:2 and 1:2 with Exod 10:14 and Matt 24:21. (The "great tribulation" in Matt 24 was primarily fulfilled in A.D. 70. The last days signs in Matt 24 have been witnessed by virtually every Christian generation from the first century until now. The "abomination of desolation" in Matt 24:15ff. is not necessarily the antichrist, but it refers to events surrounding the destruction of the temple in A.D. 70 by Rome [cf. Luke 21:20ff.]. Apart from the passages that mention Christ's second coming, Matt 24 has only secondary implications to the final tribulation. For further study on these issues see my book, *99 Reasons,* 87–93; cf. 28–29, 72–85, 180.)

times (cf. 1 Cor 10:11; Phil 4:5; Heb 1:2; 2 Pet 3:3–4; 1 John 2:18).[33] Peter's original intent in Acts 2:17–23 was to convey not a *future* prophecy, but the *fulfillment* of an old one. Joel's prophecy of the Spirit's outpouring upon the sons and daughters—bestowed with prophetic utterances, dreams and visions—occurred on the day of Pentecost. The "wonders in heaven above, and signs on the earth" along with the "fire" and "smoke" probably alludes to the wind of the Spirit that came "from heaven" and the immediate miraculous results of the tongues of fire and the speaking in different languages at Pentecost (Acts 2:1–13).

The "sun and moon" darkened before the coming day of the Lord can refer to the sun becoming dark at Christ's crucifixion.[34] F. F. Bruce writes:

> It was little more than seven weeks since the people in Jerusalem had indeed seen the sun turned into darkness, during the early afternoon of the day of our Lord's crucifixion. And on the same afternoon the paschal full moon may well have appeared blood-red in the sky in consequence of the preternatural gloom. These were to be understood as tokens of the advent of the day of the Lord, "that great and notable day," a day of judgement, to be sure, but more immediately the day of God's salvation to all who invoked His name.[35]

Peter's citation from Joel reaches its climax in Acts 2:21. What does this all mean? Why the tongues? Why the signs and wonders? Peter answers: "And everyone who calls on the name of the Lord shall be saved." In order to keep Peter's use of Joel's prophecy consistent, those who relate this passage to the end

---

[33] The phrases "in those days" and "at that time" of Joel 3:1 (cf. Mark 13:24) conjoin the entire church era (cf. Joel 2:29) from Acts 2 to future end-time events. Unlike Joel 1 and 2, Joel 3 (except for verses 4–8) appears futuristic. Joel 3:9–21 may depict the Battle of Armageddon (Rev 19) or the Battle with Gog and Magog (Ezek 38–39; Rev 20). We can see the progression of captivities and oppressors in the Book of Joel: Assyria (ch. 1—fulfilled c. 722 B.C.), Babylon (ch. 2—fulfilled c. 587 B.C.), Rome (ch. 3:1–3—fulfilled A.D. 70), and Gog or the nations (3:9–21— fulfilled in the future).

[34] The darkening of the constellations appears in Joel 2:31 and again in v. 10 and 3:15. The "Day of the Lord" appears in Joel 1:15, 2:11, and 3:14. When God brings a great judgment, these prophetic themes often recur. Clearly, they are not exclusive to the coming final tribulation.

[35] F. F. Bruce, *The Book of the Acts* (NIC; Grand Rapids: Eerdmans, 1986) 69.

times should interpret verse 21 as futuristic. However, if this passage finds its fulfilment only in the future, then no one can call on the name of the Lord and be saved until the end times! Of course, this would contradict the basic message of salvation (cf. Rom 10:9–13). Such exegetical gymnastics are unnecessary when we properly interpret Acts 2:17–21 as entirely fulfilled on the day of Pentecost, with its results continuing throughout the church era.

## VINEYARD AND THIRD WAVE DISTINCTIVES

The birth of the Third Wave movement came by way of the Fuller Evangelistic Association in Pasadena, California. In 1975 Fuller Seminary professor of church growth C. Peter Wagner invited John Wimber, then with the Yorba Linda Friends' Church, to work with him at the school. Then in 1977, shortly after Wimber's wife Carol awoke from a dream speaking in tongues, Wimber, who was struggling with charismatic issues, became an advocate for the gifts of the Spirit.[36]

That same year Wimber encouraged altar calls for divine healing at his services. This came after a period of bewilderment and disgust at the lack of authentic spiritual power he saw in the churches as a church growth consultant for Fuller Theological Seminary. He recalls those days: "There was a lot of action that was called the work of the Holy Spirit, but it was nothing more than human effort in which the Holy Spirit was asked to tag along."[37] After ten months of seeking but experiencing nothing, Wimber and Wagner saw the first healing take place (a young woman was healed of fever), and from this small beginning Vineyard theology flourished. From 1982 to 1986, Wimber and Wagner hosted course MC510: "Signs and Wonders," in which students could experiment with the supernatural gifts of the Spirit, to the Fuller faculty's dismay.

---

[36]David L. Smith, *A Handbook of Contemporary Theology* (Wheaton: Bridgepoint/Victor, 1992) 227–40; C. Peter Wagner, "Wimber, John," in *Dictionary of Pentecostal and Charismatic Movements*, ed. Burgess and McGee, 889.

[37]Tim Stafford, "Testing the Wine from John Wimber's Vineyard," *Christianity Today*, 8 Aug. 1986, 19.

Over 800 students attended the classes, breaking all prior enrollment records.[38]

C. Peter Wagner contrasts the Third Wave with two previous moves of the Holy Spirit. The first wave birthed Pentecostalism in the first decade of the twentieth century. The second wave occurred in the 1960s with the charismatic movement. The Third Wave is the current signs and wonders movement. Contrary to both charismatics and Pentecostals, the Third Wave movement considers the baptism in the Holy Spirit not as a second act of grace, but as something that occurs at conversion (1 Cor 12:13). Afterward, subsequent fillings in the Holy Spirit mark a dedicated Christian's walk.[39] Also, speaking in tongues is not necessarily included in the package. According to researcher David Barrett, as of 1987 an estimated twenty-seven million people are considered Third Wave Christians.[40]

Ken Sarles notes a Third Wave paradox:

> For the first time in American religious history a noncharismatic segment of conservative evangelicalism has adopted a charismatic view of signs and wonders without accepting the charismatic label. This astounding turn of events has created both a confusion of categories and a sense of consternation among noncharismatic evangelicals who are not part of the signs and wonders movement.[41]

At least two other aspects of the Third Wave have recently become sources of conflict due to the events at the Toronto renewal. First, the Third Wave teaches that ministering under the power of the Holy Spirit in and of itself is the "porthole of entrance into the Third Wave rather than a spiritual experience as is typical of the first two waves."[42] Does this still hold true, given the spiritual experiences Third Wavers enjoy through the Toronto Blessing? Second, the Third Wave has sought to avoid division at all costs: "Compromises in areas

---

[38] Donald Kamner, "The Perplexing Power of John Wimber's Power Encounters," *Churchman* 106 no. 1 (1992) 47.

[39] Kevin Springer, "The Third Wave," *Faith and Renewal,* Jan./Feb. 1994, 13.

[40] C. Peter Wagner, *The Third Wave of the Holy Spirit* (Ann Arbor: Vine Books/Servant, 1988) 13.

[41] Ken L. Sarles, "An Appraisal of the Signs and Wonders Movement," *Bibliotheca Sacra* 145 no. 577 (Jan.–Mar. 1988) 64.

[42] C. Peter Wagner, "Third Wave" in *Dictionary of Pentecostal and Charismatic Movements,* ed. Burgess and McGee, 843–44.

such as raising of hands in worship, public tongues, methods of prayer for the sick and others is cordially accepted in order to maintain harmony with those not in the Third Wave."[43] The Toronto Blessing, however, has offended many with its bizarre behavior. Have Third Wave participants sought to compromise by curtailing their Holy Laughter experiences for the sake of "weaker" brethren?

Nevertheless, a distinction should be made between the Third Wave movement as a whole and the Vineyard churches as a denomination. Not necessarily everything the two groups believe equally applies to both. John Wimber may not adhere to everything C. Peter Wagner teaches. Moreover, what individual Vineyard pastors teach may not always be in total agreement with what the Vineyard as a denomination teaches.

### POWER ENCOUNTERS

Vineyard theology leans much upon the writings of the late Fuller Theological professor George Eldon Ladd. Ladd described the kingdom of God not merely in terms of preaching the gospel, but also in terms of the superiority of the heavenly kingdom over the dark kingdom of Satan.[44] One of the values listed in the Vineyard's statement of faith reads: "We value the Kingdom of God. We aim to move in the signs of the present fulfillment of the kingdom, invoking the Spirit's powerful presence, ministering through the Spirit's gifts, and seeing God heal and work wonders (Mark 1:14, 15)."[45] Spiritual warfare often includes "binding" territorial spirits that oppress entire cities and casting out devils from "demonized" Christians.[46] The Vineyard rightly observes that Christ and the

---

[43]Ibid.

[44]John Wimber and Kevin Springer, *Power Evangelism* (San Francisco: HarperSanFrancisco, 1985; Rev. and exp. 1992) 29–32.

[45]Association of Vineyard Churches, "Theological and Philosophical Statements" (Anaheim: Vineyard Christian Fellowship, April 1994; revised) n.p.

[46]Thomas D. Pratt, "The Need to Dialogue: A Review of the Debate on the Controversy of Signs, Wonders, Miracles and Spiritual Warfare Raised in the Literature of the Third Wave Movement," *Pneuma* 13 no. 1 (Spring 1991) 13. For a critique on the excesses of spiritual warfare, consult Eric Villanueva, "Territorial Spirits and Spiritual Warfare: A Biblical Perspective," *Christian Research Journal* 15 no. 1 (Summer 1992) 38–39.

apostles supported their words by a demonstration of the power of God through miracles and exorcisms. They wrongly, however, build a case for Christian demonization when Scripture does not support this view.[47]

Westernized Christians must strip themselves of their secular and rationalistic worldview and once again embrace the reality of the supernatural spiritual realm as did the early Christians. Power encounters with the forces of darkness are the thrust behind Wimber's bestsellers *Power Evangelism* and *Power Healing.* Journalist Tim Stafford writes, "Wimber's essential message is 'We can do what Jesus did.' In fact, he reads it as a command: We *must* do what Jesus did."[48]

## PENETRATING THE THIRD WAVE

Fuller Seminary dropped the Signs and Wonders class in 1986. The seminary's faculty listed the following concerns in relation to their termination of the class:[49]

---

[47]For a critique on Christian demonization, consult Brent Grimsley and Elliot Miller, "Can a Christian Be Demonized?" *Christian Research Journal* 16 no. 1 (Summer 1993) 16–19, 37–38. As an active teacher and worker for Victory Outreach, I have personally seen many lives changed by the power of God. And these converts are not from average non-Christian American families. Victory Outreach specializes in reaching drug addicts, prisoners, gang members, prostitutes, homosexuals, and other hard-to-reach peoples. In all my years ministering there I have yet to see one person, having totally surrendered his or her life to Christ, who needed an exorcism because they were "demonized." You would expect that if there were such a thing as Christian demonization, these people—who know first hand what it is to experience the attacks and depravities of Satan—would need deliverance. Indeed, some do, but their deliverance takes place at their conversion. Perhaps no Christian deliverances would need to take place if repentance and a turning away from one's sin were rightly stressed at one's conversion.

[48]Stafford, "Testing the Wine," 18.

[49]Ben Patterson, "Cause for Concern," *Christianity Today,* 8 Aug. 1986, 20. Other criticisms come from Reformed minister Michael Horton, who edited a work entitled *Power Religion: The Selling Out of the Evangelical Church?* in which several chapters criticize the Vineyard's concept of power religion. Wayne Grudem, professor of theology at Trinity Evangelical Divinity School, responded to the articles in Horton's book by writing a paper entitled *Power and Truth: A Response to Power Evangelism* (Vineyard Position Paper Number 4; Anaheim: The Association of Vineyard Churches, 1993).

1. An overemphasis on the supernatural and extraordinary sets up a false dichotomy with, and prejudice against, the providential work of God through the natural and ordinary.

2. When people see power evangelism as the norm for Christian evangelism, they too easily fall prey to the error of elitism. Christians exercising the signs and wonders gifts may easily slight the evangelistic moves in past revivals that did not emphasize the supernatural.

3. Miraculous healings, particularly those in the area of deliverance, are almost magical in formulation, depending on certain words or phrases or on knowledge of the demon's name for deliverance.

4. When health and spiritual warfare are emphasized, ethics are often de-emphasized. The biblical pattern, however, values the fruit of the Spirit above the gifts of the Spirit (cf. Gal 5:22–23).

5. A feeling that Satan has "won" when a soul is not healed or delivered can be all too common; also, miraculous reports are wild and unsubstantiated.

One faculty member described the signs and wonders theology as a type of "lottery Christianity" where "there must be a few big winners—spectacular healings—and many $10 winners—cured headaches—in order to attract a crowd."[50] Others outside the Fuller faculty have also voiced their criticisms. J. I. Packer said:

> In saying that "power evangelism" is normative, do they realize they are saying that the evangelism of John Wesley, D. L. Moody, Billy Sunday, and Billy Graham is sub-biblical? . . . Christ enables us to be more than conquerors under pressure. We seek the strength to cope with divinely permitted circumstances. There are many of us for whom the role model is Joni Eareckson rather than John Wimber. We see the powers of the kingdom operating, but mainly in regeneration, sanctification, the Spirit as a comforter, the transformation of the inner life, rather than in physical miracles which just by happening prevent much of that other kingdom activity whereby people learn to live with their difficulties and glorify God.[51]

Still, the kind of emphasis on divine healing we find in the Third Wave and Vineyard movements bears little resemblance

---

[50] Stafford, "Testing the Wine," 21.
[51] Ibid., 22.

to that found in the Word Faith movement. Wimber admits
that not everyone gets healed, and that this is not necessarily
due to anyone's sin or a lack of faith. He even admits that there
are "very few" extraordinary healings that would parallel the
New Testament accounts.[52] But how then does he reconcile
this with his emphasis that Christians can do "greater works"
than Christ? Beliefs seem to be speaking louder than actions.
Ironically, this is also happening in the area of power evangelism. As Vineyard leader Todd Hunter shared, "actually for the
most part, most Vineyard people have not been sharing their
faith very much over the last 5 to 8 years."[53] A lack of any great
influx of new converts is one of the main reasons the Vineyard
is officially reluctant to call the current renewal a genuine
revival. Although we currently see an increasing number of
unbelievers getting saved through the renewal, until now most
of those who have experienced the "signs and wonders" already believe.

If the Vineyard rightly notices that many power encounters occurred when Jesus and the disciples proclaimed the
good news to the lost, why doesn't the Vineyard emphatically
follow the same practice? Namely, let's see more healings *out
on the street, out on the mission field,* and not merely in the
church house. Let's see deliverance performed on unbelievers,
not believers!

Nevertheless, none of the Vineyard's teachings are heretical. It holds to solid evangelical doctrines and values. We
cannot discredit the Toronto Blessing as false via Vineyard
doctrine. Generally speaking, we should not attempt to "res-
cue" people from this church as some do to those in Word
Faith churches.

There is much we can commend about the Vineyard.
Loving, vibrant Christians grace the movement—Christians
whose main desire is to please God. The Vineyard has also
sought to deal with many of the criticisms I have mentioned.
Recently, I attended an renewal meeting at Anaheim where
the speaker stressed repentance and evangelism. I commend
such preaching. Let's see more of the same on a consistent
basis.

---

[52] Ibid., 20.
[53] Todd Hunter, "Revival in Focus," 23 Oct. 1994 (Mission Viejo,
Calif.: Vineyard Fellowship), audio tape.

God is using the Vineyard Fellowship in unique ways, despite its excesses. Like the Holy Laughter renewal, the Vineyard churches are anything but monolithic—some are more balanced than others. A few even refrain from participating in the renewal. One of the best ways, then, to evaluate the Vineyard is by letting those who are in the Vineyard critique it themselves. Wayne Grudem, himself a Vineyard member, has candidly written on some areas in which the Vineyard's teaching and practice warrant improvement. He points out the following weaknesses:[54]

1. It needs more mature Bible teachers.

2. It needs to warn its members more against "the excesses of subjective guidance."

3. It needs to teach a more thorough doctrine of sanctification.

4. It needs more accountability among the ministers.

5. It needs more appreciation for older Christian traditions.

6. It needs to build better relationships with other denominations.

Grudem also notes that many of the Vineyard's weaknesses could be overcome by establishing better communication with other evangelicals. Sadly, some evangelicals have criticized the movement in an unfair manner. This only discourages open communication.

In summary, the Vineyard rightly addresses the error of a lack of authentic spiritual power in this era. They stress a return to the supernatural manifestations of the first century. However, when trying to offset a lopsided aspect of the church, one has the tendency of going to the opposite extreme. Charismatics and noncharismatics alike often set doctrine, intellect, and the word of God on one end of the spectrum, and experience, faith, and supernatural power on the other. This bifurcation must end.

If Wimber overemphasizes signs and wonders, many of his critics ignore or even discourage a Christianity that moves in power and spiritual gifts. Both sides have pointed out perfectly legitimate problems currently facing the Christian

---

[54]Grudem, *Power and Truth*, 62–63.

church: on one end of the spectrum we lack doctrinal discernment, on the other we lack spiritual power. A third problem is
this: both sides often wrongly see the other side as the one that
is woefully deficient or the source of the problem. Evangelical
Christianity often lacks both doctrinal discernment *and* power.
Thus we need both a reformation *and* a revival. And until we
combine instead of opposing the two, we will not see either
side reach its full potential.

Power with little intellect may have appeared effective in
some past revivals, but that does not make such an imbalance
right, nor does it mean we should follow the same example. The
world has changed; culture has changed; values have changed.
In the same way, doctrinal reform with little supernatural power
may have borne fruit during the Reformation, but we are post-
Reformation believers who face a new barrage from our Enemy.
What was sufficient then may not necessarily be sufficient now.
It is time for revival and reformation to unite!

Christ's great intercessory prayer in John 17 did not side
with either revival or reformation. It centered upon unity: "My
prayer is not for them alone. I pray also for those who will
believe in me through their message, that all of them may be
one, Father, just as you are in me and I am in you. May they
also be in us so that the world may believe that you have sent
me" (John 17:20–21).

Now that we have explored some roots of the renewal—the
Kansas City Fellowship, the Latter Rain movement, the Manifest
Sons of God, and the Third Wave, let us head back to Toronto.

## TORONTO PROPHECIES: A GREAT REVIVAL, A GREAT DIVISION, A GREAT PERSECUTION

The goal of those involved in the Toronto Blessing is consistent with that expressed in the Vineyard's official doctrinal
statement: to "bring renewal to the larger Church of Christ
around the world, both through direct ministry and through
the stimulation of our example."[55] John Wimber believes he

---

[55] Association of Vineyard Churches, "Theological and Philosophical Statements," n.p.

will witness a great revival before he dies. He sees the current move of the Spirit preparing hearts "on the journey of sanctification."[56] Therefore, "joy and laughter will bubble forth. Don't be afraid of it. It's His work. It's not people acting weird."[57]

Wimber also claims the Lord revealed to him a vision of a mountain lake that cascaded fresh water down the mountainside into a plain of vineyards below, where workers dug irrigation ditches for the water. Wimber continues, "I got the clear impression of a co-laboring. God was pouring out his blessing. But if we don't dig the channels, if we don't go out into the highways and by-ways, if we don't put evangelism forward, if we didn't do the things God calls us to do, revival won't spread. . . . In other words let's begin organizing ourselves to give this blessing away."[58]

Bill Jackson, another Vineyard minister, writes that God is shaking up and humbling his church, to the end of making it more Christ-like. The Holy Laughter phenomena indicate the Lord's presence, and thus "can best be described as prophetic signs, even as Ezekiel and Jeremiah were signs that pointed to God."[59] Certain phenomena, such as the shaking motions, precede prophecy or empowerment or both; however, adds Jackson, "certain body movements" are "indicative of demonic presence."[60]

### END-TIME PROPHECIES FROM THE CURRENT RENEWAL

If the Holy Laughter phenomena amount to "prophetic signs," then what are the prophecies themselves? As noted at the beginning of this chapter Bob Jones, James Ryle, and Stacy Campbell predict a great coming division among Christians. Paul Cain and others who came from KCF still maintain in

---

[56]John Wimber, "Season of New Beginnings," *Vineyard Reflections,* May/June 1994, 6.

[57]John Wimber, "Visitation of the Spirit," *Ministries Today,* Sept./Oct. 1994, 9.

[58]John Wimber, "Refreshing, Renewal, and Revival," *Vineyard Reflections* July/Aug. 1994, 7.

[59]Bill Jackson, "What in the World Is Happening to Us? A Biblical Perspective on Renewal" (Champaign/Urbana, Ill.: Vineyard Christian Fellowship, 1994) 9.

[60]Ibid.

varying degrees the coming of a "new breed" of Christian. Even though they deny that this new breed is the same as the Latter Rain's "manifest sons of God," the prophetic weaving of this "new breed" into end-time scenarios is strikingly similar to the Latter Rain prophecies of the manifest sons of God, though few in the renewal will readily admit this.

Perhaps the most popular prophecy from the Toronto Blessing comes from Toronto Vineyard minister Marc Dupont. The first part of the prophecy came in May 1992 and the second in July 1993. Part one discloses Toronto as a place where living water will be abundant. In this vision, as in Wimber's, an idyllic mountain lake landscape is depicted. The waterfall is seen breaking big rocks into smaller ones, to help build the kingdom, but those "stones" who resist the Spirit "will be broken down into dust." Many mainline denominations, this prophecy asserts, will be at the forefront of the movement, while many current leaders will not respond to the Spirit's call.[61]

The second prophecy predicts a quick acceleration of the moving of the Spirit. There will be two stages of this move, as in Ezekiel's vision of the valley of dry bones (Ezek 37). Like the dry bones in Ezekiel's vision that grew flesh and sinew, stage one involves Christian leaders doing seemingly impossible things. Stage two anticipates an apostolic authority with signs and wonders that will come to Toronto, and the reaching of many non-believers with the gospel. Certain leaders in the body of Christ will have authority that will transcend denominational barriers in the "government of God." Dupont places one qualification (among others): "It will only be when all of the fivefold offices of Ephesians [4:11] are in operation."[62] Dupont also predicts, with qualification,

> I may be wrong in this, but I believe that the great harvest, as some people call it, or when we begin to see just radical, radical evangelism begin to touch some of the cities and things, I don't believe it's really going to begin to happen until sometime after the year 2005, but I *do* believe that churches in the nineties that are responding to the Spirit, they're going to begin to experience the first-fruits; that they are, in their circles, going to begin to see

---

[61] Chevreau, *Catch the Fire*, 28–32.
[62] Ibid., 32–35. The fivefold ministry refers to the offices of apostle, prophet, evangelist, pastor, and teacher.

more and more radical evangelism—they're going to begin to see more and more miracles and signs and wonders.[63]

Dupont says that God will remove some leaders who oppose the Spirit's moving, in this decade that he calls "the Elijah years" of prophetic restoration. He clearly ties this decade with his understanding of end-time prophecy by claiming that Mal 3:1 applies to the 1990s: "Behold, I'm going to send my messenger and he will clear the way before me; and the Lord whom you seek will suddenly come to his temple, and the messenger of the covenant in who you delight, behold he is coming."[64] Dupont's prophecy—apart from implying the Spirit will depart from anyone who opposes the renewal—puts us back into teachings strikingly similar to the Latter Rain teaching of modern-day apostles and prophets. As noted earlier, the Assemblies of God rejected this teaching as one of the errors of the so-called Saskatchewan revival.

Larry Randolph, another prophetic leader in the current renewal, declares: "I have a promise from the Lord in a visitation that He gave me some years ago, that before this decade was over, before the year 2000, that there were going to be manifestations in churches where Jesus Himself is going to appear. We won't be able to carry on church as we used to carry on church."[65] In the mid-1980s God reportedly told Randolph that the coming renewal would begin at the end of 1993 and would last seven years.[66]

James Ryle, a Vineyard pastor from Boulder, Colorado, in his best-seller entitled *Hippo in the Garden,* prophesied a similar vision. In 1989 Ryle dreamed about a hippo in a garden. Just as a hippo looks inappropriate in a garden, so the Lord would do a new but strange thing in his church, fulfilling the prophecy of Joel in Acts 2:17–23 by "pouring out a vast prophetic anointing upon My church and releas[ing] My people as a prophetic voice on the earth."[67] It will happen in

[63] Marc Dupont, "Prophetic School—Part 3," 16 Nov. 1994 (Toronto: Airport Vineyard), audio tape.

[64] Ibid.

[65] Larry Randolph, "Pursuing Jesus Before His Gifts," 19 Nov. 1994 (Toronto: Airport Vineyard), audio tape.

[66] Larry Randolph, "Renewal And Revival Today," 18 Nov. 1994 (Toronto: Airport Vineyard), audio tape.

[67] James Ryle, *Hippo in the Garden: A Non Religious Approach to Having a Conversation with God* (Orlando: Creation House, 1993) 259.

this generation, but some will be offended by the new prophetic voice that will bring in "a great last-days harvest."[68]
Others in the movement have predicted that a time of persecution is around the corner.[69]

## HOLY LAUGHTER: THE END-TIME REVIVAL?

Dupont and others indicate the current renewal marks the
last generation before Christ returns. But the predictions don't
all come from Toronto or the Vineyard.[70] Also, as noted last
chapter, Rodney Howard-Browne has made prophetic statements that we are presently living in the "last of the last days."

Frankly, I am not impressed by the promoting of predictions that are made after the event takes place. This reminds
me of the prophecies of Nostradamus. His followers parade
the accuracy of his predictions *after* they see an event that
somewhat resembles one of Nostradamus's sixteenth-century
predictions.

I would be more impressed if Paul Cain would show us
some evidence *back from the 1950s* that his mother would live
to a very old age. I would be more impressed if Larry Randolph
could give us proof *back in the mid-1980s* that renewal would
begin in late 1993. I would be more impressed if Bob Jones's
predictions in 1984 were not so vague. Then again sometimes
chance has more to do with predictions than a genuine revelation from God. If a "prophet" predicts thirty future events, and
five of them come to pass, and the five are touted as authenti-
cating a prophet's ministry while the twenty-five false predictions are swept under the rug, this has little to do with genuine
prophecy. Even Jeanne Dixon is right once in a while.

Few can dispute the fulfillment of Rodney Howard-Browne's
prediction, given in his booklet *The Coming Revival*, publish-
ed in 1991, two years before the "outpouring." But how significant is this? Holy Laughter and similar phenomena had
followed his ministry since at least 1989. Moreover, Pentecostals and charismatics are always anticipating revivals. Also,
we have not seen a major renewal in the West since the charis-

---

[68] Ibid., 262; cf. 267–68, 291.

[69] E.g., Randy Clark, "Evidence of This Present Move," 15 Oct. 1994
(Toronto: Airport Vineyard), audio tape.

[70] Riss, *Latter Rain*, "Foreword," cites Korean Paul Yonggi Cho's
predictions of a great revival in Canada prior to Christ's return.

matic renewal more than thirty years ago; some historians claim a revival normally breaks out about every twenty to thirty years. Was Rodney Howard-Browne's prediction a genuine prophecy, or merely luck, or an educated guess? (Of course there's the bigger issue of whether this renewal is even a revival at all!)

I do believe in the prophetic gift of Spirit, but I do not believe God will reveal any further revelation about the end times (cf. Rev 22:18–19). Hence, even if some predictions about the current renewal come true, this still would not validate predictions that tie it in with the biblical end times (cf. Acts 1:7). As I will demonstrate in chapters 8 and 9, leaders from past revivals often condemned "new revelations" received by revival enthusiasts of their day. These "revelations," often including end-time predictions, led many astray.

End-time predictions with reference to revivals are nothing new. In the same manner as many who have been influenced by the Latter Rain movement, Cotton Mather (1663–1728), convinced by the increase of earthquakes and "signs of the times" in his age, predicted the Spirit's outpouring of Joel 2:28–32 would usher in the second coming, which he believed could happen around 1736.[71] An outpouring of the Spirit did indeed take place through the Great Awakening, but events related to the biblical end times did not. Ironically, though Jonathan Edwards condemned the mystical revelations of the enthusiasts, he did not escape his own share of end-time speculations. He believed the world had entered the period of the sixth vial in Rev 16 and that Christ might return in the year 2000.[72] Prophetic extremists from the Second Great Awakening sometimes joined end-time sects such as the Shakers or the Millerites.

The kind of prophecy Mark Dupont gave—anticipating new apostles and prophets—is also found in the nineteenth-century Irvingites. Edward Irving, founder of the London Irvingites, spearheaded the "apostolic" restoration of speaking in tongues. But the restoration did not end in tongues. "In due

---

[71] R. E. Davies, *I Will Pour Out My Spirit: A History and Theology of Revival and Evangelical Awakenings* (Tunbridge Wells, UK: Monarch, 1992) 269–70.

[72] Paul Boyer, *When Time Shall Be No More: Prophecy Belief in Modern American Culture* (Cambridge, Mass./London: The Belknap Press of Harvard University Press, 1992) 7.

time, the church ordained 12 'apostles' who were to be the end-times equivalent of the 12 chosen by Christ. According to their prophecies, this group would be the last apostles to exist before the rapture of the church. Eventually, however, the apostles died one by one. When the last one died in 1901, the British church collapsed and practically disappeared."[73]

Prior to the Latter Rain movement in 1948, Welsh revivalist Robert Evans had applied Joel 2 to the revival of his day, and early Pentecostals often took on the name "Latter Rain" in relation to the same passages cited by the later Latter Rain movement.[74] Grieved by the apparent sinking zeal of the first Pentecostals, the 1948 Latter Rain movement borrowed the same teachings from their predecessors and applied them to themselves.

In the manner of the current renewal "prophets' " predictions of a "final revival," certain Pentecostals at the turn of the century believed Azusa Street was the final revival. Frank Bartleman passed out a tract entitled "The Last Call." An extract from the tract reads: "And now, once more, at the very end of the age, God calls. The Last Call, the Midnight Cry, is now upon us, sounding clearly in our ears. God will give this one more chance, the last. A final call, a world-wide Revival. Then Judgement upon the whole world."[75]

Robert M. Anderson, a historian on Pentecostalism, argues that in the early days of the Azusa Street revival the central theme of the Pentecostals was "Jesus is coming soon." Speaking in tongues became the central theme only after second

---

[73]Vinson Synan, "Who Are the Modern Apostles?" *Ministries Today,* March/April 1992, 45.

In a secondary (and more acceptable) sense, apostles were "sent out ones," the founders of mission fields. Thus, St. Patrick is considered the apostle of Ireland. The leaders of theological movements were sometimes considered apostles. Luther was the "apostle of the Reformation," while Wesley was the "apostle of Methodism." Nonetheless, in the biblical sense, the apostles died out after the first century. The second century church bishops became the successors of apostolic tradition, but they generally did not see themselves on the same level as the apostles (e.g., Ignatius: c. A.D. 115, *Epistle to the Ephesians,* 2–5, 20; *Epistle to the Romans,* 3; *Epistle to the Trallians,* 3).

[74]Donald Dayton, *Theological Roots of Pentecostalism* (reprint; Peabody: Hendrickson, 1987) 26–28.

[75]Frank Bartleman, *Azusa Street* (Plainfield, N.J.: Logos International, 1980; reprint) 42.

coming expectations waned.[76] Many of the early Pentecostal journals reflected the end-time theme in their titles, e.g.: *The Last Trump, The Bridal Call,* and *The Midnight Cry.*[77]

Larry Randolph's "Elijah generation" in Malachi has similar precursors. In the late nineteenth century, men such as John Alexander Dowie were considered by some to be Elijah or to have an Elijah ministry.[78] More recently, William Branham claimed to be the prophet of the Laodicean age in Rev 3 and the coming prophet of Malachi, and his followers thought of him as the second coming of Elijah.[79] The question now remains: *will those who embrace the prophecies of Holy Laughter learn from the mistakes of history, or will they repeat them?*

## A BIBLICAL APPROACH TO THE END TIMES

Most Holy Laughter advocates would agree that date setting for the end times is unbiblical. We have seen enough date-setting fiascos in our own time.[80] But how do those who claim a final generation of "new breed" Christians already exists, and the last revival is already budding, escape the implicit time frame they themselves are setting up for the end? A generation from the current renewal that started in 1993 leaves us with the false impression that Christ will return within the next few decades. If those involved in Holy Laughter continue to promote their apocalyptic prophecies, like the prophetic extremists that have come out of past revivals and

---

[76]Robert M. Anderson, *Vision of the Disinherited: The Making of American Pentecostalism* (1979 reprint; Peabody: Hendrickson, 1992) 79, 96.

[77]Walter J. Hollenweger, *The Pentecostals* (1972, reprint; Peabody: Hendrickson, 1988) 415.

[78]Vinson Synan, *The Holiness-Pentecostal Movement in the United States* (Grand Rapids: Eerdmans, 1971) 111.

[79]See for instance, William Branham, *Only Believe the "Thus Saith the Lord"* (Jeffersonville: Spoken Word Ministry, n.d.), introduction page.

[80]In 1988 Edgar Whisenant's eighty-eight reasons for the rapture failed, in 1992 the Korean rapture movement failed, and in 1994 predictions by John Hinkle and Harold Camping both failed. For details see the author's book, *99 Reasons.* This book also refutes virtually every major candidate for the antichrist, virtually every supposed sign that we are living in the final generation, and virtually every argument prophetic teachers make in their attempts to get around Acts 1:7 and related passages.

renewals, I believe they will set themselves up for mass deception and spiritual abuse.

What will happen if Christ does not return in this generation? The long-term effects could be devastating. I believe many
in the current renewal could become disillusioned. I am sure
that many will regret decisions they may have made when they
thought the end was right around the corner. How many would
refrain from a college education because they believed Christ
would return shortly? How many would not prepare for their
children's future? How many would neglect saving for retire-
ment, or making long-term investments, and be left with nothing? No doubt many in the current renewal would discourage
people from making bad decisions that would affect their future, but they fail to recognize that, because of their prophecies,
they themselves are the source of the problem! Whether they
like it or not, they will be held responsible for such fall-outs.

It does not matter how valid one's prophetic gift might be.
It does not matter if many have the same visions, dreams, and
prophetic utterances of this end-time new breed or end-time
revival. Those involved in the Korean rapture movement were
also dedicated charismatic Christians, and many of them received the same vision and prophetic utterance that Christ
would return on October 28, 1992. What was missing from
their prophecy? The same thing that is missing from the
prophecies of this renewal—concurrence with Scripture (Matt
24:36–44; Mark 13:32–33; Acts 1:6–7).

What then will indicate that we are living in the final days
before Christ's second coming? Second Thessalonians 2 tells us
we are not to be disturbed by those who claim the end is at
hand, even if they *prophesy* that the end is at hand (2 Thess 2:2).
The end will not come until there is a great falling away and "the
man of lawlessness" is clearly revealed (2:3–4). As it now stands,
we can't even determine that this "man of lawlessness," whom
many believe to be the antichrist, is alive today.[81] Scripture is
clear: we simply do not have enough evidence to warrant the
presumptuous prophetic claims that stem from the Latter Rain
movement, the Kansas City Fellowship, or the current renewal.

---

[81] The preterist would argue that the prophecy of the "man of
lawlessness" given in 2 Thess 2 was fulfilled in the first century, when
Caesar Nero came to power. Personally, I do not hold to such a view,
but it is certainly a possible interpretation of this passage.

Although some Holy Laughter advocates do see themselves as the final generation, on a more positive note, Wimber discourages elitism, and the Association of Vineyard churches has officially discouraged tying in Holy Laughter with any end-time scheme: "We want to avoid linking the present work of the Spirit to any precise eschatological scenario (e.g., Hal Lindsey or the Latter Rain movement, etc.). . . . we have been in 'the last days' since Pentecost and we don't know when the precise last moments of time are. Consequently, we don't know if this current renewal is 'the last big one' or not."[82]

I highly commend this position, but it seems to undermine prophecies made by some of the Vineyard ministers. When James Ryle speaks of the final generation, when Paul Cain predicts a "new breed" that has prophetic ties to Joel and Revelation, when Carol Arnott warns of a great coming division, shouldn't such "prophecies" be corrected by the Vineyard elders?

Moreover, will people in the Toronto Blessing submit to the Vineyard's official statement? Months after the Vineyard's statement came out, I heard a layperson at a renewal meeting in John Wimber's church prophesy that Armageddon was at hand, and that there would be a great persecution where God would expose the phonies. The minister who headed the meeting neither publicly corrected this individual, nor cut off his prophecy. The Vineyard's official statement regarding the end times does not seem to be making much of an impact. What is the Vineyard doing, in an official capacity, to correct this? I hope the official statement is not merely a move to pacify the Vineyard's critics.

Personally, I have nothing against the Vineyard movement. I believe God is moving through this unique ministry, and I pray its participants receive my questions and criticisms in a constructive manner that will only help purify their ministry in pursuit of the genuine revival we all long for. But until some of the difficulties are addressed and resolved, I believe this otherwise fine ministry will continue to attract many more criticisms.

Similarly, discernment should be exercised within the Toronto Blessing, not only in meeting with the Enemy in "power encounters," but also in testing teachings and prophecy.

---

[82] "Board Report: Association of Vineyard Churches Sept./Oct. 1994," Anaheim: Vineyard Christian Fellowship, 2.

# THE SPIRIT BEHIND THE HOLY
# LAUGHTER PHENOMENA

Perhaps it was the heat, or the air of febrile intoxication coursing in the air, but I could fell myself growing giddy. "Can you catch for me?" a woman asked. A body came falling toward me. I rested it on the ground, and moved on. I found myself beside John Arnott, who was moving through the crowd, blessing people, who fell like ninepins. I didn't even see his hand coming as it arched through the air and touched me gently—hardly at all—on the forehead. "And bless this one, Lord . . ." I could feel a palpable shock running through me, then I was falling backwards, as if my legs had been kicked away from underneath me. I hit the floor—I swear this is the truth—laughing like a drunk.[1]

What is so unusual about London reporter Mick Brown's encounter with Holy Laughter? He is not a Christian. He says he has had a similar experience when Mother Meera, a Hindu avatar (incarnation of deity) prayed for him, but that experience, like the one in Toronto, did not last. He reports that while floored in Toronto,

People knelt down beside me in a generous spirit and started to pray over me. I became slightly worried, and started to feel a sort of obligational responsibility to them, as if I ought to suddenly spring up and say that I had found Christ. I didn't do that, and I don't know if they were disappointed because I didn't. But that's just the kind of social pressure that kind of situation brings to bear on one. Nor did I feel any kind of longer term effects.[2]

---

[1]Brown, "Unzipper Heaven," 30.
[2]Mick Brown, "What Happened Next? Toronto and the Telegraph Reporter," *Evangelicals Now*, Feb. 1995, 8.

His religious views did not change after he left Toronto (he believes in religious pluralism). On the other hand, he did not attribute what went on at Toronto to hypnotic suggestion. *Evangelicals Now* magazine, which conducted an interview with Brown after the Toronto event, asks: "Could it be that we are witnessing what in the majority of cases is an essentially non-Christian experience, which some Christians are trying their best to assimilate into their view of the Christian life?"[3]

Does Mick Brown's experience indicate that Holy Laughter is non-Christian, or is it that Mick Brown, like King Saul (1 Sam 19), had a real encounter with God but did not convert? Subjective experiences are extremely difficult to decipher. Let's see if we can find the source of the Holy Laughter phenomena.

## AN EXAMINATION OF HOLY LAUGHTER PHENOMENA

Some of the most common events taking place at a renewal are laughing, crying, fainting, trembling, convulsing, seeing visions, prophesying, jerking, running (sometimes called "Jesus laps"), falling (being "slain in the Spirit"), staggering (getting "drunk in the Spirit"), and whooping, trilling, roaring, barking, mooing and making other animal noises— which are often accompanied with gestures. To catalogue the wide variety of strange events which occur in such meetings would fill a book. Robert Hough, reporter for *Toronto Life Magazine,* asked one woman named Colleen at the Airport Vineyard, " 'In what way do you manifest?' [She responded,] 'I'm a blower.' Colleen was about five feet tall and shaped like an orange. 'A blower?' 'When the Spirit of God hits, I blow and blow and blow. Wind just jets right out of me.' "[4] Guy Chevreau writes, "A curious manifestation has been exhibited at the Airport meeting, and noted elsewhere. Those affected jump up and down in one spot, sometimes for extended periods of time. Not surprisingly, the phenomenon has been dubbed 'pogoing.' "[5] One man experiencing the convulsive phenomena proudly displayed on his T-shirt "I'm a JERK FOR JESUS!"[6]

---

[3] Ibid.
[4] Hough, "God is Alive and Well," 1.
[5] Chevreau, *Catch the Fire,* 53.
[6] Ibid., 215.

We will focus our attention on the most prominent phenomena: laughing, being "slain in the Spirit," getting "drunk in the Spirit," and emitting animal sounds.

## HOLY HA HA'S

"Don't stick your toe in to test the water! Don't wait! Jump all the way into this flowing river! Let's follow God into the greatest and most powerful move ever seen in the history of the church! . . . It's the sound of the joy of the Lord, the sound of HOLY LAUGHTER!" proclaim Charles and Frances Hunter.[7] Holy Laughter sometimes works in unusual ways. Once, over the phone, while Frances prayed for a man who had tic douloureaux and migraine headaches, the man broke out laughing and was instantly healed.[8] The Hunters also claim that a woman named Darlene listened to some Holy Laughter tapes while in labor. Instead of concentrating on her breathing, she broke out in Holy Laughter: "This happened about halfway through labor at the transition phase and lasted throughout all the labor. When a contraction came, laughter came with it, but there was NO PAIN!"[9] Not all accounts of laughing in the Spirit are that spectacular. And don't hold your breath looking for secondary witnesses to verify such reports.

What is the purpose of the laughter? Most people who experience the laughter claim it's a joyful, cathartic experience that usually takes place when one is lying down—doing "carpet time." Rodney Howard-Browne writes, "God uses laughter in our meetings to bless certain people."[10] Laughter seems tame in comparison to shrieking or convulsing or animal sounds. So what's so bad about Christians laughing? Bill Johnian says, "God's people have an unholy fear of the devil. They honestly believe that hundreds of believers can come together in the name of Jesus, worship and sing unto Him, pray and preach His word—only to have the devil come in and take over the service with a mocking laughter."[11]

Genuine laughter may result from joy, but we must be careful not to assume that it *must* do so. Holy Laughter could

---

[7]C. and F. Hunter, *Holy Laughter,* 159.
[8]Ibid., 67–68.
[9]Ibid., 118.
[10]Howard-Browne, *Manifesting the Holy Ghost,* 29.
[11]Johnian, *The Fresh Anointing,* 131.

easily break out in total chaos so that people laugh for laughter's sake and reduce a service to sheer flippancy. If Christians end up laughing at the sacredness and austerity of God—like the time the congregation laughed when Rodney Howard-Browne preached on hell—something is wrong. Holiness and repentance are easily devalued in such a setting. C. S. Lewis observed that ungodly laughter is a means of destroying genuine shame. This can result in a person not taking anything seriously in Christianity. Lewis's fictional demon Screwtape writes that flippancy "is a thousand miles away from joy; it deadens, instead of sharpening, the intellect. . . ."[12]

Christian mystic Watchman Nee expressed his concern about the Holy Laughter in his day: "What is their aim? They want to laugh, to be joyful. They do not pray, 'O God, I ask You to fill me with Your Spirit, I am satisfied with or without feeling.' Whoever wishes to be filled with God's Spirit ought to assume such an attitude."[13]

Joy is indeed one of the fruits of the Holy Spirit (Gal 5:22–23). It can, but certainly does not need to, express itself in laughter. Nothing is wrong with laughing when the Spirit touches us with joy; however, our focus should be on the Giver of that joy, not on the laughing that may or may not result from it. One writer notes, "The true fruit of joy is best seen against the backdrop of sorrow and suffering. This does not mean the Christian never smiles; it simply means that the supernatural joy of the Holy Spirit is measured by inward confidence and optimism rather than by outward expression."[14]

## "SLAIN IN THE SPIRIT": GOD'S OPERATING TABLE

For twenty minutes Carol Arnott, wife of Airport Vineyard pastor John Arnott, prayed for Stephen Strang, of *Charisma* magazine. Then it happened. Strang said, "At that point, I felt totally overcome by God's presence and fell backward onto the

---

[12]C. S. Lewis, *The Screwtape Letters;* reprinted in *The Best of C.S. Lewis* (New York: The Iversen-Norman Associates, 1969/Grand Rapids: Baker Book House, 1977) 46–47.

[13]Watchman Nee, *The Latent Power of the Soul* (New York: Christian Fellowship, 1972) 73.

[14]Zenas J. Bicket, "Joy and the Spirit-Filled Life," *Paraclete* (Spring 1977) 3.

floor—only the second time in my life that such a thing happened to me."[15]

What is the spiritual purpose of falling on the floor? Apparently, an awareness of the Spirit's presence floods the recipients, and they fall to the ground. Too often, however, falling episodes have been faked, having more to do with the minister's touch or suggestion than anything else. Some individuals who fall simply want to experience the falling effect. Others fall not because they sense a touch by God, but because they hope to receive something *from* God as they fall "by faith." In the case of a genuine touch of God, according to Morton Kelsey, the experience brings an individual "into touch with another dimension of reality, causing that person to let go of ordinary conscious control and thus fall to the ground. If not actually unconscious of ordinary reality, the individual is at least focusing attention almost entirely upon this other level of reality."[16] A more natural explanation comes from Paul Conkin:

> In any religious context, in any moment of intense feeling, the physical manifestations always involve various movements and sounds. . . . And in any such context, the body may eventually reach a state of neurological overload. The one commonality across cultural boundaries is this limit condition—fainting.[17]

In a similar way, convulsion and trembling can be caused by a strong overload of emotions such as fear or sorrow.[18]

Rodney Howard-Browne claims the Lord told him, "When they fall down under the anointing, leave them there, for that's My operating table."[19] Some lie on the floor for minutes while other "soak" for hours depending on the "surgery." Tom Waggoner writes, "While we are on God's 'operating table,' the Lord is tearing down these walls of hindrances [fear, doubts, rebellion, etc.]. In their place He is putting love, joy, peace, humility, submission, which all give great victory."[20] In short,

---

[15]Stephen Strang, "Floored in Toronto," *Charisma*, Feb. 1995, 106.

[16]Morton Kelsey, *Discernment: A Study in Ecstasy and Evil* (New York/Ramsey/Toronto: Paulist Press, 1978) 19.

[17]Paul K. Conkin, *Cane Ridge: America's Pentecost* (Madison: University of Wisconsin Press, 1990) 107.

[18]Pierre Janet, *The Major Symptoms of Hysteria* (New York: Macmillan & Co.,1907) 94–104.

[19]Howard-Browne, *Manifesting the Holy Ghost*, 23.

[20]Tom Waggoner, *Falling Under God's Power* (Springfield, Mo.: Restoration, 1978) 55.

many renewal teachers believe that the "slain in the Spirit" phenomenon can occur when God is doing a transforming work on individuals, healing and delivering them from deep-rooted problems. Aside from this "healing" phenomenon, others have visions while they "rest in the Spirit."

Joseph Cardinal Suenens, a charismatic Catholic, lists the following benefits of being "slain in the Spirit":[21]

- Inner peace

- Inner healing

- Ability to forgive or repent

- Occasional physical healings

- Healing of marriages and other relationships

- The alleviation or almost total healing of psychic problems

- A desire to get closer to Jesus through prayer and Scripture

If a person is genuinely overwhelmed by the Spirit's presence, such results are certainly possible. However, not all cases of being "slain in the Spirit" yield positive results. After Kenneth Hagin's wife, along with a fellow minister and his wife, questioned whether a levitation in one of Hagin's meetings was of the Lord, a "word from the Lord" reportedly came to Hagin, and he touched them on the forehead. They immediately hit the floor and were paralyzed: "When the three tried to move and found themselves completely immobilized, they of course, were willing to admit that Hagin's power and ministry were of God. Hagin was then instructed by the voice to 'release them' by again touching them with his finger."[22] Another strange account involved an eighty-five-year-old woman named Ella Peppard. In 1986 she died fifteen days after her hip was fractured by another person who fell on her—that person was "slain in the Spirit" when touched by evangelist Benny Hinn.[23]

---

[21] Francis MacNutt, *Overcome By the Spirit* (Grand Rapids: Chosen Books/Baker Book House, 1990) 45–46.

[22] McConnell, *A Different Gospel,* 66. The account is recorded in Kenneth Hagin's book *Why Do People Fall Under the Power?* (Tulsa: Faith Library, 1980) 11–12.

[23] "In Brief," *Christian Research Journal,* vol. 12 no. 3 (Fall 1989) 27.

*order*

Not long ago at a Pentecostal rally someone fell on me as I prayed at the altar. I was not hurt, but I was definitely upset! It is hard for me to imagine that the Holy Spirit touched that individual so as to send him flying on top of me. Order and caution certainly need to play stronger roles in environments where the "slaying" phenomenon occurs.

Waggoner relates how a lack of order can cause the slain in the Spirit phenomenon to take on the appearance of a three-ring circus. He writes, "For many people, unfortunately, the falling is an end in itself. This is a tragedy."[24] One charismatic

*People are seeking a feeling*

leader suggests, "If you find yourself lined up to be 'slain,' wanting something to be felt, something to happen, you are probably seeking a feeling, a thing, and not seeking purely to glorify God."[25]

## DRUNK ON THE "NEW WINE"

Akin to being "slain in the Spirit" is the renewal phenomenon of getting "drunk in the Spirit." Both are said to occur when a person is overwhelmed by the Spirit's presence. The only real difference is that instead of falling to the ground, the person remains on his or her feet but is too "overcome" to function correctly. Such a one thus mimics the characteristics of a drunk—staggering, acting "dopey," using slurred speech, and so on. "I am drunk, I am drunk," sings Rodney Howard-Browne, "I've been drinking down at Joel's place every night and every day. I am drunk on the new wine."[26] While it is true that the Spirit fills us with his sweet influence, renewal teachers must be careful not to grieve the Holy Spirit by attributing drunken gestures to his work.

Strange results arise from these experiences; for example, when designated drivers are pressed into service to drive people home who are too "drunk in the Spirit" to drive for themselves! One Vineyard minister claimed to be "drunk in the Spirit" for a few days. When trying to clip a baby dove's wings (a procedure that normally takes about five minutes), he took half an hour. He then noticed that his hands were covered with

[24]Waggoner, *Falling Under God's Power,* 53–54.
[25]George Maloney cited in "Slain in the Spirit: Another View," Jerry Don Venable, *Paraclete* (Summer 1988) 25.
[26]Julia Duin, "An Evening with Rodney Howard-Browne," *Christian Research Journal* (Winter 1995) 45.

blood, because he had accidentally tried to clip the wings of a full-grown male dove, who bit his hands.[27]

If people are indeed touched by God, what are they doing standing up and moving about? Why don't they prostrate themselves or lie down and let God continue his work? This would virtually do away with the drunkenness phenomenon. This phenomenon, however, allows the person to make a public spectacle of him- or herself. And often the "drunken" one is not disappointed. Many Christians love the entertainment. But put such an individual in a room alone and they quickly sober up. Jack Deere points out that people of this sort are normally insecure and lonely. They use physical manifestations to attract attention to themselves.[28] The touch of God may be real, but mimicking the stereotypical movements of a drunk in response to that touch is a purely carnal and disrespectful reaction.

### ANIMAL SOUNDS AND GESTURES

As Marc Dupont of the Toronto Vineyard began praying for one pastor, " 'He began to roar like a lion,' Dupont relates, noting that normally he would have assumed [Gideon] Chui [the pastor] needed deliverance from a demon spirit. But he believed Chui's unusual vocal expression heralded a sign from God."[29] Roaring, crowing, mooing, flapping, whooping, barking, braying, howling—along with an assortment of other "zoological" phenomena—have become part of the Holy Laughter theatrics.

But not everyone accepts the spiritual jungle jamboree. Rodney Howard-Browne criticizes animal noises by writing, "I've walked into a room and seen ministers wailing like a bunch of cats and dogs. I asked, 'What's going on here?' 'We're interceding.' 'Lord, have mercy. I thought you were dying!' There was no anointing. I could have produced an even better effect by holding a cat under my arm and squeezing the thing's neck."[30]

---

[27] Carolyn Tennant, "Toronto Blessing? Decide for Yourself" (Minneapolis: North Central Bible College, 1995) 40–41.

[28] Deere, *Surprised By the Power,* 97–98.

[29] Daina Doucet, "What is God Doing in Toronto?," 26.

[30] Howard-Browne, *The Reality of the Person of the Holy Spirit,* 15–16.

Officially, John Wimber does not endorse such activities, but neither does he prevent them from happening in the Vineyard churches. For the most part, the animal activities continue at the renewal meetings.[31] Wimber admits "there have been times in the past where we've attempted to cast demons out of people who made 'animal noises.' "[32] But based on the testimonies of seven or eight people who have experienced the roaring phenomenon, Wimber affirms the fruit has been positive. He notes that such individuals experience righteous indignation, and sense that they are prophetically "announcing" that they are taking back God's territory from the devil, and they seem "very excited about the potential for more powerful ministry in the future."[33]

Yet we must ask ourselves if the end justifies the means. Suppose an entire congregation claimed they drew closer to the Lord every time they spit on the walls of the sanctuary. Suppose they called this "holy spitting," backing it up with a few scriptures taken out of context (such as the incident of Jesus making clay out of his spittle) and giving it the meaning of a prophetic declaration of a new creation. Moreover, suppose they claimed that Scripture nowhere directly condemns "spitting in the Spirit." Would the renewal accept such an activity?

Paul captures the chaotic mood perfectly in 1 Cor 14. Regardless of how blessed the Corinthians felt when they all spoke in tongues, regardless of the positive fruit that may have come from it, Paul's bottom line remained the same: If others dropped in on your service, "would they not think you are mad" (1 Cor 14:23)? Perhaps renewal ministers need to take Scripture more seriously when, almost unanimously, people who first see the animal hysteria think, "This is madness!"

## DOES HOLY LAUGHTER BEAR GOOD FRUIT?

One of the few ways we can evaluate Holy Laughter (and related phenomena) is by the fruit produced in the lives of

---

[31] John Wimber, "John Wimber Responds to Phenomena," supplement to "Board Report: Association of Vineyard Churches Sept./Oct. 1994."

[32] Ibid.

[33] Ibid.

those who experience it. Christ said that a good tree does not produce bad fruit, and a bad tree does not produce good fruit (Matt 7:16–20). What type of fruit is coming out of Holy Laughter? Anyone who is not deaf to the testimonies of the hundreds of people touched by the renewal must concede that there is definitely good fruit arising out of the movement.

## CHANGED LIVES

Many positive changes are reported in the lives of those who experience Holy Laughter. Terry Virgo of New Frontiers writes, "Marriages have been restored in our church, the recalcitrant have been humbled, and the timid have begun witnessing boldly. Half-hearted attenders have become zealots for God."[34] Paul and Mona Johnian claim that Holy Laughter "is more than an emotional outburst or a charismatic fad. It has been accompanied by forgiveness, emotional healing, a desire to witness and the healing of relationships."[35]

## GROWTH, MATURITY, AND REPENTANCE

In many cases, Holy Laughter is reported as being a maturing influence in believers' lives. So positive is the fruit in these areas that Johnian asserts:

> The changes in our congregation convince us that the tree and its fruit are good and lasting. Along with a marked numerical growth in our church, we see in our members godly attitudes, improved health, zeal to witness, and increasing love for God and one another. . . . Since this outpouring, however, my husband and I have watched in awe as the Holy Spirit has successfully addressed in minutes what we have attempted to fix for 13 years. We have watched strong men cry aloud in repentance. We have seen 'impossible' relationships reconciled and half-hearted commitments turned to burning zeal.[36]

## SALVATION OF THE LOST

Although the Vineyard refrains from calling Holy Laughter a revival because it still lacks evangelistic impact, souls are

---

[34] Terry Virgo, "Making Sense of the Spirit's Move," in *The Impact of "Toronto,"* Wallace Boulton, ed. (Crowborough, UK: Monarch, 1995) 74.

[35] Steve Smith, " 'Holy Laughter' Hits Boston Church," *Charisma,* June 1994, 58.

[36] Johnian, "Flowing with Revival," 14.

nonetheless being saved. Steve Long, associate pastor of the Airport Vineyard, writes:

> You need to know that the most important thing happening at the Airport Vineyard is changed lives. We estimate that 5,000 people trusted Christ or reconnected with Christ during 1994. We have an altar call every meeting where individuals may respond to a gospel presentation. At this point, 10–15 people respond to trust Christ for the first time every night [and there are services 6 days a week]; some nights there are more than 50 responding.[37]

## HEALINGS

In his book *Catch the Fire,* Guy Chevreau reserves an entire chapter, entitled "An Embarrassment of Riches," for the personal testimonies of more than a dozen people whose lives have been changed by the renewal. Chevreau describes two significant cases of divine healing. One involved a girl named Heather Harvey who had dyslexia; another case involved a girl named Sarah Lilleman who was suffering from loss of sight, muscle control, and cognitive ability. Jim Beverley, professor of theology and ethics at Ontario Theological Seminary in Toronto, investigated these cases. Both girls did show drastic improvements of health after their healings took place, but the reports of the second case were riddled with errors.[38] Whether or not one wishes to call these cases miracles, the fact is that lives have been positively touched.

The list of testimonies continues to lengthen. Healings, restored relationships, repentance, zeal for evangelism, and many other positive fruits are reported over and over again. Five characteristics of the renewal's fruit are summarized by Michael Green:[39]

- A prevailing sense of joy

- An intensified love for Christ

- Healings

- Discernment and empowerment for areas of service

- Numbers of lapsed members returning to church

---

[37] Long, "An Insider's Story," 10.
[38] Beverley, *Holy Laughter,* 103–20.
[39] Michael Green, "Introduction," in *The Impact of "Toronto,"* 15.

Many critics will respond that current assessments of the renewal's fruit are based on evidence too short-term to warrant any solid conclusions. Many people similarly convince themselves that they feel better after taking a placebo; in the long run, however, such benefits diminish significantly. This may be true in some Holy Laughter cases—perhaps in many— but in every single case? How many lives must be changed before we will admit that a work is producing good fruit? How many souls must be saved? How many healings need to be verified as authentic before we admit the positive results that are coming out of this renewal? Still, we would have an incomplete picture if we failed to mention the negative results as well.

## WHAT ABOUT THE BAD FRUIT OF HOLY LAUGHTER?

### DISORDERLY CONDUCT

I do not have much respect for renewal ministers who after taking an honest look at 1 Cor 14 cannot admit that they have allowed some disorder to continue in their services. For the most part, all I have seen is renewal ministers reading their own experiences into the text. How does Paul's instruction in 1 Cor 14:40, that everything be done "in a fitting and orderly way," apply to their church? If "the spirits of the prophets are subject to the control of the prophets" (1 Cor 14:32), then why do these "prophets" continue to permit uncontrolled behavior in their congregations?[40]

---

[40]See chapter 7 for an elaboration on orderly worship. Holy Laughter teachers often appeal to the move of the Spirit in Acts 10 to demonstrate a case of acceptable "disorder"; what they do not recognize is that this account is historically unique, in that it is the first time the baptism of the Holy Spirit occurs in a Gentile community. Moreover, when Peter started preaching, Cornelius and his group were responding to the gospel for the first time. We could allow for some disorder among the unchurched. But those in the current renewal are for the most part *already churched.* They should know better. Then again, maybe the fault lies in the ministers who let disorder continue. Additionally, Acts 10 is no proof-text for allowing laughing distractions to continue while a minister preaches. The Spirit touched the entire group at once; it wasn't just a few enthusiasts laughing while the vast majority were trying to listen to the sermon. In the current renewal, the

## EMOTIONALISM, ANTI-INTELLECTUALISM, AND EXPERIENTIALISM

Joseph R. McAuliffe writes regarding the renewal:

At its worst, the meetings are hyper emotional, theologically choppy, overly subjective, elitist, unruly, divisive, and shallow. I interviewed scores of participants as to their experience at the meetings who consensually acknowledged some kind of "release" that was emotional or spiritual but not altogether explicable or intelligible. Most comments reminded me of my Woodstock era buddies attempting to describe an LSD trip: "*Like, I don't know, I mean, Wow, it's far out, it's cool, it's really unreal, I dunno man. You know?*"[41]

Experience should never be people's focus or goal in attending renewal meetings. Jesus Christ—not experience, the Holy Spirit or anything else—should be at the center of attention. Bob Hunter observed that over a three-month period, Toronto Vineyard sermons referred to prophecy 372 times, the Holy Spirit 383 times, but Jesus Christ only 143 times.[42]

## DIVISION

Although we often hear how denominations are coming together because of Holy Laughter, it is also true that individual churches are splitting apart over the issue. Moreover, the problem is only agitated when Holy Laughter preachers mock their critics or say that people who come against the movement are blaspheming the Holy Spirit. As we noted last chapter, certain Vineyard ministers prophesy that a great division awaits us in which Christians will have to choose for or against the current renewal.

## ABNORMAL BEHAVIOR

One irate person wrote *Charisma* magazine complaining that his friends have not been the same since they have expe-

---

ushers should escort such people into a private room or tell them to quiet themselves. I'm sure if the preacher would single out such individuals and tell them to remain quiet during the sermon, they would find they have the power to control themselves.

[41] Joseph R. McAuliffe, "Revival," *Chalcedon Report*, Dec. 1994, 15.
[42] Beverley, *Holy Laughter*, 159–60.

rienced Holy Laughter. They now "have a crazed look in their eyes and twitch uncontrollably."[43] Dr. Carolyn Tennant writes, "Personally, the author [Tennant] has now heard of five people who have been so affected by the laughter that they continue laughing, even after the church services, at inappropriate times. One of these is about to lose her job, the laughter has been so disruptive at work. The others are continuing to have problems."[44] Christian psychologists have documented case studies showing that extreme charismatic behavior can have damaging effects on those who manifest it.[45]

### IGNORING, MISREADING, OR DISTORTING SCRIPTURE

Holy Laughter advocates often fall short when it comes to scriptural conformity. Scriptures are all too readily tailored to support Holy Laughter, instead of correcting it. I have yet to hear those in the movement give a satisfactory explanation for why Paul's command in 1 Cor 14 to worship in an orderly way does not apply to them; they will normally just point to the fruit. Certainly, much of the fruit is good; but so was the fruit at Corinth, and Paul still had to rebuke the Corinthians for their conduct. Others will say that they really don't know what Paul meant by disorderly conduct; but inconsistently, they will often dogmatically assert that what goes on in Holy Laughter is not the disorder Paul refers to.

## COMMON QUESTIONS AND CRITICISMS

### ISN'T HOLY LAUGHTER OF THE DEVIL?

"This laughter thing shows the subtlety of Satan in diverting the Church and corrupting her message. He is working to a well devised plan awaiting 'The coming of the lawless one . . .' 2 Thess 2:9–10. Those days are upon us," affirms Philip

---

[43] Mark Myers, letter, *Charisma*, April 1995, 11.
[44] Tennant, "Toronto Blessing? Decide for Yourself," 40.
[45] For sample documentation see, David R. Copestake and H. Newton Malony, "Adverse Effects of Charismatic Experiences: A Reconsideration," *Journal of Psychology and Christianity* 12 no. 3 (1993), 236–44.

Powell of Christian Witness Ministries.[46] Is Satan the source of the renewal?

In the earlier chapters we probed the doctrines of both Rodney Howard-Browne and the Vineyard and discovered that though problems exist, the teachings expounded by these Holy Laughter advocates are still generally orthodox. I fail to see how causing a group of Christians to laugh will subtly draw them to Satan, especially when, for the most part, the renewal is only drawing them to a closer walk with Christ. If so many Christians are being fooled by Satan, this would seem to slight the sovereignty of God, who is in control of the Christian church. Moreover, those who claim the renewal is the final end-time deception of Satan are faced with the same problem faced by those who say this is the final end-time revival: how do they know these are the end times, when Christ said it is not for us to know the timing of these things before they happen (cf. Acts 1:6–7)? On the other hand, in every genuine move of God we can expect the devil to counterfeit and pervert what God is doing. I believe the end-time prophecies themselves, along with some of the excessive disorder in renewal meetings, provide fertile soil for the Enemy to cultivate his agenda.

## DON'T THE SAME PHENOMENA OCCUR IN OTHER RELIGIONS AND CULTS?

The late Bhagwhan Shree Rajneesh used to lay hands on his followers. They would go into ecstatic frenzies and experience great laughter. Rajneesh said, "just be joyful . . . god is not serious . . . this world cannot fit with a theological god . . . so let this be your constant reminder—that you have to dance your way to God, to laugh your way to God."[47] Other gurus, New Agers, and shamans report similar phenomena including animal sounds, convulsions, crying, laughing, fainting, trances, and the like.[48]

---

[46] Philip L. Powell, "From Around the World," *Contending Earnestly for The Faith*, Nov./Dec. 1994, 4.

[47] Cited from Warren Smith, "Holy Laughter or Strong Delusion?," *SCP Newsletter*, Fall 1994, 14.

[48] See for instance, I. M. Lewis, *Ecstatic Religion: An Anthropological Study of Spirit Possession and Shamanism* (Middlesex, UK: Penguin, 1971).

According to Elizabeth Hillstrom, Hindus who experience kundalini (an alleged energy that resides coiled at the base of the human spine)

> may experience extreme heat and cold and find their bodies making strange involuntary movements—muscle twitches, prolonged trembling or sinuous writhing. . . . The automatic movements of the body may be accompanied by spontaneous crying, laughing, screaming or whistling. Other common involuntary behaviors include speaking in tongues, chanting unknown songs and making a variety of animal sounds and movements.[49]

Parallels between religious manifestations, however, do not necessarily indicate the same source. The early church spoke in tongues, and so did some of the pagan cults of that time. Should the apostles have refrained from speaking in tongues simply because the other religions did so? If a Muslim prays does that mean I shouldn't? If a Hindu fasts should I break mine? We should avoid committing the fallacy of guilt by association. The spirit pervading a Hindu service is radically different from that present at a Christian charismatic service. Regardless of what we think about Holy Laughter, its teachers still preach that salvation comes only through Jesus Christ, God the Son, Second Person of the Trinity. Nevertheless, discernment is always needed.

## ISN'T HOLY LAUGHTER A FORM OF MANIPULATION THROUGH MASS SUGGESTION OR HYPNOSIS?

Franz Anton Mesmer (1734–1815), an Austrian physician, is known as the father of modern hypnotism. The reactions of his patients under hypnosis included convulsions, hysterical laughter, and fits of hiccups.[50] Is it possible that mass hypnotism or manipulation through autosuggestion is the cause of the Holy Laughter phenomena? Regarding mass hypnosis, I'd say the likelihood of this is less than one percent. Having been to several of these meetings, having been prayed over by those in the renewal, having worked a number of years in discernment ministry, and having fellowshiped with Pentecostals and charismatics my entire Christian life, I find this option to be

---

[49] Elizabeth L. Hillstrom, *Testing the Spirits* (Downers Grove, Ill.: InterVarsity Press, 1995) 122.
[50] Dixon, *Signs of Revival*, 227.

extremely unlikely. Just because Mesmer caused his patients to laugh under hypnosis, it does not follow that Holy Laughter leaders are doing the same thing. Moreover, unless every minister is being secretly trained in the art of mass hypnosis, there is no way each one could transfer the renewal back to his or her own church after going to Toronto or seeing Rodney Howard-Browne.

Mass manipulation is also highly unlikely. Rodney Howard-Browne is most often accused of this, for reasons discussed in chapter 3. Granted, Holy Laughter ministers do arouse their audiences through lively music, through sermons often related to receiving "the blessing," and through displaying dramatic testimonies of those who have received "the blessing." Crowds do tend to influence individuals. Nazi Germany is a good example. Nevertheless, although suggestion and peer pressure may exist at such meetings, wide-scale mass manipulation seems unlikely. When your favorite preacher becomes highly dramatic and uses persuasive rhetoric, is this also a form of manipulation? To be consistent, we should label either both the renewal and our own preachers as manipulative, or neither. Christian psychiatrist and author John White writes, "To manipulate a large number of people you need to exhaust them, to bombard them with levels of sensation they are not accustomed to, to expose them to concepts that frighten them, to humiliate them and make them feel guilty and hopeless, while still offering a new and magical idea."[51]

David Lewis notes that two doctors (Moss and McEvedy) used the Eysenck Personality Inventory scales to measure personality types that are prone to mass hysteria. The result from hundreds of samples showed that about twelve percent of those studied fell into the category of the highly suggestible, scoring high on both the extroversion and neuroticism axes.[52]

At a Vineyard conference at Harrogate, fall 1986, Lewis surveyed hundreds of participants with a detailed questionnaire about their spiritual experiences in the past and at the conference. Many of these had experienced laughing, weeping, shaking, holy "drunkenness," and so forth. When con-

---

[51] John White, *When the Spirit Comes in Power* (Downers Grove, Ill.: InterVarsity Press, 1988) 67–68.

[52] David C. Lewis, *Healing: Fiction, Fantasy, or Fact?* (London/Sydney/Auckland/Toronto: Hodder & Stoughton, 1990) 166–71.

ducting the Eysenck inventory on such individuals, Lewis discovered the following: "What is immediately clear from these figures is that reports of these phenomena are spread across all the different categories of people and are by no means confined to those high on both the extroversion and neuroticism scales. This argues against a theory that these phenomena are due largely to a form of mass hysteria."

Nevertheless, like Mick Brown, I felt somewhat pressured to "produce" some phenomenon when two loving workers laid hands on me and prayed for me at a renewal meeting. No doubt they would have prayed for me for hours until I laughed, cried, barked, or did something unusual. Did they not realize the Holy Spirit is so sovereign that he could touch a person without them having to manifest anything at all? After about ten to fifteen minutes, I still didn't feel anything, so I left.

Ironically, I did have a memorable experience when doing research for this book, but it was not in a renewal service. Rather, it happened in a Vineyard bookstore, of all places. No one prayed for me, but when I walked into the bookstore I sensed a sweet presence of the Holy Spirit that I had not felt in quite a while. I fell to my knees between the rows of shelves. No one else seemed to notice, or to sense what I was sensing; they must have thought I was just kneeling down looking at some books on a lower shelf. I didn't laugh, cry, scream, or what have you—I just knelt there enjoying God's presence. No significant change took place in my life that day, but I know he touched me. At other times in my life when I have felt God's presence in a similar way, sometimes the event significantly renewed me; other times it simply confirmed my relationship with him.

Even though suggestion, peer pressure, and other human motivations are present at renewal meetings, they do not preclude the Spirit's touching lives—as I believe he does—at such meetings.

## ISN'T HOLY LAUGHTER MAN-MADE?

This is a very difficult question to answer. Most Christians would like to give the multitude of believers in Holy Laughter a break by saying they don't believe it is of the devil; but they would say that, since the phenomena are so strange, they must have a purely human origin. I believe that on the one hand much of what goes on *is* human-induced. On the other hand, accounts like the move of God at the Assemblies of God radio station in Florida (see chapter 1) seem best answered by admitting a genuine visitation. I think we thus have both God and the flesh (and the devil too) working in many of these meetings. Journalist Mike Fearon states:

> If the work of the Holy Spirit takes place upon and through our humanity, and if one dimension of our humanity can be described through psychology—as I believe it helpfully can—then to say of the Blessing "it's psychological" is a truism. To go beyond it, as reductionism, and to say "I can give it a psychological explanation, therefore there is no other explanation," is actually to make an enormous logical jump, and to claim something that you haven't proved![53]

### DOESN'T HOLY LAUGHTER LEAD TO AN ALTERED STATE OF CONSCIOUSNESS?

Holy Laughter can lead to an altered state of consciousness, but this is not as threatening as it may seem. Anyone who speaks in tongues fits the same category. Peter, Paul, and other saints of the past reached altered states of consciousness when they saw visions. Any level of trance would qualify as an "altered state" as well.[54] Robert M. Anderson writes,

> Those few students of the subject who insist that a person speaking in tongues is usually in a perfectly normal state of consciousness fail to recognize that altered states of consciousness run the full gamut from near full consciousness to complete unconsciousness. Thus, many experienced tongue-speakers are able to enter a state of dissociation with such little effort that neither they nor others are aware of the change. Yet the underlying alteration of consciousness is normally there, as it is in the case of all automatic behavior.[55]

The real question is not whether one can reach an altered state of consciousness at a renewal meeting, but whether such

---

[53] Mike Fearon, *A Breath of Fresh Air* (Guildford, Surrey: Eagle, 1994) 152.

[54] For levels of trance states, see Mary Douglas, *Natural Symbols: Exploration in Cosmology* (London: Barrie & Jenkins, 1970; 2d ed. 1973) 104–5.

[55] Anderson, *Vision of the Disinherited*, 13. For characteristics of altered states of consciousness and the mechanisms that trigger it, see Dixon, *Signs of Revival*, 258–79.

a state in that particular context opens one up to the occult. I suppose occultic phenomena may occur if a person is not a true Christian. Further, occultic or demonic phenomena may account for some renewal cases; especially those of the animal manifestations variety. Such cases would be the exception, however, not the rule. Those in the renewal freely admit the demonic could be motivating certain individuals. God, the devil, and the flesh can be present in any meeting, renewal or not. Nevertheless, if Christians constantly "empty out" and "open up" their minds to the first thing that pops into their heads, they should realize that what "pops in" might be a demonic voice, instead of the Spirit of God.

### ISN'T TEACHING NEGLECTED FOR THE SAKE OF EXPERIENCE?

This is a legitimate problem I find not only in the renewal, but in Pentecostal-charismatic churches in general. Such groups always run the risk of emphasizing experience rather than the preaching of Scripture as the central focus of the service. Often, solid teaching is woefully absent. Most renewal ministers teach a bland message—often one related somehow to the renewal. Steve Long of the Airport Vineyard responds, "Sermons at our nightly meetings are not shallow, as some have said. The main and plain truths are shared each night; sin, holiness, the cross, Christ or hell, for example."[56]

Still, most people do not come to the renewal meetings to hear the sermons, but to get touched by God after the sermon is preached. Moreover, the way renewal ministers normally determine that the Spirit is moving upon the congregation is through the manifestations, not the impact of their preaching. This is quite different from many past revivals, where the message played a much stronger role. What are the future implications of this disturbing trend? Perhaps the biggest threat Holy Laughter poses is that it could become a stepping-stone for future hyper-Pentecostal and charismatic experiences which will become the norm in Christianity. As the Lord's Supper was generally replaced by the altar call in evangelical circles during the last century, so a hundred years from now the emotional-experiential motif could replace the sermon message as the center of

---

[56]Long, "An Insider's Story," 10.

attention at evangelical services. Holy Laughter could be used by the Enemy in a continuum of deception, leading eventually to the perversion of evangelicalism. The word of God seems to be taking a back seat to charismatic experiences.

## HOLY LAUGHTER: MADE BY GOD, PEOPLE, OR THE DEVIL?

AREAS OF CONCERN

I wish to address briefly a few more areas of concern before making a final evaluation of Holy Laughter. First, I think a characteristic lack of discernment remains at many of the renewal meetings. When ministers say things like "don't analyze, just receive," or "God is in the business today of offending our minds," this can only encourage anti-intellectualism and discourage discernment.

The evangelical mind is already on a downward trend. Anti-intellectualism is always a potential danger in highly emotional and experiential settings. Ironically, past revivals were often birthed at higher learning centers, as in the Haystack prayer group at Williams College or the Wesleyan Holy Club at Oxford University. Surveying Pietism, Moravianism, and Methodism, Howard Snyder observes that education played a key role in these movements as well. Snyder notes, "One may recall that historically many significant social movements, both religious and political, have sprung up in university settings or among university students."[57]

Many Holy Laughter ministers assure their listeners that when God's children ask him for bread he will not give them a stone, meaning that since they are asking him for blessing, he's not going to give them Satan. While this is generally true, we still must be cautious. God could originally bless a church, but Satan could come quickly thereafter and lead people astray with extremism. Once extremism is accredited to the work of God and accepted as the norm, or once emotionalism is sought for emotionalism's sake, Satan has discredited a once

---

[57]Howard A. Snyder, *Signs of the Spirit: How God Reshapes the Church* (Grand Rapids: Zondervan, 1989) 250.

genuine move of the Spirit. Certain publications by those in the renewal do offer some discernment guidelines for testing a manifestation. I pray these will be implemented more in renewal services.[58]

There should also be a better balance between allowing God to do as he pleases and imposing human expectations. Carolyn Tennant writes: "A pastor friend of mine had a phone call from one of Rodney Howard-Browne's associates recently. He wanted to come and hold services. . . . Then he said something very interesting: 'I can guarantee you revival. If there is not revival, then you can have your money back.' "

Tennant observes, "Now I always thought that God was the one who chose to revive! How, then, can this man 'guarantee' revival? It seems that this eliminates the sovereignty of God."[59]

The renewal must put more emphasis on repentance and evangelism. George O. Wood, General Secretary of the Assemblies of God, notes that in Luke 15 the parables of the lost sheep, the lost coin, and the prodigal son all center on the concept of rejoicing. There was great rejoicing when the lost sheep, the lost coin, and the lost son were found. Wood writes, "The true laughing revival, spoken of by Jesus Himself, is one which comes to a church doing the work of evangelism, which knows the unlimited joy of seeing lost men and women, boys and girls, come to Christ."[60]

## TREASURES IN EARTHEN VESSELS
### (2 COR 4:7; 2 TIM 2:20)

What should we make of the phenomena? In a message entitled "Transposition," C. S. Lewis relates that when a lan-

---

[58] See for instance Mike Bickle and Michael Sullivant's guidelines: Does it bring honor to the person of Jesus Christ? Does it produce a greater hatred of sin and a greater love for righteousness? Does it produce a greater regard for Scripture? Does it lead people into truth? Does it produce a greater love for God and man? Mike Bickle and Michael Sullivant, *God's Manifest Presence: Understanding the Phenomena that Accompany the Spirit's Ministry* (Kansas City: Metro Vineyard, n.d.) 2. A similar list was written by Wes Campbell entitled "Our Judging Criteria," *Prophet Sharing 1992*, New Life Vineyard Fellowship.

[59] Tennant, "Toronto Blessing? Decide for Yourself," 70.

[60] George O. Wood, *The Laughing Revival: Distinguishing the Normative and Unique Elements of Spiritual Renewal* (Costa Mesa, Calif.: Christian Education Press, 1995) 16.

guage with more words in its vocabulary translates to one with fewer words, some words from the language with the smaller vocabulary must take on several different meanings. In the case of our emotions and the sensations they cause, something similar to this takes place.[61] The sensation of crying, for instance, is not limited to one emotion. Sometimes it expresses pain, other times grief, joy, or other feelings. Could not a touch from the unsearchable glory of God result in laughter, crying, or other activities—when in our frailty and human limitations we have no other way of expressing our response? As a faulty receiver fails to transmit energy properly, so humans often fail to express properly a touch from God due to their fleshly limitations. We have this treasure in meager jars of clay (2 Cor 4:7). Holy Laughter may be the result of frail humans expressing limited and faulty reactions to a true move of the Spirit.

Sometimes the human transmitters overreact, mistaking one level of frequency of God's presence for a deeper one. The presence of God, of course, is everywhere. But this presence cannot usually be felt. At another level, however, we can sense the presence of God in a deeper way, usually at a church service, a funeral, in prayer and solitude, or just whenever God wants to touch us with a real sense of his presence. On a third level, we may experience God in an overwhelming way (cf. Rev 1:17).

I remember entering a hyper-Pentecostal service a number of years ago where bedlam had broken out. Throughout this service I did sense a faint presence of the Lord, but nothing that should have caused the overreaction that I saw. Might it be that many in Holy Laughter are really sensing God's presence, but overreacting? Could they have created their own patterns of routines in response to the Spirit's presence? When Joe senses the Spirit, he laughs uncontrollably. When Sue senses the Spirit, she cries. Another falls down. Some reactions, like Joe's, conflict with Scripture—which says we can control ourselves (1 Cor 14:32). Some reactions, like Sue's, are perfectly biblical.

Here are some closing observations. First, as mentioned earlier, I do not think the devil is ultimately behind the Holy Laughter phenomena. He is losing too many souls and seeing

---

[61]C. S. Lewis, *The Weight of Glory and Other Addresses* (Grand Rapids: Eerdmans, 1965) 16–29.

too many Christians become more aggressive in attacking his kingdom through the renewal. Second, I also do not think the phenomena are due purely to suggestion. Too many discerning Christians, who were once skeptical, are now participating in the renewal. Third, on the one hand, if it is of God, why does he allow people to overreact in disorderly ways? On the other hand, do we realistically think God would stop touching people's lives for the sake of those who overreact? Did the Spirit stop touching people at the church of Corinth when they became disorderly? The Spirit can certainly move despite human shortcomings; I think this is primarily the case with the current renewal.

Moreover, I think it is the minister's responsibility, not God's, to make sure a church is running in an orderly way; and for the most part, renewal ministers have failed in this responsibility. It is certainly possible that the Spirit could one day grieve over the disorder and chaos so much that he refrains from touching the congregation. Congregants would then be left to continue mimicking the bodily exercises they manifested when God really was touching them. My bottom line is much in agreement with the Vineyard's official position. This is not a revival but a renewal. Not only God is present; so too are the flesh and the devil. Unlike most in the Vineyard, however, I believe that renewal ministers have not honestly come to grips with their churches' disorderly conduct.

PART 2

# BIBLICAL AND HISTORICAL PRECEDENTS

# 6

# HOLY LAUGHTER: A BIBLICAL APPROACH

"It's kind of a Samson anointing for strength. I don't know what sort of noises Samson made when the Spirit of God came on him and he carried the gates to the top of the hill. . . . he probably made this great roar and tore those things out of the ground and carried them to the top of the hill as he was empowered."[1] So says John Arnott, pastor of the Toronto Vineyard, regarding the manifestation of animal noises at his church. He relates how Samson escaped the Philistines in Judg 16:1–3, "And in any battle scenario, a part of the bravado that goes along with it is all of the yelling and stuff, isn't it? So it's a natural impulse when people are going to war. . . . I think that [roaring] is an impartation of power and strength and kind of like a declaration of war."

Many Holy Laughter ministers cite biblical references to support phenomena such as laughter, trembling, falling, and roaring. They teach that the presence of God causes people to react physically in extraordinary ways. Their critics also employ Scripture, claiming that the Bible condemns such practices. Some of these critics call the phenomena strong delusions of Satan, fulfilling the end-time predictions of a coming apostasy (e.g., Matt 24:24; 2 Thess 2:9).[2] One writer warns, "The 'laughing

---

[1]John Arnott and Guy Chevreau, "Pastors' Meeting," 19 Oct. 1994 (Toronto: Airport Vineyard), audio tape.

[2]See for instance, K. B. Napier, "Toronto Update," *British Beacon: Christian News and Views* (Nov. 1994) 2–3; Alan Morrison, "Falling for

revival' could one day merge with what the New Age calls the coming day of 'planetary Pentecost.' "[3]

Many, however, fail to establish why such phenomena are apostate. Merely saying that God will permit false prophets to perform lying wonders in the last days is not enough. Such an answer begs the question by presupposing that Holy Laughter is demonstrably occultic. The critics must show *why* the renewal teachers are false prophets, and why Holy Laughter is occultic. And they have failed to do this adequately.

Others claim that although Holy Laughter phenomena are not necessarily occultic, there is no biblical evidence to support them. The Vineyard Christian Fellowship discourages proof-texting the phenomena.[4] They do believe that some of the manifestations, while unconventional, still have some biblical basis (e.g., being "slain in the spirit"), but they consider other manifestations such as animal noises as extrabiblical. They encourage pastors to avoid creating a doctrine out of such manifestations. John Wimber writes:

> In the excitement of the infilling and empowering, and moving of the Spirit, some people momentarily do things that they really ought not to do. They say or do things that they think are in vogue, like "Fall, fall, fall. . . ." or "Roar, roar, roar. . . ." Frankly, that is excusable—for now—but the methodology of the ministry to one another needs correction.[5]

Nevertheless, the Vineyard also claims, "The absence of a proof-text, however, does not necessarily disallow an experience. If so, none of us could go to Disneyland, use computers to write messages, or have worship bands."[6] Ultimately, Wimber's bottom line on Holy Laughter is: "The Lord is being

---

the Lie," *Evangelical Times* (Oct. 1994) 15; "Dr. John MacArthur: Songtime USA Radio Interview," audio tape (transcript by Todd Hunter; Internet: hunter44@io.org).

[3]Smith, "Holy Laughter or Strong Delusion?" 13.

[4]The official Association of Vineyard Churches position on Holy Laughter is presented in two documents entitled "Board Report: Association of Vineyard Churches Sept./Oct. 1994," and a supplementary insert paper entitled "John Wimber Responds to Phenomena." These were distributed to all Vineyard pastors on October 14, 1994. These documents summarize consensus views of the Association of Vineyard Churches Board Meeting of September 1–2, 1994.

[5]John Wimber, "Refreshing, Renewal, and Revival," 3.

[6]"Board Report: Association of Vineyard Churches Sept./Oct. 1994," 1.

exalted by His own means. He just does things differently than you or I would (see Is. 55:8). Let's keep the message Christ-centered."[7]

But other renewal ministers do not hesitate to cite proof-texts supporting Holy Laughter. Perhaps the most prominent apologetic work of this sort comes from a paper entitled "What in the World Is Happening to Us?: A Biblical Perspective on Renewal" by Bill Jackson from the Champaign/Urbana Vineyard in Illinois. Although there are no primary scriptures directly attesting to these phenomena, Jackson writes, "There are, however, a number of secondary (remember, secondary does not mean invalid or unimportant) texts that illustrate that these were some of the responses people had during moments of divine visitation."[8] British renewal minister Gerald Coates writes, "There is plenty of biblical material covering these manifestations of the Holy Spirit and reactions to his presence."[9]

Does Scripture support Holy Laughter phenomena? It may be difficult to answer this question since we are primarily addressing experience, not doctrine. Guy Chevreau writes: "In seeking to evaluate what is taking place at the Airport Vineyard, we must understand that the manifest presence of God IS highly subjective. It IS experiential. It IS, often, emotional. And, it IS typically messy."[10] Still, we shall attempt to unravel some of the "mess."

## SLAIN IN THE SPIRIT

Ezra Coppin stood by skeptically whenever he saw "holy rollers" fall down in ecstatic bliss, allegedly overwhelmed by the Spirit's presence. Having been raised a Baptist, he was suspicious of being "slain in the Spirit" (also called "falling" or "resting in the Spirit"); that is, until it happened to him. After it did, he wrote a book describing several accounts of the falling

---

[7]Wimber, "Visitation of the Spirit," 9.

[8]Jackson, "What in the World?" 3. This work has spawned many other apologetic papers adopting the same basic arguments.

[9]Gerald Coates, " 'Toronto' and Scripture," in *The Impact of 'Toronto,'* 47.

[10]Chevreau, *Catch the Fire*, 67–68.

phenomenon. Aware that Satan counterfeits God's enter-
prises, he criticizes extreme accounts of the phenomenon
but resists any blanket condemnations or endorsements. Ultimately, he believes that since God can do whatever he pleases,
being slain in the Spirit can generally be a sign of his divine
presence.[11]

Like Coppin, we must not deny God's sovereignty. Who can
dare deny that he has the ability to knock someone down with
his overwhelming presence? The question is, does this ability
of God validate an expectation of being slain in the Spirit as a
normal part of one's Christian experience? Morton Kelsey
responds:

> Religious descriptions do not always tell us what was happening
> inside the person, and this makes it hard to be sure about a
> complex experience like slaying in the Spirit. There was obviously
> nothing in biblical times exactly similar to a modern service in
> which people come forward, are touched, and fall down; on the
> other hand, there are many references in the Old and New Testa-
> ments to people who fell before God and seemed to be struck
> down by His Spirit.[12]

Let us examine the most prominent texts related to this
subject. Genesis 15:12–21 is often cited to support being slain
in the Spirit. The passage tells of Abraham falling into a deep
sleep. The Lord reveals to him some prophetic events such as
the upcoming slavery of his people in Egypt. Jackson writes
that, "the Hebrew word [for sleep] *radam* is the same word
that is used when God put Adam to sleep when he made Eve in
Gen 2:21."[13] In the current renewal, however, most people
who fall down remain conscious. The deep sleep of Abraham
and Adam seems to indicate they were *unconscious*. (It would
have been terribly painful for Adam to be conscious while God
took out one of his ribs!) Neither passage claims they fell down
overcome by the Spirit's presence.

Similarly, renewal advocates parallel Matt 17:6 with Luke
9:32 to show that the disciples were "heavy with sleep" when
Jesus was transfigured before them. This allegedly means
they were overwhelmed by Christ's unveiled glory. But the
disciples did not feel drowsy as a result of God's presence or

---

[11] Ezra Coppin, *Slain in the Spirit: "Fact or Fiction"* (Greenforest,
Ariz: New Leaf Press, 1976) 11, 13, 20, 96.
[12] Kelsey, *Discernment,* 526.
[13] Jackson, "What in the World?" 3.

Christ's unveiled glory. Norval Geldenhuys observes, "The disciples, who had for some time been sleeping because it was night and they were fatigued, later on, probably owing to the glow of the heavenly vision, awoke and saw the Savior with the two celestial messengers [Moses and Elijah] while His divine glory radiated from Him."[14] They did fall "facedown to the ground" when God appeared in a cloud overhead. They prostrated themselves before the Almighty because they were "terrified." Contrary to what we would expect if they had been spiritually slain, "Jesus came and touched them. 'Get up,' he said. 'Don't be afraid' " (Matt 17:7).

## FALLING DOWN IN GOD'S PRESENCE

Holy Laughter advocates also use other passages that generally depict the same thing—people falling down in the presence of the Lord. Ezekiel, for instance, falls facedown when he sees God's glory (Ezek 1:28; 3:23; 43:4–5; 44:4). Such contexts commonly depict the Hebrew custom of prostrating oneself before man or God out of reverence or worship (cf. Ruth 2:10; 2 Sam 14:22; Ezek 43:3). Here, the falling on one's face involved fear and reverence common in Middle Eastern settings, not ecstatic bliss.

In Matt 28:1–4, the guards at Christ's tomb shook and became as "dead men" when the angel of the Lord appeared (Matt 28:1–4). Apparently, they fainted from overwhelming fright. But unlike most of today's occurrences, here it was *unbelievers* who swooned in the visitation, not Christians. Nevertheless, the accounts in Ezekiel and Matthew do not preclude the real possibility of God's overwhelming presence having such a physical effect.

Two other passages present a further challenge. In Dan 8:17 and 10:9, Daniel fell down and was "stunned" when he encountered the angel of God. In Rev 1:17, John fell at the feet of the glorified Christ "as though dead." After both Daniel and John were told not to fear, they received a prophetic revelation.

---

[14]Norval Geldenhuys, *The Gospel of Luke* (NIC; Grand Rapids: Eerdmans, 1983) 281.

Notably, fear and reverence are not the only causes of Daniel's prostration. In 8:17–18, Daniel's state of being "terrified" *(ba'ath)* "commonly means 'overwhelm' without in itself specifying the cause. The context often indicates something other than fear (e.g., 1 Sam 16:14–15)."[15] The Hebrew word "stunned" *(radam)* in Daniel 10:7 can be translated as a deep sleep (as we saw earlier in Gen 15:12) or a "stunning effect of awe and dread," or perhaps a "trance."[16]

One should also take into consideration the state of Daniel's company: "terror overwhelmed them that they fled and hid themselves" (10:7). Does God's presence instill such a reaction of holy fear in reference to today's phenomenon?

John's prostration in Rev 1:17 is reminiscent of Daniel. Fear and overpowering awe struck John when he beheld Christ's glory. As in Daniel, this is a unique and sovereign act of God upon one of his saints, prior to inspired revelation. Such biblical encounters were not presented as being normative, as are the ecstatic, "make me feel good" experiences in our own time.

### THE WEIGHT OF GLORY

We now turn to 2 Chron 5:13–14. At the dedication of Solomon's temple, the priests could not perform their duties because the shekinah glory of God filled the temple. Jackson claims:

> It never says that the priests fell but it does indicate that under God's glory they were essentially immobilized, physically unable to perform their duties. What happened seems to be connected to the Hebrew word for "glory" *(kabod)* which means "a weight." The phenomenon of falling in God's presence might be understood as being overcome by the weight of God forcing them to the floor.[17]

Similar biblical occurrences involve God being so overwhelmingly present that the priests could not *enter* the temple (Exod 40:34–35; Rev 15:8). Hence, God's powerful presence indeed filled his temple, but in these passages, his presence drove people *out* of his house!

---

[15]John E. Goldingay, *Daniel* (WBC; Dallas: Word Books, 1989) 199.
[16]Brown, Driver, Briggs, *Hebrew-English Lexicon*, 922; Goldingay, *Daniel*, 291.
[17]Jackson, "What in the World?" 3.

Similarly, Paul and his companions may have been "flattened" by the weight of God's glory in Acts 9. Here we read that Paul fell to the ground when Christ appeared to him in a bright light. We must remember, though, that the fear and surprise of being surrounded by a light that was "brighter than the sun" played a significant part in this fall (Acts 26:13). The light rendered Paul blind for three days, resulting in his conversion (Acts 9:9). Steve Eutsler writes: "In the case of Paul, the Lord gave him direction as to how to receive the revelation of His will. Something distinctive was given each time [someone fell in God's presence]. The application is clear. *Each prostrated believer should receive an extraordinary revelation of the Word or will of God, if his experience is genuine.*"[18]

We find an unusual case in 1 Sam 19:18–24. Here Saul and his men are overcome by the Spirit of God at Naioth when they enter Samuel's school of the prophets. Saul lies down, stripped of his garments "all day and night" as he prophesies.[19] He appears to have been in an ecstatic state or "possession trance."[20] The Spirit had overwhelmed Saul before, but this time it was recorded that he fell to the ground (cf. 1 Sam 10:10–13). Is this a legitimate example of being slain in the Spirit? The utterances of the prophets in this account certainly depict phenomena similar to those seen in modern revivals, but there are some significant differences.

Saul, in a state of rebellion against God, was persecuting David when this event took place. *In order to protect David,* the Spirit of God came upon Saul and his men. And no true repentance took place: "One would think that such a religious catharsis might have freed Saul of his bitterness. But obviously the experiences touched only the periphery of his emotional trouble. Like many an unstable person who attend a religious revival, the effect is superficial."[21] We must also remember that in this account Saul stripped off his

---

[18] Steve Eutsler, "The Doctrine of Prostration," *Paraclete* (Summer 1988) 19.

[19] Ralph Klein suggests from two Masoretic glosses that the messengers also stripped (*1 Samuel* [WBC; Waco: Word Books, 1983], 199).

[20] Simon B. Parker, "Possession Trance and Prophecy in Pre-Exilic Israel," *VT* 28, 3 (1978) 271–275.

[21] George Caird and John C. Schroeder, *The Interpreter's Bible* (New York/Nashville: Abingdon/Cokesbury Press, 1953) 2:988.

clothes.[22] It may not be a good idea to encourage such reactions to the Spirit's moving today! Some scholars claim the question arising from 19:24, "Is Saul also among the prophets?" suggests the negative answer, "No, Saul is no prophet; he is insane."[23]

One final proof-text cited to support being slain in the Spirit is John 18:6. When the soldiers were about to arrest Jesus, they asked him if he was Jesus of Nazareth. Jesus replied, "I am he." As soon as he said "I am he," the soldiers fell backward to the ground.

The "I am he" in this passage may indicate a reference to the divine name (cf. John 8:24, 28, 58; Exod 3:14), but we must note that other times when Christ said "I am he" no one fell. Why this exception? Leon Morris explains the passage this way:

> The effect of Jesus' bearing is now brought out. His fearlessness, the gloom with its atmosphere of mysteriousness, His numinous words, all combined to produce a moment of terror, or perhaps awe. The soldiers retreated and fell to the ground. It is possible that those in front recoiled from Jesus' unexpected advance, so that they bumped those behind them, causing them to stumble and fall.[24]

However one understands this passage, one thing is evident: as with the case of Saul, no transformation took place. The soldiers got right back up and arrested Jesus.

FALLING DOWN: PAST AND PRESENT

While a number of the passages we have examined have been misinterpreted or misapplied, God's presence can certainly overwhelm a person so that he or she falls to the ground. Although we do not find an *exact* one-to-one scriptural correlation with today's phenomenon of being slain in the Spirit, we do see some *similarities* in 1 Sam 19:18–24, Dan 8:17 and 10:9, John 18:6, Acts 9:26, and Rev 1:17.[25] We should also note that

[22]According to Robert P. Gordon, Saul's nudity may have been only partial ("Saul's Meningitis According to Targum 1 Samuel 20:24," *VT* 37, 1; 1987:39).

[23]Klein, *1 Samuel,* 199.

[24]Leon Morris, *The Gospel According to John* (NIC; Grand Rapids: Eerdmans, 1971) 743–44.

[25]In all the accounts except John 18:6, those who were touched by God apparently fell forward, not backward, as commonly seen in today's phenomenon.

on some occasions demons threw people to the ground (Mark 3:11; 9:20; Luke 8:28).

Since the Spirit of God is sovereign, we should be cautious not to claim presumptuously that the Spirit *cannot* move in this way—there is enough indirect biblical support to warrant the possibility that such a phenomenon as falling is valid. Moreover, it would be incorrect to say that being overwhelmed by God's presence is entirely unbiblical or anti-biblical. Nor can we rule out *every* instance of being slain in the Spirit as human-induced (or demon-induced) as opposed to God-induced.

On the other hand, such incidences as those in which "gifted" preachers conduct "assembly line" slaying in the Spirit (where church members sequentially fall down when the preacher lays hands on or blows on them) discredits God's sovereignty. This has more to do with mimicking, suggestion, and peer pressure than with God's Spirit. Why does the Spirit need a minister to suggest when a person must fall? And why would the Spirit need the nudging hand of the minister to help him "floor" an individual? Jerry Don Venable writes: "If 'slain in the Spirit' is a gift to be sought, then all other manifestations in the Bible would be the same, such as Moses' rod turning into a serpent, stopping the moon and sun as Joshua did, etc. These manifestations are sovereign acts of God, not gifts."[26] While God can certainly overwhelm individuals with his presence, it is unbiblical to think that he needs human help to do this.

To keep order and avoid injuries, some ministers employ "catchers" to lay down falling individuals neatly and cover the legs of women with dresses. Although this is orderly, it lacks authenticity.[27] If the Spirit genuinely overwhelms someone so that he or she falls down, will he allow that person to be injured?

However, many Christians, including those experiencing Holy Laughter, would testify that they fell because God alone touched them. We cannot deny that at least in some of these cases, individuals may really have been touched by the Spirit

[26] Jerry Don Venable, "Slain in the Spirit: Another View," *Paraclete* (Summer 1988) 25.

[27] For John Wimber's perspective on catchers, consult Wimber, "Season of New Beginnings," 7.

of God. But such instances of falling down are not as normative as often portrayed. John White recalls only three instances where he experienced the overwhelming presence of God: "On the first two occasions I was somehow able to remain kneeling, in spite of appalling weakness and trembling. I mumbled adoration and confessions incoherently between my sobs. On the third occasion I lay on my face, a quivering mass of adoring jelly. I, therefore, am unable lightly to dismiss what I see of certain phenomena in the present, or what I read about in the past."[28]

## CRYING AND SHAKING

The Holy Laughter apologists cite a number of biblical references to justify the shaking and crying sometimes observed in their congregations. Since the trembling phenomena is closely related to falling down, certain passages used to defend being slain in the Spirit are applied here as well (e.g., Dan 10:7; Matt 28:4–6). Other common passages cited to support trembling are Ps 99:1: "The LORD reigns, let the nations tremble; He sits enthroned between the cherubim, let the earth shake" (cf. Pss 2:11; 114:7); Jer 5:22: " 'Should you not fear me?' declares the LORD. 'Should you not tremble in my presence?' "; Jer 23:9a: "My heart is broken within me; all my bones tremble . . . "; Hab 3:16: "I heard and my heart pounded; my lips quivered at the sound; decay crept into my bones and my legs trembled"; and Acts 7:32b: "Moses trembled with fear and did not dare look." Bill Jackson cites a strange example in Acts 4:31.[29] After the disciples prayed, they were filled with the Spirit, and the place where they had gathered was "shaken." (Note that the "place" was shaking, not the people!)

Crying can be observed in national or group repentance, as supported by passages like Neh 8:9 and Acts 2:37. (But the latter passage refers only to the Jews being "cut to the heart" after hearing Peter's sermon on Pentecost. There is no mention of crying.) Other passages used to support crying are Ezra 10:1; 2 Chron 34:27, Isa 22:12, and Luke 6:45.

---

[28] White, *When the Spirit Comes,* 24.
[29] Jackson, "What in the World?" 6.

Passages on trembling refer to people or objects (such as the earth) trembling before the Lord or before the judgment he brings. In every case the source of the shaking is human fear and reverence before God. As long as the same motivation undergirds the phenomenon in the renewal today, I find nothing wrong with it. Quite different are the extreme cases of shaking I have personally witnessed at a renewal meeting, which were violent to the point of convulsion. This was indistinguishable from an epileptic fit. What if someone really had a seizure in such a setting? I am convinced that many church members and ministers would have thanked God for touching that individual! Beyond this, John White notes that shaking can also be an indication of a demonic trance.[30]

Scripture does not support "convulsing" in the Spirit, or phenomena that resemble an epileptic seizure. Conversely, nothing is wrong with genuine crying and trembling in the Lord's presence, *unless it distracts others*. Mindless and disorderly activities must be discouraged. Christians are called to be sober-minded and self-controlled (1 Thess 5:6, 8; 1 Tim 2:15; 3:2; Tit 2:2, 4, 6; 1 Pet 1:13; 4:7; Rom 12:3 cf. Prov 25:28). Being sober-minded entails not merely maintaining moral self-control, but also being in one's right mind (cf. Mark 5:15; contrast Acts 26:24–25 with 1 Cor 14:23). Being in a state of madness (Greek: *mainomai* and *exestemen*) is the exact opposite of self-control and sobriety *(nepho* and *sophronoumen)*. When one is not in a proper frame of mind, this can result in having no control over oneself.

## DRUNKENNESS IN THE SPIRIT

At one local Rodney Howard-Browne meeting which I attended at Melodyland (Anaheim, California), a lady staggered around the altar as if drunk, becoming the new source of church entertainment for several minutes. As one of the ushers

---

[30]White, *When the Spirit Comes*, 99. Some have argued that Scriptures such as Isa 21:3–4 ("My mind reels, sudden convulsions seize me" NEB) refer to a sanctioned convulsive activity. This passage, however, specifically indicates that it was pain, of the magnitude of child birth, which resulted in this extreme writhing.

gently assisted her back to her seat, she ran away from him, making gestures that made it seem like he was trying to "pick her up." The audience got a big laugh out of this. Do such occurrences really glorify God? Some apparently think so. David Hoffman's response exemplifies the opinion of those who support being "drunk in the Spirit":

> If someone were to walk into this meeting not understanding what was happening, they'd definitely think we had been drinking or on some sort of drug! The manifestations of being "drunk in the Spirit" in the book of Acts is [sic] the same manifestation that we are experiencing today. I for one say, "Bless you Jesus for your works among us."[31]

Rodney Howard-Browne, who considers himself the "Holy Ghost bartender," speaks of the phenomenon as making one "more aware of the Holy Spirit than: friends, neighbors, loved ones, or natural surroundings . . . That's what it means to be filled with the new wine of the Spirit: to be drunk, inebriated, and intoxicated with His presence."[32] Reportedly, God told him, "I want you to pray for the fire that fell on you in 1979 to fall on other people—the same fire, the same drunkenness, the same filling."[33] There are three primary passages cited by those who support this phenomenon.

## JEREMIAH 23:9: "LIKE A DRUNKEN MAN"

In Jer 23:9b, Jeremiah describes himself as being "like a drunken man overcome by wine because of the LORD and his holy words." The context describes the prophet's sorrow on account of false prophets who seduce God's people. As drunkenness causes staggering, so Jeremiah staggered, overwhelmed by the sins committed in his homeland, and the judgment God would bring on the false prophets and priests (23:9–12). Jeremiah often refers to the judgment of God in terms of this metaphor of drunkenness (Jer 13:13; 25:1–29; Lam 4:21). Such descriptions are entirely foreign to the "holy drunkenness" touted by renewal leaders. Today's participants almost uni-

---

[31] David Hoffman, with Marc Dupont (ed.), "A *Biblical* Look at Renewal Manifestations" (El Cajon, Calif./Toronto: Mantle of Praise Ministries Inc., 1994) 7.
[32] Howard-Browne, *The Reality of the Person of the Holy Spirit*, 20.
[33] Howard-Browne, *Manifesting the Holy Ghost*, 18.

formly behave like carefree, sluggish drunkards with little concern for God's wrath or the sins of his people.

## ACTS 2:13: "THESE MEN ARE FULL OF NEW WINE"

In Acts 2:13, when the disciples spoke in tongues on the day of Pentecost, the mockers accused them of being drunk. According to Bill Jackson: "They would have been accused of such because they were acting like drunks, i.e., laughing, falling, slurred speech by some, boldness through lack of restraint, etc."[34] Rodney Howard-Browne writes, "Why did they think the believers were drunk? Because they must have acted like drunk people."[35]

Since Acts does not give enough details about why the mockers thought the disciples were "drunk" we should refrain from any dogmatism on this verse. The passage does not give us sufficient evidence to support that the disciples were "acting like drunks" in the "sluggish" Holy Laughter sense of the word. What then are some better explanations?

One explanation is that the mockers were fellow Israelites who could not understand the new languages of the disciples (cf. Acts 2:14). To them this phenomenon sounded like gibberish—similar to that used by drunks or by the worshippers of Dionysus who drank themselves into an ecstatic state and then made prophetic utterances.

Another plausible explanation comes from a first-century account in Philo's treatise *On Drunkenness:* "But whatever soul which is filled with grace is at once in a state of exultation, and delight, and dancing: for it becomes full of triumph, so that it would appear to many of the uninitiated to be intoxicated, and agitated, and to be beside itself."[36]

Despite the fact that it is a depressant, alcohol can have a stimulating effect in the early stages of drunkenness. The disciples, who were filled with the Holy Spirit, may have been labeled as drunkards because of their great joy and apparent exuberance. Even today when certain people are touched by God or get saved, their friends and family interpret their new

---

[34]Jackson, "What in the World?" 6.
[35]Howard-Browne, *The Reality of the Person of the Holy Spirit,* 25.
[36]Philo, *On Drunkenness* 36.146 in *The Works of Philo* (1854; trans. C. D. Yonge; Peabody: Hendrickson, 1993) 219–20.

enthusiasm as a sign that they are on drugs or have lost their mind. At any rate, we must remember that "it was the 'mockers' who said they were drunk, which is hardly a reliable source for listing symptoms of drunkenness!"[37] Moreover, Peter's sermon that immediately follows does not reflect the words of someone "drunk in the Spirit."

### EPHESIANS 5:18: NOT DRUNK WITH WINE, BUT FILLED WITH THE SPIRIT

In Eph 5:18 Paul contrasts being drunk with being filled with the Spirit. Holy Laughter ministers claim that this suggests those who were filled with the Holy Spirit acted like drunks. The Greek word "be filled" *(plerousthe)* is technically an imperative passive plural. It literally means "Let yourselves continually be filled" with the Spirit. Obviously Paul did not want the entire Christian community continuously to act like drunks! In the words of Gordon Fee:

> The richness of the metaphor comes in part from its contrast to being drunken with wine and in part from the verb "be filled." Together they do not picture a person who is "drunk on the Spirit," as it were, as if there were virtue in that, but a person—and in this case, a community!—whose life is so totally given over to the Spirit that the life and deeds of the Spirit are as obvious in their case as the effects of too much wine are obvious in the other.[38]

In essence, Paul is not equating being filled with the Spirit to any particular "drunk in the Spirit" experience. Rather, being filled with the Spirit involves a continuous and unfabricated lifestyle resulting in community worship and service (Eph 5:18–22). The overall context is calling for self-control. The children of light are contrasted with the children of darkness (Eph 5:8–14). This common Pauline theme exhorts the children of light to "take off" the works of the flesh and self-indulgence while "putting on" the fruits of the Spirit and self-control. One of the works of darkness and self-indulgence is drunkenness (Gal 5:19–22; 1 Thess 5:4–8; Rom 13:12–14; Col 3:5–17). The children of light are not to be yoked together with darkness (2 Cor 6:14–18). They must practice self-control,

---

[37] Intercessors for Britain, "The Toronto Experience," Fact sheet dated 15 Sept. 1994; Merryside, UK.

[38] Gordon Fee, *God's Empowering Presence: The Holy Spirit in the Letters of Paul* (Peabody: Hendrickson, 1994) 721.

which is also needed for prayer and spiritual warfare (Eph 6:10–18; 1 Thess 5:8, 17–22; Rom 13:12).

In Paul's mandate against getting drunk with wine, "debauchery" *(asotia)* is the same word used to describe loose living and a sense of wild, uncontrollable behavior (*asotia* is translated as "wild" in Titus 1:6 NIV; cf., Luke 15:13; 1 Pet 4:3–4).[39] It seems inconceivable that Paul would be encouraging the Ephesians to act like "holy drunkards" when in his overarching narrative he is contrasting disorderly self-indulgence with orderly self-control.

In a similar vein, Peter Gosnell argues that Eph 5:18–20 is an exhortation for meal-time propriety. The Hellenistic culture of the Ephesians participated in mealtime symposia where drinking and lively discourse converged. But "without proper direction, such meals easily degenerated into mindless frenzy."[40] In contrast, the Christian community was to eat their meals without letting their fellowship devolve into drunkenness (cf. 1 Cor 11:17–21) or unwholesome conversation (Eph 4:29–5:7). They were to be filled instead with the Spirit and sing spiritual songs to the Lord. As Gosnell asserts, "Controlled discussion is to be preferred to drunken dissipation."[41]

Out of the three passages we have examined, only Acts 2:13 seems to indicate that the Holy Spirit affected the disciples in such a way that they could be accused of drunkenness. But the modern Holy Laughter interpretation of this Spirit-drunkenness lacks scriptural support. It is perhaps the least appealing reading of this passage, because it comes closest to violating the biblical standards of sobriety and self-control. Being "drunk in the Spirit" is acknowledged as tending to lead to excesses, even by those who generally support it. Dave Roberts writes, "For those who are prone to be influenced by the 'flesh and the devil,' there may be temptations in this phenomenon that can lead to a

---

[39] Also see Cleon L. Rogers's teaching on *asotia* in "The Dionysian Background of Ephesians 5:18," *Bibliotheca Sacra* (July-Sept 1979) 255–57. Rogers claims that Paul is exhorting the Ephesians against the backdrop of Dionysus, the god of wine, whose wild worship prevailed in the Graeco-Roman world.

[40] Peter W. Gosnell, "Ephesians 5:18–20 and Mealtime Propriety," *Tyndale Bulletin* 44.2 (Nov. 1993) 368.

[41] Ibid., 369.

pseudo-drunkenness and what church leader Terry Virgo describes as 'unhelpful foolishness.' "[42]

Dennis Legget writes, "Christians are indeed called to live under the influence of the Spirit. Whereas wine depresses, dehumanizes, and leads to an uncontrolled life, the Spirit enlivens, stimulates, and humanizes by producing self-control in the life that is becoming more like Christ."[43]

---

## LAUGHING IN THE SPIRIT

---

"When it hit me in my belly, I began to laugh uncontrollably . . . laughter comes out of your belly, not out of your head. Your head says, 'What are you laughing at?' Your heart says, 'Shut up!' It bubbles. It was so overwhelming, I couldn't stop it," avows Rodney Howard-Browne regarding Holy Laughter.[44] There's nothing wrong with a good laugh, but does Scripture support the idea that the Holy Spirit causes people to laugh uncontrollably? Let's look at some of the most prominent Holy Laughter texts.

In Gen 17–18 we read that both Sarah and Abraham laughed when God promised Sarah she would give birth to a son in her old age. The child's name "Isaac" means "laughter." God worked out his divine plan through Isaac, who was revealed as a type of Christ in Gen 22. Mona Johnian writes, "Why indeed would the Creator from whom all creation has issued pour out joy and laughter for the healing of such a sick generation? Simple. The plan of redemption itself was birthed in laughter."[45]

This passage, Gen 17–18, essentially has nothing to do with Holy Laughter. Abraham and Sarah laughed in unbelief. Some Vineyard pastors have reportedly taught that this incident represents God's sovereignty to heal the barrenness of his people. But such an explanation is merely an *application* of this text. The account does not intrinsically warrant this interpretation.

---

[42] Roberts, *"Toronto" Blessing,* 133.
[43] Dennis Legget, "Be Filled with the Spirit," *Paraclete* (Fall 1989) 11.
[44] Howard-Browne, *Manifesting the Holy Ghost,* 16.
[45] Johnian, *The Fresh Anointing,* 15.

Dave Roberts notes that in Ps 126 God's people were filled with laughter, and Eccl 3:4 teaches that there is "a time to weep and a time to laugh."[46] The former passage depicts laughter from the Jewish captives returning to Jerusalem in joy and triumph. The latter simply affirms the human emotion of laughter. Neither refers to laughter prompted by the Spirit.

In John 17:13 Jesus prays that the joy of the disciples may be full. Many other passages speak of joy in the presence of the Lord (Isa 9:3; Ps 16:11; 25:6; Acts 13:52, cf. Prov 17:22). The problem lies, however, in equating fullness of joy with "holy laughter." Granted, the overflowing of joy may result in laughter, but there is no *necessary* connection between the two.

A number of other passages mention laughing, but none of them attribute it to a move of the Spirit. Jesus says, "Blessed are you who weep now, for you will laugh" (Luke 6:21). But if this refers to Holy Laughter, what does he mean when he later says, "Woe to you who laugh now, for you will mourn and weep" (Luke 6:25)? Would this not condemn Holy Laughter? It is better to admit that neither passage applies to the phenomenon. Bildad, when exhorting Job, says that if Job were blameless, "He [God] will yet fill your mouth with laughter and your lips with shouts of joy" (Job 8:20–21). Since the book of Job is highly poetic, we cannot draw much even from this passage. Nothing in this text implies the uncontrollable laughter found in today's phenomenon. The Bible affirms only that God's children, like all other human beings, participate in laughter.

Nevertheless, this does not rule out the possibility that God could move upon an individual so that the person was filled with extreme joy. A natural way to express that joy would be laughter. The crux of the matter, however, is sobriety. Scripture clearly enjoins Christians to be sober-minded (1 Pet 1:13; 5:8; Tit 2:2; 3:11; 1 Thess 5:6–8; cf. Eccl 7:3–4; Jas 4:10–11). The Greek word commonly used here is *nēphō*, "be sober." In Hellenistic literature, it refers to abstaining from wine. In the New Testament, however, it is used figuratively to exhort freedom from all forms of mental and spiritual drunkenness, excess, passions, rashness, and so forth. It encourages being

[46]Roberts, *"Toronto" Blessing*, 129.

well-balanced and self-controlled.[47] Excessive, uncontrollable expressions of Holy Laughter stand in stark contrast to this. Also, since the "spirit of the prophets is subject to the prophets" (1 Cor 14:32–33), we must question the legitimacy of the experience of those who claim they cannot control themselves when the Spirit causes them to laugh.

### ROARING AND OTHER ANIMAL NOISES

Animal noises are perhaps the most controversial phenomena in the Holy Laughter renewal. John Wimber admits that the "roaring" phenomenon has caused disagreement within the movement. He says, "I cannot endorse or even encourage this experience in our movement and ministry."[48] He admits that in the past the Vineyard would cast out demons from people who made animal noises.[49]

Dave Roberts admits that in the past, animal noises in the charismatic movement would normally have prompted an exorcism.[50] John Arnott responds, "Our first inclination is 'That's demonic.' But that is too simplistic a view. It should be the flesh or more probably, if you know the person and their heart and their integrity, it just may be the Holy Spirit putting an empowering, like a warrior, on them."[51] Arnott combines Amos 3:8 ("The lion has roared—who will not fear? The Sovereign LORD has spoken—who can but prophesy?") with Rev 4:6–7 (John's prophetic vision of the four beasts with the faces of a lion, an ox, a man, and an eagle) and suggests the animal noises are precursors to prophetic utterances. In the Vineyard church at St. John, New Brunswick, he claims, the four animals of Rev 4 once manifested at the same time:

> One of our congregation's been acting like an eagle flying around the room. We can't get them to stop, what do we do? And we

---

[47]W. Bauer, W. F. Arndt, F. W. Gingrich, and F. W. Danker, *Greek-English Lexicon of the New Testament and Other Early Christian Literature* (2d ed. Chicago: University of Chicago Press, 1979) 538–39.

[48]Wimber, "John Wimber Responds to Phenomena," n.p.

[49]Wimber, "Refreshing, Renewal, and Revival," 2, 6. See also John White, "Young Lady, Old Hag," in *Power Encounters among Christians in the Western World,* Kevin Springer, ed. (San Francisco: Harper & Row, 1988) 81–82.

[50]Roberts, *'Toronto' Blessing,* 134.

[51]Arnott and Chevreau, "Pastor's Meeting," audio tape.

thought, you know, throw a rabbit out in the middle of the floor and maybe they'll come down [Laughter]. . . . But we saw all four of them going at once. It scared people so bad that many of them ran right out of the meeting. I was amazed, myself. This one little keyboard player lady, about 115 pounds, she's on all fours just snorting and pawing the ground like an angry bull.[52]

Scriptures such as Amos 3:8 and Rev 4:6–7 simply do not encourage or imply any human mimicking of animal noises or gestures. The passage in Amos illustrates that as the roar of the lion causes those who hear it to be attentive, so Israel needs to be attentive to God's word.

Some appeal to Christ's identity as the "lion of Judah" and relate roaring to the prophetic with passages such as Hos 11:10: " 'They will follow the LORD; he will roar like a lion. When he roars, his children will come trembling from the west. They will come trembling like birds from Egypt, like doves from Assyria. I will settle them in their homes,' declares the LORD." The context refers to Israel's regathering into their land after being dispersed abroad. Note that it's the Lord who "roars," not the Christians. This refers to a loud authoritative call, much like the blowing of a trumpet (Isa 27:13; Rev 10:3). We cannot draw any conclusion about literal lion roaring among Christians from this passage, any more than we could reason that Christ is Satan because he is the lion of Judah in Rev 5:5 and Satan is a roaring lion in 1 Pet 5:8!

If we support the use of animal noises on the basis of Scripture, what would stop us from eventually casting off all interpretative constraints? Why stop at the four animals in Rev 4? Why not moo like the cow in 1 Sam 6:12? Why not slither like the snake in Prov 30:19? Why not crow like the rooster in Matt 26:75? (No doubt these phenomena have already been tried!) The possibilities are virtually endless once we have banished all objectivity from our interpretation of the Bible, seeking only to make Scripture fit our subjective experiences. Of course, once we do this, we have reduced the Bible to meaninglessness—it means whatever we want it to say. Then profane activities such as "holy burping," "holy spitting," and who knows what else, become fair game. As the late Walter Martin would say, one could ignore the context of individual scriptures, isolate verses, and string them together

---

[52] Ibid.

to support any desired belief. "Judas hanged himself" (Matt 27:5) can be added to "Do likewise" (Luke 3:11) to support suicide.

John Wimber has a more honest approach regarding animal sounds when he admits "there is no biblical or theological framework for such phenomena. I don't see anywhere in the New Testament where Jesus and/or the apostles encouraged such phenomena or encountered such phenomena. Therefore, I think these kinds of things have to be put in a category of 'non-biblical' and 'exotic.' "[53]

## HOLY LAUGHTER: BIBLICAL, EXTRABIBLICAL, OR UNBIBLICAL?

We have examined the major biblical texts used to support the Holy Laughter phenomena. Many passages have been misused to support the phenomena of the current renewal. Other Scriptures actually describe phenomena *like* those found in the current renewal, but these occurences are not normative. There are four observations I wish to address from our study.

*First, the Bible relates a variety of reactions on the part of people who were touched by God's presence.* Some fell down; some trembled; some had visions; and so on—Daniel even felt sick.

*Second, the presence of God can overcome both saints and sinners.* God's presence touched not only Daniel and John the apostle, but King Saul and Saul of Tarsus too. The event changed Saul of Tarsus forever. He became the Apostle Paul. Nonetheless, King Saul, even after being touched by God's Spirit, did not repent.

*Third, God's presence can come in various forms or modes.* The presence of God was sometimes manifested as the glorious shekinah cloud: such was the manifestation to the children of Israel in the wilderness, and perhaps with the Hebrew priests at the dedication of Solomon's temple. Other times God chose to manifest his presence through visions, as in the case of Ezekiel. At still other times he appeared as the Angel of

[53] Wimber, "John Wimber Responds to Phenomena," n.p.

the Lord. On the day of Pentecost, the Spirit was accompanied with tongues of fire.

*Finally, as with King Saul, there are times when no apparent manifestation or vision takes place, but people are touched by his presence nevertheless.* Throughout biblical history, God has revealed his presence in a variety of ways, and there have been a variety of human reactions to his presence.

Perhaps the Holy Laughter critics' most common objection is that the phenomena connected with this renewal have no biblical support. (Nonetheless, they should admit that similar phenomena have some biblical precedent, if not normative force.) But the question to answer is: even if Scripture did not give us any remote similarities to the current renewal phenomena, would this necessarily mean they cannot be from God? Wes Campbell says:

> Now here's the fundamental question: if you remember nothing else, remember this. What law of interpretation of the Bible do you operate on? Unless it's expressly stated, does that mean you can't do it? Or unless it's forbidden and contrary to Scripture, does that mean that you can do it? In other words, is your interpretation of the Bible this: if it doesn't contradict the flow of Scripture and has spiritual fruit and it is in the bounds of the principles of Scripture, it's allowed. Or, if it isn't mentioned, it's not allowed? That's the fundamental thing right there. And I'll tell you this: every single person that believes the Bible—that says "If you can't show it to me in the Bible, I don't do it"—every single one of them will violate that principle somewhere in their life. Every single one of them. Because the Bible was not written to be read in that narrow context.[54]

Campbell continues by citing John 21:24–25, which states that Jesus did many miracles not recorded in Scripture. He concludes that there are things not found in the Bible which are nevertheless true. In essence, he is correct. All truth *is* God's truth, be it a mathematical equation, Aristotle's logic, or the statement "The U.S. abolished slavery in the nineteenth century." In a similar way, worship should not be limited to forms that are directly found in Scripture. If we were so limited, we would have to ban all microphones, cassette tapes, electric guitars, ties, three-piece suits, and even leather-bound red-letter edition study Bibles, because such things are not found in Scripture.

---

[54]Wes Campbell, "Spiritual and Physical Manifestations of the Holy Spirit," 15 Oct. 1994 (Toronto: Vineyard Fellowship), audio tape.

In any case, the phenomena we have studied here are clearly not biblically normative; *but then again, neither is a genuine revival* (nor an alleged precursor to a revival). So we must always use discernment and test all things (Acts 17:11; 1 John 4:1). In the same passage where Paul enjoins us to "test everything," he also exhorts, "Do not put out the Spirit's fire; do not treat prophecies with contempt" (1 Thess 5:19–21). Perhaps Paul understood that God's ways are not always like our ways. Perhaps he understood that God sometimes offends our sense of propriety.

Martin Lloyd-Jones once said, "The greatest sin of the evangelical church . . . is that we want to put God in a little box and tell him what he is permitted to do and what he's not permitted to do."[55] If we are to critique the Holy Laughter phenomena correctly, we must do so without assuming that it is wrong because it violates our own personal sense of propriety. Moreover, it is not enough to say there is no biblical evidence for it. We must show why it is contrary to Scripture, or why it undermines the Christian faith, or why it offends the biblical sense of propriety in worship.

---

[55]Virgo, "Making Sense," 72.

# HOLY LAUGHTER, THE
# CORINTHIAN CHURCH, AND
# PROPRIETY IN WORSHIP

Two passages in 1 Cor 14 stand out regarding propriety in worship. Chapter 14:32–33 reads, "The spirits of the prophets are subject to the control of the prophets. For God is not the God of disorder but of peace." Verse 40 of the same chapter reads, "But everything should be done in a fitting and orderly way." Holy Laughter supporters respond to these passages in several ways. John Wimber has stated that there are many, culturally diverse usages of the word "order"; he concludes that our interpretation of what is decent and orderly has been colored by our Western world view.[1] Dave Roberts writes, "For some then 'decently and in order' means a responsible flexibility, a willingness to live between the opposite poles of detailed organization and complete spontaneity."[2]

Some interpretations have been tailored not to conflict with the phenomena present at Holy Laughter services. In the process, "decency and order" have essentially been reduced to whatever a pastor or congregation wants them to mean. In another place Roberts references the soldiers' falling down before Jesus in John 18:6 and notes that despite what 1 Cor 14:32 says, God sometimes completely overcomes

---

[1]Wimber, "Refreshing, Renewal, and Revival," 5.
[2]Roberts, *"Toronto" Blessing*, 154–55.

someone.[3] Terry Virgo cites the account in Acts 10 in which
Cornelius and his household burst out in tongues in the middle
of Peter's preaching; his conclusion: "Often a new move
clashes with previous experience."[4] Peter's sermon was inter-
rupted by the Spirit of God; couldn't this, then, happen today
at a Holy Laughter meeting?

Such Scripture references are of course biblical, but they
are not normative for Christian teaching and conduct. The
circumstances surrounding Acts 10, for example, are unique.
This was the first time the Gentiles as a group accepted the
Gospel. In this one-time event, Peter was ministering to a
group of non-Christians, not Christians as in the case of the
renewal meetings. I doubt if Peter would have put up with
Christians interrupting his sermons every time he preached!
He, like Paul, exhorted Christians to be sober-minded and
self-controlled (1 Pet 1:13; 4:7; 5:8). George O. Wood, General
Secretary of the Assemblies of God, notes how Peter's shadow
healed people in Acts 5:15. He invites us to imagine a contemporary minister having a healing "shadow ministry":

> Suppose, further, that the word got around, and other ministers
> also began claiming to have "the shadow ministry." Suppose that
> yet others came along and said, "All ministers can have the
> shadow ministry, and all who want to be healed should get them-
> selves into the shadow." Finally, imagine that books and clinics
> began to teach the entire body of Christ the importance and need
> for "shadow ministry," along with practical steps of having
> "shadow ministries" in every local church. . . . What the "shadow
> ministry" of Peter illustrates is that the Holy Spirit may act
> sovereignly through an individual for a limited time and in a
> unique manner, but such working on His part may not be de-
> signed as normative in the experience of the church.[5]

Like the imagined promoters of "shadow ministries," the
Holy Laughter promoters often turn abnormal phenomena
into something normative. True, some phenomena *like* that
found in Holy Laughter can be found in Scripture, but like
Peter's healing shadow, they seem to be neither normative nor
even intended ever to be repeated. Thus, Holy Laughter advocates have not adequately presented us with a biblical model
of propriety in worship.

---

[3]Ibid., 138.
[4]Virgo, "Making Sense," 73.
[5]Wood, *The Laughing Revival*, 3–4.

Before we can conclude with sufficient confidence whether or not Paul would have considered the Holy Laughter phenomena as disorderly, we must understand Paul's motivations in insisting that worship be done "decently and in order." At the time that Paul wrote 1 Cor 11–14, it seems that some of the Christian women at Corinth had carried over into their worship aspects of their former pagan practice of Dionysiac worship. Let us first look at Dionysiac rituals, and then relate this background to events in the church at Corinth. After this we will compare the problems of disorder in the church of Corinth with Holy Laughter.

## DIONYSIAN WORSHIP AND MAENADS

In Graeco-Roman cultures, the god Dionysus was the son of Zeus. Dionysian devotees drank wine and believed that Dionysus manifested himself *through* the wine. Since the wine itself changed (in their belief) into a drink potent with divine power, the cult's drunkenness transcended mere intoxication—it involved spiritual ecstasy.[6] Converts also ate the raw flesh of a fawn or bull that had been torn apart by the maenads (from the Greek word *mainas* or "raving woman"[7]) who were among the followers of Dionysus. Other Dionysian ritual practices included reversing the sex roles in one's outward appearance, swinging a virgin in a chair hung on a tree, crowning one's head with snakes, playing the flute and cymbal, holding the thyrsus (a long stick with ivy leaves), and wild dancing.[8]

In Phrygia, Asia Minor—the same region that birthed the prophetic Montanist movement of second century A.D.,[9] which

---

[6]Harold R. Willoughby, *Pagan Regeneration: A Study of Mystery Initiations in the Graeco-Roman World* (Chicago: The University of Chicago Press, 1929, 1960) 71–75.

[7]C. Kerenyi, *Dionysos: Archetypal Image of the Indestructible Life* (Princeton: Princeton University Press, 1976) 176.

[8]John Dillon, "Dionysus," in *Anchor Bible Dictionary* 2.202; C. Kerenyi, *Dionysos,* 156–59; Luther H. Martin, *Hellenistic Religions: An Introduction* (New York/Oxford: Oxford University Press, 1987) 95; Elaine Fantham, Helene Foley, Natalie Kampen, Sarah Pomeroy, and H. A. Shapiro, *Women in the Classical World: Image and Text* (New York/Oxford: Oxford University Press, 1994) 90–91.

[9]After the ecstatic Montanists arrived in Phrygia their prophetic ministry was condemned by the bishops. Montanists claimed a fuller

may have been influenced by Dionysiac precursors—aspects of Dionysian worship intermingled with those of the *Magna Mater* or Cybele cult that worshipped the Great Mother of Anatolia. Practices included the playing of tambourines and cymbals, reed-bearing, flogging, mourning, abstinence, and castration of the male devotees.[10]

The maenads participated in ecstatic Dionysian dances. One of the oldest and most prominent texts on maenadism appears in Euripedes's *Bacchae* (c. 450 B.C.), which claims that the maenads "at the appointed hour, began to move the thyrsus into bacchic dances" as they danced their way to a state of ecstatic frenzy.[11] As a maenad, a Corinthian housewife could escape boredom and responsibilities by dancing into a mindless state. As W. K. C. Guthrie asserts, "The greatest gift of Dionysus was the sense of utter freedom, and in Greece it was the women, with their normally confined and straitened lives, to whom the temptation of release made the strongest appeal."[12]

Thus, Corinthian women were participating in a religion that gave them a sense of power through possession by the god of wine himself. Dionysiac worship therefore appealed to the lower and slave classes.[13] Once the Dionysian faithfuls reached their final state of ecstasy *(ekstasis)*, miraculous and supernatural phenomena allegedly took place. In the first century, Philo describes this ecstasy in terms of alienating the mind.[14] In this state, devotees sometimes received visions or imagined the ground turning to milk and

---

revelation with apocalyptic messages. The prophets of the movement received these revelations while in a state of ecstatic frenzy. However, Epiphanius, the church father, claimed that true prophets retained their reason when they prophesied. See Burgess, *Ancient Christian Traditions*, 14, 49–53.

[10] Marvin M. Meyer, ed., *The Ancient Mysteries: A Source Book* (San Francisco: Harper & Row, 1987) 113; W. K. C. Guthrie, *The Greeks and Their Gods* (Boston: Beacon Press, 1954) 154.

[11] Euripedes, *Bacchae* 720–30; reprinted in Ross S. Kraemer, ed. *Maenads, Martyrs, Matrons, Monastics* (Philadelphia: Fortress Press, 1988) 12–13.

[12] Guthrie, *Greeks and Their Gods*, 148.

[13] Mary R. Lefkowitz and Maureen B. Fant, *Women's Life In Greece and Rome* (London: Gerald Duckworth & Co., 1982) 250–51.

[14] Augustus Clissod, *The Prophetic Spirit in Its Relation to Wisdom and Madness* (London: Longmans, Green and Co., Pasternoster Row, 1870) 27–28.

honey.[15] Dionysian worshippers with their chanting, shrieking, promiscuity, and wild, disarrayed maenads, became so popular that by the time Livy wrote his *History of Rome* (second century B.C.), "They were an immense group, and were now almost a second nation."[16]

What effect did all of this have on the church of Paul's time? Ancient sources of or around the first century affirm that Dionysiac worship was a popular ritual among women. Was it practiced in the vicinity of Corinth? The ancient geographer Pausanius makes it evident that Dionysian worship was accessible to the people at Corinth.[17] Additionally, the legendary Medea, depicted as a maenad, was said to have killed her two children at Corinth.[18] Two caves excavated at the Isthmus in Corinth were recognized as a meeting place for a guild of Dionysian devotees.[19] As well, a plaque discovered in a 1964–65 excavation bore the name of Dionysus as one of the gods worshipped at the Sanctuary of Demeter and Kore at Acrocorinth. Richard and Catherine Kroeger affirm, "The sanctuary was in use during Roman times as well as in the Hellenistic era and was heavily patronized by women."[20]

---

[15]Guthrie, *Greeks and Their Gods,* 149.

[16]Livy, *History of Rome* 39.8–19, reprinted in D. G. Rice and J. E. Stambaugh, *Sources for the Study of Greek Religions* (Missoula: Scholars Press for SBL, 1979) 200.

[17]Pausanius, *Description of Greece* 6.7.5 (trans. W. H. S. Jones, LCL, 1954). In Pausanius' second book he describes the city of Corinth. In the same region, he mentions that Sikyon, northern Peloponnese, lies beyond the sanctuary of the Fortune and Dioscuri where resides the temple of Dionysus. At Sikyon, near Corinth, lies the temple of Dionysus where there stands an image of the wine god made of gold and ivory and surrounded with marble images of women worshippers called "Bacchanals" (worshippers of Bacchus, the Roman name for Dionysus). These women were "maddened *(mainesthai)* by his inspiration." If worshippers at Corinth did not have their own temple, they could worship at the Dionysian temple in Sikyon or travel to the one at Delphi.

[18]Richard and Catherine Kroeger, "An Inquiry into Evidence of Maenadism in the Corinthian Congregation" (SBLSP 65, vol. 2; Missoula, Mont.: Scholars Press, 1978) 332.

[19]Oscar Broneer "Paul and the Pagan Cults at Isthmia," *HTR* 64 (1971) 178–79.

[20]R. and C. Kroeger, "Evidence of Maenadism," 335.

## DIONYSIAC WORSHIP AND WOMEN IN THE CHURCH OF CORINTH

Are maenadic elements of the Dionysian sect or similar cults reflected in the Corinthian epistles? Paul's language certainly warrants this conclusion. He speaks of the Corinthian saints as possessing a "secret wisdom" (*sophian en mystērion*, 1 Cor 2:7) and being entrusted with the "secret things of God" (*mystērion theou*, 1 Cor 4:1). Such language reflects Paul communicating to a culture steeped with the secret rituals of mystery religions such as the Dionysian sects.

The Corinthian Christians were no strangers to the religious practices that preoccupied many at Corinth. They once participated in the pagan practices of their culture (1 Cor 6:9–11). They were well aware of the idolatry surrounding them. It was such a pressing issue to the budding church that Paul devoted an entire section of one Corinthian epistle to the subject (1 Cor 8–10). As former worshippers of pagan deities, the Corinthians, says Paul, were once "carried away" by dumb idols (1 Cor 12:1–2). In reference to this passage, Arnold Bittlinger writes, "This is probably an allusion to the practice of pagan ecstatic cults where the initiate was seized and violated by demonic power."[21] Because the church was relatively new, Paul exhorts the Corinthians to refrain from compromising with their former practices and rather to pursue holiness in light of the new Christian era.

In 1 Cor 13:1 the "sounding brass" and "tinkling cymbal" may be reminiscent of a maenadian entourage. The Phrygian worship of Cybele, extremely popular in the first century, "where Maenads wearing ivy throw back their heads, where they practice the sacred rites with sharp yells,"[22] made use of cymbals, tambourines, and pipes. Like the maenads, the members of the Corinthian congregation tended to come from the lower end of the social spectrum. There were among them "not many wise," and "not many noble"; they were the "foolish things of the world" (1 Cor 1:25–27). Apparently, as converts from "empowering" cults, the Corinthians had found in the

---

[21]Arnold Bittlinger, *Gifts and Graces: A Commentary on 1 Corinthians 12–14* (trans. Herbert Klassen; Grand Rapids: Eerdmans, 1967) 15.
[22]Catullus, *Poems* 63 (trans. Sisson/Meyer).

power provided through operating in the gifts of the Holy Spirit an appealing alternative. Yet they had at times abused this power through impropriety in worship (1 Cor 11–14).

## ON SEX ROLES AND DISHEVELED HAIR IN 1 COR 11

As he encourages propriety in worship, we find Paul exhorting the Corinthian women to have a covering for their hair (1 Cor 11:2–16). He considered it a disgrace for a woman to have "uncovered" hair; it was honorable for men to have short hair and women to have long hair. As Cynthia Thompson points out, Paul's writing on this subject is in harmony with first-century Graeco-Roman iconography, which depicts men with short hair and women with long hair. But knowing exceptions even within his own tradition (such as Samson), as well as the permissiveness implied in his words, Paul, like his contemporary Plutarch, was simply stressing the conviction that men and women should have distinctive hairstyles.[23]

What prompted the apostle to discuss sex roles and women's hair in relation to proper worship in the church? Perhaps the text reflects a concern that Christians not be affected by the reversal of male and female roles represented in maenadic dances and Cybele castration. Dionysian festivities involved wearing the apparel of the opposite sex. This would be associated with the "effeminacy" that Paul denounces in 1 Cor 6:10–11.[24] The reversal of sex roles could also be one of the reasons why Paul considers it "shameful" for a woman to cut her hair (1 Cor 11:5–6).

More hints of a Dionysian backdrop appear in Paul's exhortation for women to wear a head covering (1 Cor 11:4–5). The Greek word for "uncovered" *(akatakalyptō)* refers to hair that is either "loosed" instead of bound up (cf. Num 5:16–18),

---

[23]Cynthia Thompson, "Hairstyles, Head-coverings, and St. Paul: Portraits from Roman Corinth," *Biblical Archaeologist* (June 1988) 103–5. Paul did not dictate to the Corinthian women how to wear their hair (p. 112). Thompson claims that Paul gave them the right *(exousia* 1 Cor 11:10) to choose their hairstyles for themselves. David W. J. Gill writes: "Paul is rather emphasizing the need for men and women to fulfill their current roles in society. The church was to permeate society not to rebel against it." See D. W. J. Gill "The Importance of Roman Portraiture for Head-Coverings in 1 Corinthians 11:2–16," *Tyndale Bulletin* (Nov. 1990) 257.

[24]R. and C. Kroeger, "Evidence of Maenadism," 333.

or "unveiled" instead of veiled.[25] Cynthia Thompson displays a number of first- and second-century coins, statuette heads, and large hair pins—and some of these artifacts came from Corinth—to argue that first-century Corinthian protocol dictated that women wear their hair bound or braided up with a chignon at the back of the neck. A woman's long hair was her "wrapping" (*peribolaion* 1 Cor 11:15).[26]

It was in sharp contradiction to the normative custom of the time, then, that the maenads disarrayed and tossed their hair in a frenzied dance as they prepared to receive visions or prophetic utterances. One of the many mural paintings from the House of Mysteries in Pompeii (first century A.D.) displays a Dionysian ritual involving the flagellation of a woman with disheveled hair.[27] Depicting events dating back to at least A.D. 85, Juvenal's *Sixth Satire* (6.314–41) describes the secret rites of the Good Goddess (considered by some to be the daughter or wife of the Roman god Faunus). Juvenal depicts a scene in which, at the sound of the flute, the maenads of Priapus "howl in frenzy from music and wine and toss their hair."[28]

In view of the maenadism that still influenced certain Christian converts' manner of worship in the church, Paul writes that if a woman prays or prophesies with her hair uncovered or loosened, she dishonors her head (1 Cor 11:5). Certain women (and men) in the Corinthian church had been converted from the mystery cults, but had brought some of their pre-Christian cultic practices with them into the church. Apparently, after entering an ecstatic state and speaking in tongues, as also practiced by cults of that time,[29] some of the

---

[25] Gordon Fee, *The First Epistle to the Corinthians* (NIC; Grand Rapids: Eerdmans, 1987) 509–10; Wilhlem Mundle, "Hide, Conceal," in *New International Dictionary of New Testament Theology,* 2:212.

[26] Thompson, "Hairstyles and St. Paul," 106–9, 112.

[27] Everett Ferguson, *Backgrounds of Early Christianity* (Grand Rapids: Eerdmans, 1993) 247.

[28] Juvenal, *Satires* 6.316–19 (trans. H. Creekmore) reprinted in Kraemer, *Maenads, Martyrs, Matrons, Monastics,* 39.

[29] R. and C. Kroeger, "Evidence of Maenadism," 334. Plato describes divination in terms of a detached state of mind *(mainomai),* visions and involuntary speech (e.g., *Timaeus* 72A–B). Other frenzied cults of the time uttered a mixture of intelligible and unintelligible speech. See Nils Ivar Johan Engelsen, "Glossolalia and Other Forms of Inspired Speech According to 1 Corinthians 12–14" (dissertation; Princeton: Yale University, 1970).

women would prophesy in church with their hair disheveled. They had transferred the freedom, power, and ecstasy they found in Dionysiac worship into their new Christian faith. This problem led Paul to write this particular passage.

When the subject of prophecy arises in 1 Cor 14, Paul emphasizes that the Corinthians should do all things in an orderly manner (14:40). If ignorant or unbelieving people find a disorderly conduct, they will think "you are mad" (1 Cor 14:23). The word used here, *mainesthai,* means "to rave," "be mad," or "be out of one's mind." It is the same word used to describe the Dionysian frenzy of the maenad.[30] Thus, Paul may be warning the Corinthians that their charismatic activities in worship could reach a level whereby the outsider would think members of the church were "possessed of a religious frenzy in the manner of the Dionysian and Cybele cults."[31]

Once again, Paul stressed propriety in worship knowing the maenadic background of some of the church members. Corinthian Christianity must not become another ecstatic mystery cult. Members were not to rebel against the protocols of their society, as long as such norms did not violate Christian belief or practice. Since many members came from a lower social level, they may have craved power and release in charismatic worship. The Corinthian church therefore needed an orderly format in which to operate their spiritual gifts. Unlike the miracle-working maenads, those who operated in the power gifts of the Holy Spirit served a God of order, not confusion.

## FIRST CORINTHIANS 14, DIONYSIAC WORSHIP, AND HOLY LAUGHTER

In many ways the maenads in Dionysian worship engaged in some of the phenomena we see in the current renewal. Holy Laughter participants are not the only ones who have experienced outbursts of ecstatic joy. Dionysus offered freedom to

---

[30]Johannes Schattenmann, "Ecstasy," in *New International Dictionary of New Testament Theology* (ed. C. Brown; Grand Rapids: Zondervan, 1986) 1:528–29.

[31]R. and C. Kroeger, "Evidence of Maenadism," 334.

cast off restraints and was "the god of joy," offering joyful
cathartic experiences that "purged the individual of those in-
fectious irrational impulses which, when dammed up, had
given rise, as they have done in other cultures, to outbreaks of
dancing mania and similar manifestations of collective hysteria; it relieved them by providing them with a ritual outlet."[32]
As the "Liberator," Dionysus "enables you for a short time to
*stop being yourself*, and thereby sets you free."[33]

Seneca, the famous Stoic of the first century A.D., wrote a
tragedy of Medea in which one scene depicts her as a maenad.
For "as a maenad uncertainly directs her frenzied steps when
now she raves at the oncoming of the god . . . so she runs now
here, now there, with frantic rush, marks of distracted passion
in her face. Her cheeks aflame, she pants with deep sobs for
breath, shouts aloud, weeps floods of tears, beams with joy;
she assumes the proof of every passion."[34] This scene could
well depict what happens in Holy Laughter. Like Holy Laughter enthusiasts, the Dionysian enthusiasts would sometimes
convulse as though having a seizure—but they would consider
this to be a mark of demon possession.[35] They would also
experience falling down, and having trances or visions.[36]
Women prophesying and whipping their hair in an ecstatic
frenzy could be seen in maenadism just as today in Holy
Laughter.

This does not mean, however, that the spirit of Dionysus
has positioned himself as the Holy Spirit in the current renewal. Paul does not think the disruptive behavior he is responding to in Corinth is the result of another spirit's activity.
In fact, the disorderly behavior that Paul rebukes in 1 Cor
11–14 is similar to—and in some ways exactly the same as—
what happens in a typical Holy Laughter meeting! In other
words, *if the Apostle Paul were living today, he would admon-
ish those involved in the Holy Laughter renewal to get rid of
their disorderly conduct just as he did the Corinthians almost
2,000 years ago.*

---

[32] E. R. Dodds, *The Greeks and the Irrational* (Berkeley/Los Angeles:
University of California Press, 1959) 76.
[33] Ibid.
[34] Seneca, *Medea* (trans. Frank J. Miller) 380–87.
[35] Dodds, *The Greeks and the Irrational*, 66.
[36] Ibid., 272.

According to 1 Cor 14:11–12, we are to seek to edify the church. As applied today, this means that selfish forms of worship ought to be discouraged—that is, activities such as roaring, barking, or laughing so as to distract those trying to listen to a preacher. If Paul discouraged speaking in tongues unless an interpreter made the message intelligent, how much more should we discourage uncontrollable laughter and animal sounds that often have no interpretation at all. Gordon Fee writes:

> Thus, since they [the Corinthian church] have such a zeal for the manifestation of the Spirit, they should direct that zeal in corporate worship away from being "foreigners" to one another toward the edification of one another in Christ. The point of the corporate worship is not personal experience but building the body of Christ . . . the building up of the community is the basic reason for corporate settings of worship; they should probably not be turned into a corporate gathering for a thousand individual experiences of worship.[37]

In a more orderly manner, the Vineyard will sometimes have prayer counselors who carry name tags and pray for others instead of seeking self-ecstasy. I believe such counselors should also be trained to stop people from becoming too disorderly in their worship, or to escort such people to a private room where in privacy they can bark, roar, laugh, and scream to their heart's content. Often such theatrics wear off much more quickly when a person realizes that he or she is not the center of attention.

### CONTROL YOURSELVES

We should never become a stumbling block to believers or unbelievers who will think our conduct borders on that of a lunatic (1 Cor 14:22–23). Unlike the maenad, the Christian should always be in control of him- or herself. The prophetic Spirit of God touches our human spirit, and our spirit is subject to us (1 Cor 14:32). Thus, the Bible contradicts Holy Laughter advocates who say such a move of the Spirit is uncontrollable.[38] You *can* stay in control.

Patrick Dixon describes his encounter with Holy Laughter. As people prayed for him, he fell to the ground and felt a

---

[37] Fee, *First Epistle to the Corinthians*, 666–67.
[38] E.g., C. and F. Hunter, *Holy Laughter*, 104.

tingling sensation all over his body. Then came the laughing: "It was as if the whole room was filled with laughing gas or some other powerful intoxicant. I laughed until my body was more than half off the floor, and then some more until it hurt and I started to wheeze. *I suppose with some effort I could have forced myself to stop* [emphasis mine]."[39] Others also admit they could have stopped themselves, but they just didn't want the Spirit to refrain from touching them. Such reports confirm that Scripture is true; those involved in Holy Laughter *can* control themselves (1 Cor 14:32).

On the other hand, Rodney Howard-Browne writes, "True, true, the Scripture does say that the spirit of the prophet is subject unto the prophet, but I want you to realize this: These are not prophets, and they are not prophesying!"[40] This kind of argument creates a false dichotomy. There is no logical reason to exhort order only among those with a prophetic gift, while permitting the rest of the congregation to wreak havoc. Moreover, Paul charges that *anyone* in the Corinthian congregation with any type of utterance, including tongues, keep order (14:26–33). Why would Paul charge the church to be orderly if the members could not control themselves? If only the "prophets" could control themselves, then Paul's words that "*everything* should be done in a fitting and orderly way" (14:40) are meaningless.

Some Holy Laughter advocates would focus on the word "everything" to suggest that anything, including roaring, barking, and holy drunkenness, should be permitted—as long as these things are done in an orderly way. Yet when we attempt to distinguish between phenomena such as orderly roaring and disorderly roaring, the argument breaks down. No one sets a standard beyond a minister's own relative judgment. If "everything" means absolutely everything, does that then mean that anything goes as long as it is done in an orderly manner? How does one spit on the inner wall of a sanctuary in a fitting and orderly way? Allowing conduct in a worship service to include "everything" in an unqualified sense only leads us to profanity, bedlam, and utter nonsense. And given Paul's constant exhortation to Christians to be self-controlled and sober-minded, this sort of disorder is not

---

[39] Dixon, *Signs of Revival*, 284.
[40] Howard-Browne, *The Reality of the Person of the Holy Spirit*, 31.

biblically supportable (cf. Rom 12:3; 1 Thess 5:6, 8; 1 Tim 2:15; Titus 2:2, 4, 6).

The Vineyard Board seems to agree that more control is necessary in renewal meetings:

> It must edify the body of Christ. In order to edify, it must be intelligible. . . . it is the responsibility of the leader to ensure that it is made intelligible to all ([1 Cor. 14:] vv. 16,17). If it is not prophetic or intelligible or is disrupting the preaching of the Word, it is to be controlled and kept from dominating the attention of the group.[41]

Such an understanding would seem to preclude most Holy Laughter phenomena since they are unintelligible. Given the maenadic underpinnings of the 1 Cor 14 passage, some Holy Laughter phenomena would definitely qualify as disorderly conduct, the very thing Paul intends to correct. I am utterly convinced that if Paul were living today, he would say that a lot of what goes on in the renewal meetings is disorderly.

## DISORDER AND THE HOLY SPIRIT

Why then would the Spirit move in such a disorderly phenomenon as Holy Laughter? I could answer this question by asking a similar one. Why did the Holy Spirit move in the disorderly church at Corinth? Regarding 1 Cor 14:12, Gordon Fee argues that the Corinthians' zeal for "spirits" is "Paul's way of speaking about the Spirit's manifesting himself through their [the Corinthians'] individual 'spirits.' "[42] In other words, Paul never doubts that the Holy Spirit is in fact touching the lives of the Corinthians, despite their disorder. Although other cults spoke in tongues and prophesied, Paul never questions that, despite the disorder, the Corinthians are still speaking in tongues and prophesying by the Spirit of God. Ironically, Paul encourages speaking in tongues and prophesying (14:1, 39).

When God wants to touch lives, disorder is not going to stop him. He could move despite disorderly conduct, and given the example at Corinth, he has at times chosen to do so. Apparently, if he could touch people in such a way as to significantly change their lives for the better, this is more

---

[41]Todd Hunter, "Board Report," Sept./Oct. 1994 (Anaheim: Association of Vineyard Churches) 3.

[42]Fee, *God's Empowering Presence*, 227.

important to him than not touching those same people for the sake of a more orderly service. People's lives are a higher priority than propriety in worship. So, if God moves in a Holy Laughter service, this does not necessarily mean he approves of all their behavior.

God is not a God of disorder, as is the god Dionysus, but a God of peace (1 Cor 14:33, 40; cf. 2 Cor 12:20). Hence Christians, especially ministers in charge of the service, should strive for decency and order in renewal meetings. Christians should abandon ecstatic outbursts of meaningless utterances, convulsions, shrieks, and other mindless activities. As followers of the God of peace, they should strive to win the favor of others, and strive not to offend them.

Having said this, I must make an important qualification. Unlike certain Holy Laughter critics, Paul did not make fun of, condemn, or ostracize those who were disorderly, nor did he attribute their conduct to the work of the devil. He exhorted and corrected the Corinthians as fellow saints of God whom he loves, compliments and expects to see in heaven one day (1 Cor 1:1–9; 4:15). They were graciously endowed by the Spirit of Christ in every kind of utterance (which would include the prophetic) so that they lacked no gracious gift (1 Cor 1:5–7). Paul himself had set the example by claiming that his own message came not by great rhetoric, but by demonstration of the Spirit's power (2:4–5; cf. 4:19–20). Although they had at one time been bound to sinful vices, they now had been sanctified and baptized by the Holy Spirit (6:9–11; 12:13). Both corporately and individually, they were now considered the temple of the Holy Spirit (3:16; 6:19–20).

As a loving father, then, Paul rebuked the Corinthian Christians, and exhorted them to be more orderly. Yes, they were immature Christians, but the Holy Spirit still touched them anyway. They were not cultic, occultic, or deliberate frauds (cf. 1 Cor 3:1–3; 14:20). If we are to be imitators of Paul (1 Cor 11:1), we should follow his example when dealing with disorderly conduct in the Holy Laughter renewal.

# 8

# REVIVAL PHENOMENA: EIGHTEENTH CENTURY

Groaning, trembling, fainting, crying, barking, and the other assorted phenomena occurring in Holy Laughter have also occurred in the most prominent revivals of recent history. Toronto Vineyard author Guy Chevreau dedicates an entire chapter of his book *Catch the Fire* to Jonathan Edwards and the Great Awakening of eighteenth-century America. Chevreau—along with Bill Jackson, Ed Piorek, and other renewal advocates—likens the phenomena that occurred then to those happening today in Toronto.

Officially, the Vineyard position is not as optimistic:

> We also need to be careful in our use of revival history and tradition to justify manifestations. People like Jonathan Edwards are helpful in that they give us examples of how godly men, who submitted themselves to the Scriptures as their final authority, sorted out similar issues. But in fairness to them, we don't know exactly what they would say about the current phenomena.[1]

Revivals of the past have normally been defined in several ways. Ministers connected with the Great Awakening often spoke of that revival in terms of "effusion," "baptism," and "outpouring of the Spirit."[2] More recently, Martyn Lloyd-Jones

---

[1]"Board Meeting," Association of Vineyard Churches, Sept./Oct. 1994, 1.

[2]Iain H. Murray, *Revival and Revivalism: The Making and Marring of American Evangelicalism 1750–1858* (Edinburgh, UK/Carlisle, Pa.: The Banner of Truth Trust, 1994) 20.

has written, "A revival of religion is nothing but a great outpouring of the Spirit of God upon the church, a kind of repetition of what happened on the day of Pentecost."[3] J. I Packer
writes, "Revival I define as a work of God by his Spirit through
his word bringing the spiritually dead to living faith in Christ
and renewing the inner life of Christians who have grown
slack and sleepy."[4] Let us take a look at the phenomena of
some of the past revivals. Are they similar to any of what we
see in the current renewal?

## REVIVAL PRECURSORS

Space does not permit us a lengthy study here on the
history of phenomena in revivalism. We shall focus our attention on the major revivals and revivalists from the time of the
Great Awakening to the present.[5] It is important to note, however, that revival phenomena are not unique to the period
following the Great Awakening, nor are they simply a Protestant occurrence. Catholic mystic Teresa of Avila (1515–82) became famous for going into ecstatic trances.[6] Convulsions and
other strange manifestations occurred in the convents of the
Middle Ages where nuns "began by hundreds to howl, bark,
or mew."[7]

Other groups arose during or after the time of the Reformation, such as the Camisards, the Jansenists, the Convulsionaries, and those simply called enthusiasts. Members of
these groups often fell into a state of trance, convulsed,
whirled, spoke in tongues, and so forth. The French Prophets

---

[3]Martyn Lloyd-Jones, *The Sovereign Spirit: Discerning His Gifts*
(Wheaton: Harold Shaw, 1985) 52.

[4]J. I. Packer, *A Quest for Godliness* (Wheaton, Ill.: Crossway Books,
1990) 36.

[5]For an overview of phenomena and outpourings of the Spirit
throughout church history consult R. A. Knox, *Enthusiasm: A Chapter
in the History of Religion* (Notre Dame: University of Notre Dame Press,
1950; 1994 ed.); James Gilchrist Lawson, *Deeper Experiences of Famous
Christians* (Anderson, Ind.: The Warner Press, 1911; 1970 ed.); Davies,
*I Will Pour Out My Spirit*, 55–93.

[6]MacNutt, *Overcome by the Spirit*, 34–36.

[7]Janet, *Major Symptoms of Hysteria*, 262.

were sometimes taken up in ecstatic laughter.[8] The Convulsionaries danced in the cemetery of Saint-Médard, where one "heard nothing but groaning, singing, shrieking, whistling, declaiming, prophesying, caterwauling."[9]

The Anabaptist enthusiasts, whom Jonathan Edwards condemned, had ecstatic experiences resulting in divine revelations: "When under the influence of the Spirit, their countenances were contorted, they made deprecatory gestures, fell on the ground as if in a fit, and finally lay stretched out as if they were dead."[10] The Quakers received their name because early practitioners "quaked" in the presence of God. One description reports: "many fall into dreadful Tremblings in their whole Bodies and Joints, with Risings and Swellings in their Bowels; Shrieking, Yellings, Howlings and Roarings."[11]

Contemporaneous with the Second Great Awakening of the late eighteenth and early nineteenth century, aberrant and heretical groups such as the Irvingites in England and the Shakers and Mormons in America encountered their own ecstatic experiences. Mormon leader Brigham Young not only spoke in tongues, he also interpreted them. "Shouting, jerks, and dancing" could be seen at Mormon gatherings.[12]

## JONATHAN EDWARDS AND RELIGIOUS AFFECTIONS

Jonathan Edwards is the revivalist most often cited in defense of the current renewal's affinity with past revivals. Ironically, unlike the Vineyard, Edwards was a cessationist who believed of "the gift of tongues, of miracles, of prophecy," that "these extraordinary gifts have ceased"[13] since the close of the canon of Scripture after the first century. Nevertheless, Edwards defended the Great Awakening from the charges of its critics.

---

[8] Knox, *Enthusiasm*, 360, 525.
[9] Ibid., 377.
[10] Ibid., 124.
[11] Ibid., 356.
[12] Synan, *Holiness-Pentecostal Movement*, 25–26.
[13] Jonathan Edwards, *Charity and Its Fruits; or Christian Love as Manifested in the Heart and Life* (New York: Robert Carter & Brothers; intro. by Tyron Edwards, 1856) 42–43.

## DESCRIBING THE AWAKENING PHENOMENA

In *A Narrative of Surprising Conversions* (1736), Edwards describes phenomena from the revival:

> It was very wonderful to see how persons' *affections* were sometimes moved—when God did as it were suddenly open their eyes, and let into their minds a sense of the greatness of his grace, the fullness of *Christ*, . . . their joyful surprise has caused their hearts as it were to leap, so that they have been ready to break forth into laughter, tears often at the same time issuing like a flood, and intermingling loud weeping. Sometimes they have not been able to forbear crying out with a loud voice, expressing their great admiration.[14]

Convulsions, fainting, and crying also appeared during the Great Awakening with one man that was "subject to such terrors as threw him to the ground, and caused him to roar with anguish; and the pang of the new birth in him were such that he lay pale and without sense, like one dead."[15] In May 1741 Edwards describes the revival at Northampton where many were overcome by love, joy, and praise and "many others at the same time were overcome with distress about their sinful and miserable estate and condition; so that the whole room was full of nothing but outcries, faintings, and the like."[16] Edwards continues, "and there were some instances of persons lying in a sort of trance, remaining perhaps for a whole twenty-four hours motionless, and with their senses locked up; but in the mean time under strong imaginations, as though they went to heaven and had there a vision of glorious and delightful objects."[17]

But Edwards notes that "when the people were raised to this height, Satan took the advantage, and his interposition, in many instances, soon became very apparent: and a great deal

---

[14]Jonathan Edwards, *A Narrative of Surprising Conversions* reprinted in *Jonathan Edwards on Revival* (Edinburgh, UK/Carlisle, Pa.: The Banner of Truth Trust, 1994) 37–38. See also Jonathan Edwards, *Some Thoughts Concerning the Revival* reprinted in *The Great Awakening*, C. C. Goen, ed. (New Haven and London: Yale University Press, 1972) 305–13.

[15]Edwards, *Thoughts Concerning the Revival*, 307.

[16]Edwards, *An Account of the Revival of Religion in Northampton in 1740–1742, As Communicated in a Letter to a Minister of Boston* reprinted in *Jonathan Edwards on Revival*, 150.

[17]Edwards, *Account of the Revival*, 153–54.

of caution and pains were found necessary to keep the people, many of them, from running wild."[18]

Edwards warns that Christians must keep an eye out for the devil, who has manifested himself several times during the revival, for "we may observe that it has been a common device of the Devil to overset a revival of religion, when he finds he can keep men quiet and secure no longer, then to drive 'em to excesses and extravagances. He holds them back as long as he can, but when he can do it no longer, then he'll push 'em on, and if possible, run 'em upon their heads."[19] In any extraordinary event, like creation itself when the Spirit moved upon the waters, we should expect "tumult, confusion and uproar, and darkness mixed with light, and evil with good."[20]

Part of the problem is that the "weakness of human nature has always appeared in times of great revival of religion, but a disposition to run to extremes and get into confusion; and especially in these three things—enthusiasm, superstition, and intemperate zeal."[21] But despite human frailties and extremism, God has chosen to work through the Awakening. Since this outpouring is so great, "no wonder that the Devil is more alarmed and enraged and exerts himself more vigorously against it."[22]

> Whatever imprudences there have been, and whatever sinful irregularities; what ever vehemence of the passions and heats of the imagination, transports and ecstasies; and whatever error in judgement, and indiscreet zeal; and whatever outcries, and faintings, and agitations of body: yet it is manifest and notorious, that there has been of late a very uncommon influence upon the minds of a very great part of the inhabitants of New England, from one end of the land to the other, the [revival] has been attended with the following affects: viz. a great increase of a spirit of seriousness, and sober consideration of the things of the eternal world; . . . a disposition to treat matters of religion with solemnity, and as matters of great importance; a disposition to make

---

[18]Ibid., 154. Edwards notes that the revival of 1741–42 was less tainted with the mixture of corruption than the revival in 1735–36. Still, in 1742 some people crept in who did more damage than good by means of their "raptures and violent emotions of affections." This led Edwards to state that the degree that one has been graced by God cannot be judged by the degree of one's joy, zeal, or affections.

[19]Edwards, *Thoughts Concerning the Revival*, 410.

[20]Ibid., 318.

[21]Ibid., 318–19.

[22]Ibid., 325.

these things the subject of conversation; and a great disposition to hear the Word of God preached, and to take all opportunities in order to it; and to attend on the public worship of God, and all external duties of religion in a more solemn and decent matter; so that there is a remarkable and general alteration in the face of New England in these respects.[23]

## DISCERNING REVIVAL PHENOMENA

Of far greater importance than any bodily effects to Edwards are the positive moral and spiritual effects of the revival: local taverns closing down, rebellious youths living more godly lives, and so forth.[24] Sinners were converted and Christians renewed in great numbers, for many had been convicted of their sins due to this great outpouring from the Lord.[25] In essence, the Great Awakening had changed New England. With regard to the positive fruits, Edwards concludes, "Now if such things are enthusiasm, and the fruits of a distempered brain, let my brain be evermore possessed of that happy distemper!"[26] If Christians keep their minds and moral conduct "in an agreeableness to the rules that Christ has given us," then "our fears and suspicions arising from extraordinary bodily effects seem wholly groundless."[27]

In defense of the revival, Edwards wrote *The Distinguishing Marks of a Work of the Spirit of God* (1741) in which he gives a list of signs which are *not* evidence that a work is *not* from the Holy Spirit. He elaborates that if a work (1) is unusual, (2) is attended by bodily effects such as groanings, tremblings, and outcries, (3) occasions attention and talk about religion, (4) constitutes great impressions on the mind, (5) incorporates various means, such as good examples, for its success, (6) has imprudence or irregular conduct, (7) is intermingled with delusions from Satan, (8) has some who fall into errors, or (9) earnestly promotes judgment from

---

[23] Ibid.

[24] Pride and its negative effects were the number one hindrance to revivals, according to Edwards. See *Thoughts Concerning the Revival*, 441.

[25] Edwards, *Narrative of Surprising Conversions*, 21. See also *The Distinguishing Marks of a Work of the Spirit of God* reprinted in Goen, ed., *Great Awakening*, 80–83.

[26] Edwards, *Thoughts Concerning the Revival*, 341.

[27] Ibid., 301.

God's law, none of these signs indicates that a work is *not* of God.[28]

The things that *do* mark a work as being of the Spirit are that (1) it confirms the message of Christ and the gospel, (2) it operates against the kingdom of Satan by turning men away from sin, (3) it prompts a greater regard for Scripture, (4) it leads to truth instead of falsehood, and (5) it leads to a spirit of love. Ecstasy, which Edwards considered different than the enthusiasm of the erroneous religions of his day, can go together with a true move of the Spirit.[29] Edwards concludes that if the fruits produced include a saint such as David Brainerd, evangelist to the American Indians, the critics can call "true experiential religion" whatever they will.[30]

Generally considered Edwards's most elaborate work on the effects of the revival on human nature, *The Religious Affections* (1746) stood as a work unrivaled in the psychology of religion until William James's *Varieties of Religious Experiences* appeared in 1902. In Edwards's book, he once again confirms that in a move of God there can be a mysterious mixture of good and bad, true and counterfeit, just as the saving grace of God works within the corrupted, hypocritical heart of the

---

[28] Edwards, *Distinguishing Marks*, 89–108.

[29] Jonathan Edwards, *The Life of David Brainerd,* Norman Pettit, ed. (New Haven and London: Yale University Press, 1985) 6–7. See also Jonathan Edwards, *The Religious Affections* (Edinburgh, UK/Carlisle, Pa.: The Banner of Truth Trust, 1961, rep. 1991) 57. During the Great Awakening, the enthusiasm that was denounced was understood as antinomianism and the reception of "divine impulses and visions, the special calls from God, the particular inspirations" (Edwin Scott Gaustad, *The Great Awakening in New England;* New York: Harper & Brothers, 1957; 77). See also David S. Lovejoy, *Religious Enthusiasm and the Great Awakening* (AHSS; Englewood Cliffs, N.J.: Prentice-Hall, 1969) 1–4.

[30] David S. Lovejoy, *Religious Enthusiasm in the New World: Heresy to Revolution* (Cambridge, Mass./London: Harvard University Press, 1985) 192. In later years Edwards became more pessimistic. In 1750, in the preface of Joseph Bellamy's book *True Religion, As Distinguished from Formality on the One Hand, and Enthusiasm on the Other,* Edwards wrote that the "false religion" resulting in the "increase of stupidity, corrupt principles, a profane and atheistical spirit, and the triumph of open enemies of religion" had obscured or obstructed all great "revivals of religion." This, argues Goen, was triggered by his dismissal as the pastor of Northampton that same year (Goen, ed., *Great Awakening* 87–89).

saint.[31] Satan sows tares among the wheat by mingling false
affections—such as false joy, comfort, or fear—with the work
of the Holy Spirit, intending to delude souls and discredit the
work of God.

In Edwards's thought, the affections "are not simply the
emotions, passions, or even the 'will,' but more fundamen-
tally, that which moves a person from neutrality or mere as-
sent and inclines his heart to possess or reject something."[32]
Once the false affections are corrected, Satan could try to
persuade the saints that all affections should be guarded
against, thus making the Christian faith a "lifeless formality."
Edwards offsets any imbalance by writing:

> True religion consists so much in the affections that there can be
> no true religion without them. He who has no religious affection
> is in a state of spiritual death, and is wholly destitute of the
> powerful, quickening, saving influences of the Spirit of God upon
> his heart. As there is no true religion where there is nothing else
> but affection, so there is no true religion where there is no relig-
> ious affection.[33]

It is therefore no sign, either for or against a revival, that
religious affections are highly evident. All affections have
some effect on the human body: the greater the affection, the
greater the effect. Edwards says, "I know of no reason why a
being affected with a view of God's glory should not cause the
body to faint, as well as being affected with a view of Solomon's glory."[34] Such bodily effects as trembling, groaning,
crying, and fainting "are fit and suitable figures to represent
the high degree of those spiritual affections which the Spirit of
God makes use of them to represent."[35]

According to Edwards, the apostles note in their sufferings
two affections raised by true religion: love and joy. Holy joy
rises by faith, and is different from carnal joys that debase the
mind. It is given in large measure through persecution, and
fills the saint's mind with "the light of God's glory."[36] The

---

[31] Edwards, *Religious Affections*, 16–17; cf. "To The Rev. James Robe
of Kilsyth, Scotland," reprinted in Goen, ed., *Great Awakening*, 535–37.

[32] Sydney E. Ahlstrom, *A Religious History of the American People*
(New Haven and London: Yale University Press, 1972) 303.

[33] Edwards, *Religious Affections*, 49; cf. 69, 213–14.

[34] Ibid., 60; cf. 54–55.

[35] Ibid., 62.

[36] Ibid., 23.

difference between true joy and hypocritical joy is that the latter rejoices in self, while the former rejoices in God.[37]

Truly gracious affections (1) are confirmed by the witness of the Spirit in our spirit, (2) are concerned with divine things, not with self-interest, (3) are founded on moral excellency, (4) arise from an enlightened mind to understand divine things, (5) have a strong conviction for divine things, (6) are accompanied with humiliation, (7) involve true conversion, (8) follow the characteristics of Christ, (9) make one sensitive to the Lord, (10) are symmetrical and proportional, exercising a well-balanced instead of an impulsive or frivolous range of emotions, (11) lead one to a stronger desire for divine things, and (12) produce fruit in Christian practice.[38]

In essence, Jonathan Edwards believed that affections are a normal, expected part of the Christian experience. According to Edwards, the Holy Spirit prompts gracious affections, which draw one to engage in godly activities. In this context, bodily effects such as fainting, convulsing, and so on may or may not be a result of the gracious touch of God. One must compare these effects with the attributes of gracious affections on a case-by-case basis to determine the touch of God. The main point is that one must ultimately depend on and look to God, not bodily effects or religious affections. For Edwards, revival is an extraordinary work of God, reinvigorating the community and promoting Christian piety.[39] God permits the mixed work laden with Satan's tares to continue, so that we all might know that spiritual fruit arises not from any human goodness, but by his grace.[40]

In 1990, J. I. Packer almost prophetically concluded,

> We shall be wise not to conclude too hastily that what Edwards is saying here has no message for us. We should be foolish to imagine that if God poured out his Spirit today, we should be able straightway to recognize what was happening. Revival has always come in unexpected ways, through unexpected and often unwelcomed people. We should not rule out the possibility that one day we shall ourselves stand nonplused before an ebullient and uproarious spiritual movement, wondering whether it is of God, and finding ourselves strongly impelled by our instinctive distaste for its surface crudities and stupidities in theology, worship, and

---

[37] Ibid., 175.
[38] Ibid., 124–308.
[39] Packer, *Quest for Godliness*, 318.
[40] Ibid., 324.

morals to look no further, but write it off at once. At such times, we shall need to bear in mind what Edwards has told us about the mixed character of revivals and the principles of judgement that should be applied in such a case.[41]

## PHENOMENA FROM THE GREAT AWAKENING

The Great Awakening (ca. 1734–43) was arguably the greatest outpouring of the Spirit in the post–Reformation West. Beyond the Awakening per se, religious emotionalism swept most of western Europe between 1730 and 1760, also influencing the Quietism which pervaded Roman Catholicism. Joseph Tracy writes,

> It was a time, too, of agitable nerves. There had been two centuries of tremendous nervous excitement. There had been the Reformation, the peasant's war, and the religious wars in Germany . . . the rise of Puritanism, the republic, and the times of the Covenanters in Great Britain; the rise of Protestantism, the religious wars, and the persecution of the Huguenots in France, ending with the appearance of the "French Prophets" in the Cevennes, some of whom were still holding forth among their followers in London.[42]

Many participants in the "revival of religion" understood the new birth as a "felt" religion, resting on the sensing of the presence of God. However, despite the important role played by religious affections, most saw that it was inadequate to base one's faith on a purely emotional experience.[43] Nevertheless, "as some hearers were struck down, others were lifted up, and in countless meeting houses the moaning and groanings of the condemned were offset by cries of ecstasy, even holy laughter, of those experiencing pangs of the 'New Birth,' demonstrations which could only convince opponents how deeply embedded enthusiasm was in the whole process of revival."[44]

---

[41] Ibid., 325.

[42] Joseph Tracy, *The Great Awakening: A History of the Revival of Religion in the Time of Edwards and Whitefield* (Boston: Charles Tappan/New York: Dayton & Newman/Philadelphia: Henry Perkins, 1845) 217.

[43] Alan Heimert and Perry Miller, eds., *The Great Awakening: Documents Illustrating the Crisis and Its Consequences* (AHS; Indianapolis/New York: The Bobbs-Merrill Company, Inc., 1967) xxviii, lii.

[44] Lovejoy, *Religious Enthusiasm*, 181.

Sydney Ahlstrom notes that the Great Awakening was marked by "flamboyant and highly emotional preaching," and physical responses such as "fainting, weeping, shrieking" due to the conversion experience. As well, "praying, devotional reading, and individual 'exhorting' took on new life."[45] The preaching of George Whitefield combined wit, intensity, imagination, expressive gestures and Spirit-led messages in setting the mood for a revival experience.[46] Crying was a common phenomenon at his meetings.[47] In Charlestown, South Carolina, the Anglican Commissary sought to discredit Whitefield by citing instances of abusive enthusiasm through church history. They compared the "grand itinerant" to " 'the Oliverians, Ranters, Quakers, French Prophets,' and even the notorious Dutartres who had outraged Carolinians a few years earlier with their trances and visions, their incests and murders."[48]

The phenomenon commonly called the "jerks" reached its peak in the First Great Awakening in 1740, though it became more prevalent in the Second Great Awakening. John Wesley accepted the convulsive activity as an indication of the divine presence, but Whitefield attributed the manifestation to demonic influence: "Satan now begins to throw many into fits."[49] Critics pointed to the crying, convulsing, roaring, laughing, and other phenomena as signs that this was not a move of God. Jonathan Edwards pointed out, as we have seen, that the bodily effects of affections neither authenticated nor disproved a moving of the Spirit.

Perhaps the most outspoken critic of the revival was Charles Chauncy, a Congregational minister (and future Unitarian) and great-grandson of a Harvard president by the same name.

---

[45]Ahlstrom, *Religious History,* 287–88.

[46]Lovejoy, *Religious Enthusiasm,* 184–85.

[47]See for instance, George Whitefield, *Journals,* 1740, e.g., "Philadelphia," reprinted in Richard L. Bushman, *The Great Awakening: Documents on the Revival of Religion, 1740–45* (Institute of Early American History and Culture; Williamsburg, Va.; New York: Atheneum, 1970) 26–27.

[48]Lovejoy, *Religious Enthusiasm,* 188.

[49]Tracy, *The Great Awakening,* 224. In his *Journal* (July 29, 1750) Wesley describes his own encounter with "holy trembling": "I shook from head to foot, while tears of joy ran down my face. . . . I no sooner knelt by him than the consolation of God come upon men, so that I trembled and wept much" (Knox, *Enthusiasm,* 527).

In a Harvard commencement sermon (1742) he warned against enthusiasm as a "kind of religious Phrenzy." After citing Paul's exhortation to orderly conduct, Chauncy says,

> And whoever the persons are, who will not acknowledge what the apostle has here said is the *commandment of* God, and act accordingly, are influenced by another spirit than that which moved in him, be their impressions or pretenses what they will. The disorder of EXHORTING, and PRAYING, and SINGING, and LAUGHING, *in the same house of worship, at one and the same time,* is as great as was that, the apostle blames in the *church of Corinth.*[50]

Chauncy prefaced his caveat with an open letter to revivalist James Davenport, who had been under criticism for his extremism. In June, 1742, Davenport was declared by the General Assembly of Connecticut to be a threat to the peace and order of the community. He was sent to Long Island as one "under the influence of enthusiastical impressions and impulses, and thereby disturbed in the rational faculties of his mind."[51] Anti-intellectualism also ran its full course in Davenport's teachings, as in 1743 he conducted a book burning campaign in New London, Connecticut.[52] His ministry demonstrates that the Great Awakening did have its excesses.

Chauncy also lowered his cannon at Jonathan Edwards in his tract, *Seasonable Thoughts on the State of Religion in New England. Religious Affections* was Edwards's (later) response. E. S. Gaustad writes, "Whatever had been the extravagances of Davenport, the blunders of Whitefield, or the telling charges of Chauncy, there was a residual good—the revival of the unconcerned and the conversion of the unredeemed—that Edwards could not betray and would not disavow. Here he drew his line of defense and from it he never retreated."[53]

## JOHN WESLEY AND REVIVAL PHENOMENA

Even as Edwards preached in America, England was also experiencing the moving of the Spirit, particularly through the

[50] Charles Chauncy, "Enthusiasm Described and Caution'd Against," reprinted in Heimert and Miller, *The Great Awakening: Documents,* 242; cf. 234.

[51] Heimert and Miller, *The Great Awakening: Documents,* 258.

[52] Lovejoy, *Religious Enthusiasm,* 183.

[53] Gaustad, *Awakening in New England,* 97.

person of John Wesley. Here, the phenomena were similar to those being experienced in America—crying, convulsing, fainting, and the like. On May 30, 1739 Wesley wrote in his *Journal:*

We understood that many were offended at the cries of those on whom the power of God came: Among whom was a physician, who was much afraid, there might be fraud or imposture in the case. To-day one whom he had known many years, was the first . . . who broke out "into strong cries and tears." He could hardly believe his own eyes and ears. He went and stood close to her, and observed every symptom, till great drops of sweat ran down her face, and all her bones shook. He then knew not what to think, being clearly convinced, it was not fraud, nor yet any natural disorder. But when both her soul and body were healed in a moment, he acknowledged the finger of God.[54]

On June 15, 1739, some sinners who heard the word of God cried and fell down while others convulsed, "torn with a kind of convulsive motion in every part of their bodies, and that so violently, that often four or five persons could not hold one of them. I have seen many hysterical and many epileptic fits; but none of them were like these, in many respects." Wesley continued, "I immediately prayed, that God would not suffer those who were weak to be offended. But one woman was offended greatly . . . when she also dropped down, in as violent an agony as the rest."[55] Twenty years later the phenomena were still showing up in some of his services. On May 20, 1759, a number of people (including children), under conviction of the Spirit, cried and convulsed. "This occasioned a mixture of various sounds; some shrieking, some roaring aloud."[56]

Wesley also experienced his share of encounters with counterfeit phenomena. His brother Charles often discouraged bodily excitements because they were so easy to imitate: "Many counterfeits I have already detected."[57] On May 20, 1739 one man, seized by "the evil one," began to "roar out, and beat himself against the ground, so that six men could scarcely

---

[54] John Wesley, *Journals* reprinted in *The Works of John Wesley* (3d ed.; Peabody: Hendrickson, 1986; reprint) 1:189; cf. 2:511–12. See also "Renewal Phenomena and the Wesleyan Tradition," *Christian Info News*, Dec. 1994, 4.

[55] Wesley, *Works of John Wesley*, 1:204.

[56] Ibid., 2:483; cf. 4:26–27.

[57] Cited from Henry Johnson, *Stories of Great Revivals* (London: The Religious Tract Society, 1906) 77. Knox, *Enthusiasm*, 521; cf. 522–24.

hold him."[58] Regarding demonic manifestations, Wesley observes, "Satan is letting his prey go, with the utmost reluctance. The bystanders fall to prayer; if there is no immediate deliverance the interrupter is carried out, and prayer goes on, often till late at night."

In May, 1740 Wesley also met with a laughter that arose from the devil:

> I was a little surprised at some, who were buffeted of Satan in an unusual manner, by such a spirit of laughter as they could in no wise resist, though it was pain and grief unto them. I could scarce have believed the account they gave me, had I not known the same thing ten or eleven years ago. Part of Sunday my brother and I then used to spend in walking in the meadow and singing psalms. But one day, just as we were beginning to sing, he burst into a loud laughter. I asked him, if he was distracted; and began to be very angry, and presently after to laugh as loud as he. Nor could we possibly refrain, though we were ready to tear ourselves in pieces, but we were forced to go home without singing another line.[59]

On May 20th Wesley reports that many were offended by a "spirit of laughter. . . . One so violently and variously torn of the evil one did I never see before. Sometimes she laughed till almost strangled; then broke out into cursing and blaspheming; then stamped and struggled with incredible strength. . . . At last she faintly called on Christ to help her. And the violence of her pangs ceased."[60] Two church-goers laughed virtually without ceasing for two days. They were delivered in a moment when prayer was made for them.[61]

Wesley never, however, made revival phenomena the center of his meetings. For him, the only acceptable form of enthusiasm was one that operated by God's grace.[62] He did not judge a person by the bodily effects they manifested, but by "the whole tenor of their life."[63] Wesley's theology of Christian

---

[58]Wesley, *Works of John Wesley*, 1:196
[59]Ibid., 1:271–72; cf. "Second Letter to Bishop Lavington," in ibid., 9:27; Luke Tyerman, *The Life and Times of the Rev. John Wesley, M.A.* (5th ed.; London: Hodder and Stoughton, 1880) 1:293–94.
[60]Wesley, *Works of John Wesley*, 1:272.
[61]Ibid., 1:273.
[62]"Enthusiasm," *Christian History* 2 no. 1 (1983) 27. As he got older, Wesley came more and more to distrust physical manifestations (Davies, *I Will Pour Out*, 229).
[63]Wesley, *Works of John Wesley*, 1:195.

experience was guided and informed by his "quadrilateral" of Scripture, tradition, experience and reason.[64]

Contrary to the ecstatic prophets, who would allow themselves to lose control and become demon-possessed, Wesley cites 1 Cor 14:32 in asserting, "For the spirits of the prophets are subject to the prophets—But what enthusiast considers this? The impulses of the Holy Spirit, even in men really inspired, so suit themselves to their rational faculties, as not to divest them of the government of themselves, like the heathen priests under their diabolical possessions."[65] Wesley believed that, if genuinely touched by the Spirit—even to the point of experiencing religious ecstasies—Christians do not become idiotic. They keep their reason, refusing to embrace uncritical intuition.

His negative experiences with laughter seem to have colored his perspective when he writes that "wherever pride, indolence, or levity revives, all the fruits of the Spirit are ready to die."[66] Wesley warns against self-manipulation and disorderly passions. Among his guidelines for testing the nature of affections against self-deception, he cites Phil 1:10–11, noting that three properties must be present for an affection to be valid:

> (1) It must bear fruits, the fruits of righteousness, all inward and outward holiness, all good tempers, words, and works; and that so abundantly that we may be filled with them. (2) The branch and the fruits must derive both their virtue and their very being from the all-supporting, all-supplying root, Jesus Christ. (3) As all these flow from the grace of Christ, so they must issue in the glory and praise of God.[67]

---

[64] Gregory S. Clapper, *John Wesley on Religious Affections: His Views on Experience and Emotion and Their Role in the Christian Life and Theology* (Metuchen, N.J. & London: The Scarecrow Press, 1989) 2.

[65] Cited from Clapper, *Wesley on Religious Affections*, 82.

[66] Ibid., 88.

[67] Ibid., 84–85.

# 9

# REVIVAL PHENOMENA: NINETEENTH AND TWENTIETH CENTURIES

## THE SECOND GREAT AWAKENING

The Second Great Awakening (ca. 1795–1830), sometimes called the frontier revival, had its share of ecstatic phenomena, most notably at the camp meetings in Cane Ridge, Kentucky. Revivalist Barton W. Stone describes the phenomena of falling, often accompanied by screaming or crying; jerking in quick spasmodic motions backward and forward or side to side, sometimes almost touching the ground before and behind; dancing, which was often aroused by jerking; barking or grunting that arose from sudden jerking motions; laughing in a loud, hearty voice; running in an attempt to escape the bodily affectations, which the recipients were seldom able to do; and heavenly singing not from the mouth or nose, but entirely from the breast.[1]

One "barking exercise" involved those who "gathered on their knees at the foot of a tree, barking and snapping in order to 'tree the Devil.' "[2] Sometimes short posts were made to cling to in order to steady oneself between the spasms while

---

[1]"Piercing Screams and Heavenly Smiles," *Christian History* 14 no. 1 (1995) 15. See also Ahlstrom, *Religious History*, 434–35.

[2]Bernard A. Weisberger, *They Gathered at the River: The Story of the Great Revivalists and Their Impact upon Religion in America* (Boston/Toronto: Little, Brown and Company, 1958) 35.

on the ground. Some revivalists were outraged by conservative Christians who, trained in medicine, treated "fallen 'mourners' like victims of a fit, instead of rejoicing over the imminent conversion."[3] The widespread incidence of "jerking" epitomized the phenomena of this revival. Methodist evangelist Peter Cartwright describes the "jerks":

> No matter whether they were saints or sinners, they would be taken under a warm song or sermon, and seized with a convulsive jerking all over, which they could not by any possibility avoid, and the more they resisted the more they jerked. If they would not strive against it and pray in good earnest, the jerking would usually abate. I have seen more than five hundred persons jerking at one time in my large congregations. . . . I always looked upon the jerks as a judgement sent from God, first, to bring sinners to repentance; and, secondly, to show professors that God could work with or without means, and that he could work over and above means, and do whatever seemeth him good, to the glory of his grace and the salvation of the world.[4]

Cartwright adds, "'To see those proud young gentleman and ladies, dressed in their silks, jewelry and prunella, from top to toe, take the *jerks*, would often excite my risibilities. The first jerk or so, you would see their fine bonnets, caps, and combs fly; and so sudden would be the jerking of the head, that their long loose hair would crack almost as loud as a waggoner's whip."[5] Itinerant mystic Lorenzo Dow added that there was no pain in jerking, except when someone resisted.

At Cane Ridge, Cartwright claimed a man who resisted the jerks tried to drink them off with whiskey, but then a severe jerk broke his neck. This brought a great conviction of sin on the people at the camp.[6] Another mocker sat on his horse as he watched people swoon, only to suddenly fall himself from his saddle and lie on the floor unconscious for thirty hours.[7] Prior to his conversion and ordination as a minister, James B. Finley went to Cane Ridge and saw 500 people collapse—also feeling his own knees buckle. In desperation he ran out of the woods to get a shot of brandy. Upon re-entering the meeting,

---

[3]Ibid., 35, 39.

[4]Peter Cartwright, *Autobiography of Peter Cartwright,* selection reprinted in *Religion in America,* George C. Bedell, Leo Sandon, and Charles J. Wellborn (New York: Macmillan, 1982) 159.

[5]Cited from Lawson, *Deeper Experiences,* 173.

[6]Ibid., 174.

[7]Weisberger, *They Gathered at the River,* 32–33.

he felt convicted of every sin he had committed, and he retired that night in a haystack. When he returned home the next day, he burst into tears. The day following that, he went to the woods to pray, but shouted and fell prostrate. When he awoke, "he had a sudden feeling of release, and he went on home, uncontrollably laughing, weeping and shouting most of the way."[8]

But along with a number of Methodist ministers, Cartwright discouraged the jumping, barking, and running exercises. He called it a "great evil" when some people would fall into trances, sometimes for days or a whole week—reportedly without "food or drink"—seeing visions of heaven or hell, and predicting the end of the world.[9]

Problems at the open camp meetings included promiscuity and intoxication. The Reverend John Lyle also noticed a negative sub-culture arising out of the revival, among those who liked their religion "hot." Critics accused Lyle of coming against the revival whenever he preached on orderly conduct, or questioned the significance of the bodily exercises. It became evident that many considered the phenomena as the focus of the revival. Lyle himself struggled with this issue, tempted to feel that if excitement and seizures appeared at his meetings, people would give him a positive "self-congratulation" for his sermons.[10] Ministers struggled in the area of giving intellectual sermons that usually didn't convict the heart as much as simple heart-felt preaching. Opponents of the revival saw this emotional preaching as the cause of the strange bodily effects.[11]

"New Light" congregations were the "holy rollers" of the nineteenth century, sometimes characterized by chaotic worship of the wildest proportions. Some services devolved into rolling in hoops, jerking, wild convulsing, and assuming a "doglike posture and growling and barking for hours."[12] Reverend McNemar, a New Light minister, encouraged the spiritual

---

[8]Ibid., 33–34.

[9]Bedell, Sandon, Wellborn, *Religion in America*, 159–160.

[10]Conkin, *Cane Ridge*, 122–23. See also Murray, *Revival and Revivalism*, 183–85.

[11]Arthur B. Strickland, *The Great American Revival: A Case Study in Historical Evangelism with Implications for Today* (Cincinnati: Standard Press, 1934) 111.

[12]Conkin, *Cane Ridge*, 130.

gifts of prophesy and exorcism. The religious fervor seemed to him a sign that Christ was coming soon. When three Shakers visited him, they persuaded him to join their apocalyptic sect with Mother Ann Lee as the incarnation of the Holy Spirit and the second appearance of Christ.[13] Lorenzo Dow, like Mormon founder Joseph Smith, claimed to have seen both Jesus and God, along with the angel Gabriel. God allegedly told him that the British would destroy Washington in the War of 1812.[14]

Unlike Kentucky and the surrounding areas, however, the Northeast generally did not experience the wild phenomena. Ministers such as Ebenezer Porter, Jeremiah Hallock, and John B. Preston reported orderly worship in stillness and silence.[15] Conversions were legion. The Baptists increased in great numbers, and the Methodists grew from 15,000 in 1785 to 850,000 by 1840.[16] Bedell, Sandon, and Wellborn observe that the Second Great Awakening helped instill, in American culture, pietism—a personal and subjective experience in religion—while an emphasis on personal salvation led to an ethos of individualism and self-reliance. Finally, a distinctly anti-intellectual reductionism arose in the combining of pietism with individualism: "If every man is his own priest, then there is no need for elaborate institutional creeds or complex theologies. Religion is within the intellectual reach of every man, which in practice means that theology is reduced to simple, basic convictions easily preached and easily understood."[17]

Sydney Ahlstrom lists the following motifs that arose in western Christianity out of the Second Great Awakening: *Perfectionism*—sanctification and "second blessing" as part of the salvation experience; *Millennialism*—preparation for the end times and individualistic interpretations of prophetic books; *Universalism*—Christ's salvation available to all, contrary to the limited atonement teaching of Calvinism; and *Illuminism*—stress on the "new light" or new teachings and on further revelation of God's purposes.[18] These issues set the

---

[13]Ibid., 131; Davies, *I Will Pour Out,* 126.
[14]Weisberger, *They Gathered at the River,* 47.
[15]Murray, *Revival and Revivalism,* 137–41.
[16]Weisberger, *They Gathered at the River,* 46.
[17]Bedell, Sandon, Wellborn, *Religion in America,* 162–63.
[18]Ahlstrom, *Religious History,* 476.

mood for nineteenth-century evangelicalism, a religious movement that affects us profoundly to this day.

---

## CHARLES FINNEY AND NINETEENTH-CENTURY REVIVALISM

---

### CHARLES FINNEY

On the tail end of the Second Great Awakening came Charles Grandison Finney (1792–1875). Preaching his convicting messages in the urban Northeast, Finney taught that God had revealed laws for revival. If the church faithfully applied these laws, they could experience revival at any time. Finney's compassion for the lost encouraged him to make the revival service one in which a sinner makes a decision for Christ. He understood revival as a "renewed conviction of sin and repentance, followed by an intense desire to live in obedience to God. It is giving up one's will to God in deep humility."[19]

His own conversion was no less dramatic. After receiving the forgiveness of his sins, he seemed to have met Jesus face to face, and to have wept at his feet. He then experienced what he considered a baptism of the Holy Spirit:

> The Spirit came upon him "like a wave of electricity going through me. Indeed it seemed to come in waves and waves of liquid love; for I could not express it in any other way. It seemed like the very breath of God. I can recollect distinctly that it seemed to fan me, like immense wings. . . . I wept aloud with joy and love; and I do not know but I should say, I literally bellowed out the unutterable gushings of my heart. The waves came over me, and over me, one after the other, until I recollect I cried out, 'I shall die if these waves continue to pass over me.' I said, 'Lord, I cannot bear any more;' yet I had no fear of death."[20]

James E. Johnson notes, "Since his own conversion had been so unusual, the revival pitch of emotion was almost a habit with him."[21] One Universalist, plotting to kill Finney,

---

[19] Charles G. Finney, *How to Experience Revival,* formerly *Finney on Revival,* E. E. Shelhamer, compiler (Springdale, Pa.: Whitaker House, 1984) 7.

[20] Citation from Lawson, *Deeper Experiences,* 179–80.

[21] James E. Johnson, "Charles G. Finney and a Theology of Revivalism," *Church History* 38 no. 3 (Sept. 1969) 348.

brought a pistol to one of the revivalist's services. In the midst of Finney's preaching, the man fell from his seat in great anguish, crying that he was "sinking in hell." The service broke into a prayer meeting.[22] On another occasion Finney preached in a place called Sodom, New York, where the people, smitten by conviction, fell to the floor and cried for mercy. Finney said, "If I had had a sword in each hand, I could not have cut them down as fast as they fell. Nearly the whole congregation were either on their knees or prostrate."[23]

But Finney would have none of the excessive phenomena of the past revivals. He taught that promoting an "unhealthy degree of excitement" was a great error that "exposes the sinner to great delusions. Religion consists in the heart's obedience to the law of the intelligence, as distinguished from its being influenced by emotion or fear."[24] Nevertheless, he remained sensitive to the fact that some may be genuinely overwhelmed with grief and cry out loud. If such things are stifled, he said, some Christians would feel that this was quenching the Spirit. But emotion, if unchecked, might cause the entire congregation to be overcome with excitements or "animal feelings."

Finney thus believes that there are cases in which God really does overwhelm a person, but the principle he follows is, "we need fear no kind or degree of excitement which is produced simply by perceived truth, and is consistent with the healthful operation of the intellectual power. Whatever exceeds this must be disastrous," giving Satan an opportunity to mix "the spirit of fanaticism with the spirit of a religious revival."[25] Conversion, which Finney understands as repentance (in terms of a "change of mind" and obedience to God), is what changes an individual, not emotions or excitement. "It is not what you feel that matters," Finney contended, "but what you do."[26]

---

[22] Charles G. Finney, *Charles G. Finney: An Autobiography* (popular ed.; London/Melbourne/New York/Toronto: The Salvation Army Book Department, 1868) 54–55.

[23] Lawson, *Deeper Experiences,* 184.

[24] Charles G. Finney, *Reflections on Revival,* Donald W. Dayton, compiler (Minneapolis: Bethany Fellowship, 1979) 38.

[25] Ibid., 48, 52; cf. 42.

[26] Leonard I. Sweet, "The View of Man Inherent in New Measures Revivalism," *Church History* 45 (1976) 214–15.

But Finney was not without his critics. Calvinist ministers took exception to this staunch Arminian's prefabricated form of revivalism. It seemed to do away with the sovereignty of God. Richard Lovelace writes:

> If evangelists conceive of the rebirth of their hearers as a responsibility resting solely on them, so that instead of being midwives to works of sovereign grace they must somehow convince human wills to turn to God by every means at their disposal, then they will quite naturally make use of any means which works. A theology of conversion like Charles Finney's, which conceives of revival as galvanizing the emotions of an audience in order to move their will toward obedience, will necessarily lead to manipulation: multiple repetitions of hymns during lengthy invitations, hard-sell salesmanship aimed at immediate decisions and the rest of the trappings of much post-Finneyan evangelism.[27]

Regardless of his use of questionable means, Finney's "anxious bench" method of calling sinners to public confession resulted in an estimated 250,000 conversions.[28] Finney's general discouragement of the revival excesses seemed to set the trend for the revival of 1857–58, as well as the Moody revivals that followed: the Third Great Awakening was generally free from excessive emotionalism. A few people might have jumped and shouted for joy here and there, and there were still some sinners who prostrated themselves, trembling in fear of God, but there was no "outbreaking of trembling, jerking, screaming, groaning, fainting, prostration, or dancing for joy."[29]

## DWIGHT L. MOODY

Dwight L. Moody's meetings were characterized by outstanding music, conversion, and "silent weeping." In 1873, while he was ministering in England, young converts from

---

[27]Richard F. Lovelace, *Dynamics of Spiritual Life: An Evangelical Theology of Renewal* (Downers Grove, Ill.: InterVarsity Press, 1979) 252.

[28]Shelhamer, *How to Experience Revival*, 5.

[29]J. Edwin Orr, *The 1857–58 Awakening: "The Event of the Century,"* (n. l.: J. Edwin Orr, 1985) 229. F. M. Davenport notes, however, that in Belfast some believed they had received the "stigmata" on their bodies, as certain Roman Catholic saints had reported. Others disclosed new revelations they had received when sleeping (Frederick M. Davenport, *Primitive Traits in Religious Revivals: A Study in Mental and Social Evolution* (London/New York: Macmillan & Co., 1905, 1910 reprint) 90.

Moody's ministry spoke in tongues and prophesied.[30] But this was definitely the exception, not the rule. Although Moody taught that the Spirit was a continuing source of power after conversion, and that Christians should seek to be filled with the Spirit to be empowered for Christian service, he was by no means a proto-Pentecostal.[31]

### MARIA WOODWORTH-ETTER

Maria Woodworth-Etter was a different story. Her "gay nineties" ministry spilled over into twentieth-century Pentecostalism with charismatic gifts, faith healing, trances, visions, tongues, and the gift of prophecy. Some were slain in the Spirit at her meetings.[32] She prophesied that in 1890 San Francisco would be devastated by an earthquake and tidal wave; it was reported that thousands fled from the Bay area as a result of her prediction.[33]

## THE WELSH REVIVAL

The Welsh Revival (1904–5) was characterized by spontaneity, singing, and seemingly disordered services with no planned agendas. That prayer and worship were the center of many of the meetings accounted for much of the spontaneity. People prayed and praised God for hours on end, so that sometimes there would be no preaching message at all. And prayer marked the life of perhaps the revival's most popular minister, Evan Roberts, who for months prayed four hours a day.[34]

---

[30]Edgar J. Goodspeed, *A Full History of the Wonderful Career of Moody and Sankey in Great Britain and America* (New York: H. S. Goodspeed and Co., 1876) 62 cited in Wesley P. Steelberg, "The Place of Emotions in Christian Experience," in *Conference on the Holy Spirit Digest*, Gwen Jones, ed. (Springfield, Mo.: Gospel Publishing House, 1983) 2:302.

[31]For Moody's view of being filled with the Spirit, see Dwight L. Moody, *Secret Power* (Ventura, Calif.: Regal Books, 1987 reprint).

[32]Wayne E. Warner, *The Woman Evangelist: The Life and Times of Charismatic Evangelist Maria B. Woodworth-Etter* (Studies in Evangelicalism 8; Metuchen, N.J., and London: Scarecrow Press, 1986) 144–45.

[33]Wayne E. Warner, "Woodworth-Etter, Maria Beulah," in Burgess, McGee, eds., *Dictionary of Pentecostal and Charismatic Movements*, 901.

[34]Edith Blumhofer, "The Welsh Revival 1904–1905," *Paraclete* 20 no. 3 (Summer, 1986) 1.

The Welsh Revival, although tamer than Cane Ridge or
Azusa Street, reported accounts of crying, shrieking, and falling. David Matthews, an eyewitness, wrote: "A young woman
sprang to her feet in terrible soul-agony—Maggie Evans, if my
memory serves me right. At this moment, the silent form of a
young man rolled off his seat into the aisle. He appeared to be
only semi-conscious . . . he lay prostrate for a considerable
time on the floor of the church, sweating profusely."[35]

Jessie Penn-Lewis, a friend of Roberts, believed that the
devil manifested his counterfeits in the revival: "Let the seeker
after 'Pentecost' demand 'signs' of the coming of the Spirit in
outward physical manifestations, such as shakings, shoutings,
laughter, prostration, etc., and *look for these as* evidences of
the Holy Spirit's presence in power, more than simple faith in
the Word of God, and the Adversary is able to fulfil his desire."[36] One example of this overeager search for manifestations was an incident in which a man roared and groaned,
beating the ground—a demon had entered him. Another man
took this as a move of the Spirit in a service, and repeated
similar activities at other meetings he attended. He would
thus "ruin every meeting he was in."[37] Yet in ironic similarity
to the Vineyard, Penn-Lewis believed "It has become an indis-
putable fact that evil spirits can enter the *body of a true child
of God,* who unwittingly opens the door to the devil in igno-
rance of his devices."[38]

Upset with Penn-Lewis's criticisms, David Matthews responded by wondering what Penn-Lewis thought about the
early excesses of her own tradition—the Quakers. He was bewildered when Roberts participated with Penn-Lewis in her
criticisms of the revival:

> His collaboration with Mrs. Penn-Lewis in producing the book,
> *War on the Saints,* was a gratuitous denial of the reality of much of
> the fine work done by the revival while it proceeded on its irresist-
> ible course. How anyone who had witnessed the miracles of grace
> wrought during this wonderful manifestation could possibly as-
> cribe so much of it to Satanic influences poses a conundrum. Is

[35] David Matthews, *I Saw the Welsh Revival* (Chicago: Moody Press,
1951) 19.
[36] Jessie Penn-Lewis, *The Warfare with Satan and the Way of Victory*
(Bournemouth, UK: The Overcomer Book Room, 1906; 6th ed. 1951) 92.
[37] Cited from Thomas, *No Laughing Matter,* 46–47.
[38] Penn-Lewis, *Warfare with Satan,* 93.

there any human being in existence anywhere who would foolishly deny the possibility of unpleasant occurrences during revival time?[39]

Criticisms of the revival came from other sources too. The Reverend Peter Price called Evans's work in the Welsh Revival a "sham Revival, a mockery, a blasphemous travesty of the real thing."[40] Reverend J. Vyrnwy Morgan criticized the lack of order and castigated those who attributed some of the bodily agitations to the work of the Spirit. He claimed the bodily agitations of Robert Evans "were awful to behold. They filled the hearts of children with fear, bewildered and astounded men of mature years, and caused hysterical women to faint."[41]

But the vast majority of those touched by the revival did not share J. Vyrnwy Morgan's views. On the whole, the Welsh Revival made a positive impact on the community. All classes and denominations participated in the revival. Taverns closed down, crime rates objectively went down, severe financial losses were reported in the liquor trade, and new converts numbered over 100,000, with 80,000 remaining in membership at Welsh churches as of 1914.[42] G. Campbell Morgan considered the Welsh Revival a "divine visitation."[43] Its emphasis on the Holy Spirit paved the way for Pentecostalism. Some heard speaking in tongues for the first time at Welsh Revival meetings.

## AZUSA STREET: THE BIRTH OF PENTECOSTALISM

More extravagant in phenomena was the Azusa Street Revival in Los Angeles (1906–9), which gave birth to the Pentecostal movement. Although speaking in tongues was the central phenomenon, crying, laughing, falling down, convulsing, prophesying, and even levitations were reported among

---

[39] Matthews, *I Saw the Welsh Revival*, 122–24.
[40] J. Edwin Orr, *The Flaming Tongue: The Impact of Twentieth Century Revivals* (Chicago: Moody Press, 1973) 23.
[41] J. Vyrnwy Morgan, *The Welsh Religious Revival: 1904–5: A Retrospect and a Criticism* (London: Chapman & Hall, 1909) 234.
[42] Orr, *The Flaming Tongue*, 17.
[43] Blumhofer, "Welsh Revival," 4.

early Pentecostals.[44] Eyewitness Frank Bartleman recalls the
early days of Pentecostalism this way:

> I would rather live six months at that time than fifty years of
> ordinary life. . . . Some one might be speaking. Suddenly the Spirit
> would fall upon the congregation. God himself would give the
> altar call. Men would fall all over the house, like the slain in battle,
> or rush for the altar en masse, to seek God. The scene often
> resembled a forest of fallen trees. . . . the shekinah glory rested
> there. In fact some claim to have seen the glory by night over the
> building. I do not doubt it. I have stopped more than once within
> two blocks of the place and prayed for strength before I dared go
> on. The presence of the Lord was so real.[45]

Bartleman writes that God often spoke to him. In 1905 he
told him, "The depth of revival will be determined exactly by
the depth of the spirit of repentance."[46] Despite misconcep-
tions, the revival was far from being a circus. Repentance was
in fact one of the key themes stressed in its meetings; Bartleman often refers to it. His compassion for unrepentant sinners
is exemplified in his repeated references to anguishing over
lost souls,[47] or "soul travail": "Real soul travail is just as defi-
nite in the spirit, as natural human birth-pangs. The simile is
almost perfect in its sameness. No soul is ever born without
this. All true revivals of salvation come this way."[48] Conviction
was so pervasive around Azusa, said Bartleman, that "When
men came within two or three blocks of the place they were
seized with conviction."[49]

But the Pentecostals had many critics, including respected
Christians such as R. A. Torrey, who said it was "emphatically
not of God"; G. Campbell Morgan, who called it "the last vomit
of Satan"; and H. A. Ironside, who called it, among other
things, "hysteria," "hypnotism," "hallucinations," "mental in-
stability," and "disgusting . . . delusions and insanities."[50]

---

[44]Harvey Cox, *Fire from Heaven: The Rise of Pentecostal Spirituality
and the Reshaping of Religion in the Twenty-First Century* (Reading,
Mass.: Addison-Wesley Publishing Co., 1995) 68; Richard N. Ostling,
"Laughing for the Lord," *Time,* 15 Aug. 1994, 38; Synan, *Holiness-Pentecostal Movement,* 106–7.
[45]Bartleman, *Azusa Street,* 60.
[46]Ibid., 19.
[47]Ibid., 17, 26, 33, 95–96.
[48]Ibid., 17.
[49]Ibid., 53.
[50]Synan, *Holiness-Pentecostal Movement,* 145.

When Charles Parham, one of the founders of Pentecostalism, visited Azusa, he rejected the "fanaticism" and "chattering, jabbering, and sputtering" which he felt was not the same as speaking in tongues but was no language at all. Moreover, he denounced the leaders as "spiritualists" and "hypnotists."[51]

When he attempted to establish his own authority over the meetings, however, Parham was asked to leave. It is probable that Seymour rejected Parham's authority because of reports that the latter was a homosexual; the following year, Parham was arrested on charges of sodomy. In later years the underlying motivation behind his rejection of the revival became all too apparent. As a segregationist who also taught that the Anglo-Saxon race were the chosen of God (Anglo-Israelism)— and later an avid supporter of the Ku Klux Klan—Parham could not tolerate the interracial atmosphere at Azusa:

> There was a beautiful outpouring of the Holy Spirit in Los Angeles. . . . Then they pulled off all the stunts common in old camp meetings among colored folks. . . . That is the way they worship God, but what makes my soul sick, and make[s] me sick at my stomach is to see white people imitating unintelligent, crude negroism of the Southland, and laying it on the Holy Ghost.[52]

The secular media also took their biased shots at the Azusa Street revival. Just hours before the great San Francisco quake hit on April 18, 1906, rocking the entire coast of California, the *Los Angeles Daily Times* reported the revival with phrases such as "new sect of fanatics," "gurgle of wordless talk," and "wild gesticulations." Those at Azusa Street practiced "fanatical rites," in which the congregation "work themselves into a state of mad excitement in their peculiar zeal. Colored people and a sprinkling of whites compose the congregation, and night is made hideous in the neighborhood by the howlings of the worshippers. . . ."

Pastor William J. Seymour was portrayed as an "old colored exhorter, blind in one eye" who is the "major-domo of the company," and hypnotizes "with his stony optic fixed on some luckless unbeliever. . . . Then it is that pandemonium breaks loose and the bounds of reason are passed by those who are

---

[51]Ibid., 112–13.

[52]*Apostolic Faith* (Baxter Springs, Kan.), 3 (April 1925) 9–10; citation from Anderson, *Vision of the Disinherited*, 190. See also Synan, *Holiness-Pentecostal Movement*, 180; J. R. Goff, Jr., "Parham, Charles Fox," in Burgess, McGee, eds. *Dictionary of Pentecostal and Charismatic Movements*, 660–61; Hollenweger, *The Pentecostals*, 22.

'filled with the spirit,' whatever that may be. 'You-oo-oo gou-loo-loo come under the bloo-oo-oo boo-loo,' shouts an old colored 'mammy,' in a frenzy of religious zeal."[53]

Of Brother Joseph Smale's church the *Daily Times* reported, "Muttering an unintelligible jargon, men and women rolled on the floor, screeching at the top of their voices at times, and again giving utterance to cries which resembled those of animals in pain. There was a Babel of sound. Men and women embraced each other in the fanatical orgy."[54] Another newspaper reports one young man behaving "with much groaning and foaming at the mouth and distortion of his body and limbs . . . "; the report continues that Azusa's "negro leader [Seymour]" commanded " 'come out of him thou unclean spirit.' After three hours of labor and much repetition of the command the penitent 'turned and writhed on the floor barking and snarling like a dog when finally the unclean spirit departed and he immediately received the gift of tongues.' "[55]

What was the problem? Many Pentecostal members were young, uneducated, and mostly lower-class people; many were also minorities and immigrants. Few had any Bible schooling which would allow them to teach and interpret Scripture properly; but tragically, few Bible colleges would allow the "holy rollers" in their classes, especially if they were black. Yet these early Pentecostals were not totally without discernment. They recognized and condemned excesses, as Bartleman demonstrates:

> Religious enthusiasm easily goes to seed. The human spirit so predominates, the show-off, religious spirit. But we must stick to our text, Christ. He alone can save. The attention of the people must be first of all, and always, held to Him. A true 'Pentecost' will produce a mighty conviction for sin, a turning to God. False manifestations produce only excitement and wonder. Sin and self-life will not materially suffer from these. . . . Any work that exalts the Holy Ghost or the 'gifts' above Jesus will finally land up in fanaticism. Whatever causes us to exalt and love Jesus is well and safe. The reverse will ruin all.[56]

---

[53] "Weird Babel of Tongues," *Los Angeles Daily Times*, 18 April, 1906, 1.

[54] "Rolling on Floor in Smale's Church," *Los Angeles Daily Times*, 14 July, 1906, Pt. ii–1.

[55] "Tongues of Fire—Gift of Languages and Holiness Union," *Daily Oregon Statesman*, 4 Oct. 1906, 6.

[56] Bartleman, *Azusa Street*, 86.

The moving of the Spirit from Pentecost spilled over to the charismatic renewal in the 1960s and 1970s. Holy laughter and other phenomena were reported at various meetings.[57] Kathryn Kuhlman became famous for the phenomenon of slain in the Spirit that appeared at her meetings.[58] Francis MacNutt notes, "A striking difference is that the falling phenomenon in the eighteenth and nineteenth centuries largely followed upon *preaching*, while today it most often accompanies *prayer for healing* with the laying on of hands."[59]

---

## REVIVALS AND REVIVAL PHENOMENA: AN ASSESSMENT

---

Having surveyed the major revivals and revivalists in the last two chapters, we can now give some general principles for discernment in the current renewal.

### 1. REVIVALS OF THE PAST WERE MARKED BY THE CENTRALITY OF THE PRESENCE OF GOD AND THE PREACHING OF THE WORD OF GOD

The central focus of past revivals was the presence of God in his word spoken by his messengers. When one sensed the divine presence, this led one to repent and seek sanctification before a holy God. Miracles or bodily phenomena were usually only incidental. This being the case, it seems unlikely that the Spirit would be grieved or quenched if a minister of today "checked" the phenomena to some degree. Hardly any phenomena were needed or welcomed at the Moody revival meetings, yet multitudes were converted. In the Second Great Awakening, when Asahel Nettleton heard groaning and screaming, "I hastened to the spot, and with kind but decided severity, called them to order. . . . They seemed to be very much

---

[57]See for instance, MacNutt, *Overcome by the Spirit*, 79; C. and F. Hunter, *Holy Laughter*, 22–25.

[58]See for instance, Jamie Buckingham, *Daughter of Destiny: Kathryn Kuhlman . . . Her Story* (Plainfield, N.J.: Logos International, 1976) 41, 224–29.

[59]MacNutt, *Overcome by the Spirit*, 113.

grieved and shocked by my conduct. It took a number of days to restore order; but when it was done, the work of God advanced, silently and powerfully, until all classes, old and young, were moved all over town."[60]

The focus of the current renewal, despite the advocates' vehement claims to the contrary, is still the phenomena, not the preaching of God's word. (In the case of the Welsh Revival, another necessary ingredient may have superseded preaching—prayer. However, Evan Roberts's neglect of preaching may have been the reason why the Welsh movement never reached its full potential as a revival.)[61] Sadly, the current renewal is still typically marked with dull speakers, poor preaching, and trite messages. Richard Lovelace writes, "The common denominator of all of these [revival] aberrations is a reliance on subjective experience divorced from the objective control of reason and the written word of God."[62]

## 2. REVIVALS OF THE PAST CALLED FOR THE RENEWAL OF THE CHURCHGOER, THE REPENTANCE OF THE SINNER, AND THE CHANGE OF SOCIETY

The Great Awakenings not only stirred up the Christian community, but affected the unbelievers. The First Great Awakening caused social change of a magnitude that influenced the American Revolution. The nineteenth-century revivals helped change public opinion against slavery, and influenced the temperance movement. The Welsh Revival also transformed the sinners of its community. If we are to see this renewal become a revival, this quality of personal and societal change must be evident.

A typical setting for revival is a general low tide of Christian spirituality or a high tide of immorality, or both. The Jesus People movement and charismatic renewal of the 1960s and 1970s rose in a time of the hippie counterculture and the drug and the sexual revolutions. Edwards and Finney also noted the low morality of their day. It is for such times as these that God raises up his leaders. As James Burns asserts, "Revivals are

---

[60] *Nettleton and His Labors* cited in Murray, *Revival and Revivalism*, 210.
[61] Davies, *I Will Pour Out*, 223.
[62] Lovelace, *Dynamics of Spiritual Life*, 265.

necessary for the spurring of man to high endeavor, and for the vitalizing of his life."[63]

## 3. REVIVAL EVENTS ARE DESCRIPTIVE, NOT NECESSARILY PRESCRIPTIVE

Even if it could be proven that laughter, animal sounds, falling, and the like were the central theme of past revivals—which they were not—this would not warrant our encouraging them. Ultimately Scripture, not history or experience, is our final authority. And Scripture never portrays bodily phenomena as *normative* for revival meetings.

On the other hand, we cannot necessarily rule out phenomena simply because some revivalist in the past condemned it. Just because Wesley or Penn-Lewis thought laughter in church was a satanic attack, it does not follow that the laughter experienced in the current renewal is satanic. Based on their descriptions of victims pounding the ground and blaspheming God, there is every reason to believe that what they experienced was different from what is being experienced today. In certain cases, we simply do not know what they would have thought of the current renewal phenomena.

J. I. Packer warns us to avoid two basic fallacies.[64] The first mistake is the *antiquarian fallacy*. We commit this error if we take a concept from a past revival and make it a norm to which all future revivals must conform. Thus, neither the Welsh Revival's spontaneity nor Moody's silence should become a norm for any future movements of the Spirit. We must always remember that the Spirit is sovereign, not the revivals. He is also creative, so we must never limit him to our own biased standards of worship.

The second error is *the romantic fallacy*. We commit this error if we think that revivals are perfect and will solve all our problems. They did not do so in the past and it is not likely they will do so in the future. Even the best of the past revivals had their excesses and shortcomings; we are still dealing with fallen humanity. Packer likens saints to sleepers who awake out of their sleep but are unaccustomed to God's spirituality.

---

[63] James Burns, *Revivals: Their Laws and Leaders* (Grand Rapids: Baker Book House, 1960) 24.

[64] Packer, *Quest for Godliness*, 316–18.

They are half-blinded by the light and thus stumble into pride, delusions, extremism, and so forth. Satan is always perverting God's work; "A revival, accordingly, is always a *disfigured* work of God, and the more powerful the revival, the more scandalising disfigurements we may expect to see."[65]

## 4. AS ENTHUSIASM WAS DENOUNCED BY REVIVALISTS PRIMARILY FOR THE NEW REVELATIONS THOSE UNDER ITS SPELL CLAIMED TO RECEIVE, SO WE MUST DISCOURAGE NEW REVELATIONS TODAY

As Reverend McNemar was led astray in the Second Great Awakening through prophecy and his belief in Christ's immediate return, so there are those today who claim prophetic scenarios that lead to false doctrines or end-time predictions. This is one of the errors of the Latter Rain movement, and it continues to be a problem today. New doctrine that is contrary to Scripture should be avoided. Teachings that set or imply end-time dates should also be looked upon with caution. False doctrine and false prophecy are two of Satan's most oft-used vehicles of deception, and they appear especially often during times of revival.

## 5. PRAYER, WORSHIP, EVANGELISM, AND THE READING OF SCRIPTURE ARE MARKS OF A TRUE REVIVAL

Such activities as studying Scripture, witnessing for Christ, and gathering for prayer should always be on a church's agenda whether or not there is a revival or renewal taking place. Earnest prayer, especially for the lost, characterizes true revival. Prayers of "earnest desire, submission, dependence, diligent use of means, humility, perseverance, and such trustful expectancy . . . " should be our starting point.[66] Worship and reading of scriptures help us keep our mind on God, while evangelism keeps our mind on the work of God in reaching the lost.

---

[65] Ibid., 317–18.
[66] Walter P. Doe, *Revivals: How to Promote Them* (New York: E. B Treat & Co., 1884, 1895) 379.

After declaring that genuine revivals are not identified by great excitement, great numbers, or great opposition, nineteenth century revival expert William Sprague claims that they are identified by conformity to the word of God, self-examination prior to emotion, and enduring fruit.[67] He asserts:

> It may be safe to admit even in the wildest scenes, the possibility of some genuine conversions; because there may be some truth preached, and some believing prayer offered, which God may regard and honor, notwithstanding all the error and delusion with which it may be mingled. But in general it is perfectly fair to conclude that when men become dissatisfied with plain Bible truth, and simple Bible measures, and undertake to substitute doctrines or devices of their own, any excitement which may be produced, however extensive, however powerful, is of an exceedingly dubious character. If the effect partake of the same character with the cause, it must be of the earth, earthy.[68]

## 6. REVIVALISM MANIFESTS A MIXTURE OF GOD, THE FLESH, AND THE DEVIL

As Edwards and others have claimed, there is a mixture that infiltrates the work of God in revivalism. What was originally pristine can become soiled by Satan's sowing tares of human weakness. According to Richard Lovelace, Satan sows tares in three ways.[69]

First, he attempts to destroy revival by persecution or accusation that will discredit the movement or limit its potential. As the early Christians were persecuted and slandered as cannibals for partaking in the Lord's Supper, so those participating in true revival may anticipate that Satan will do similar things to discredit them.

Second, to reinforce its defects and thus provoke accusations, Satan will attempt to infiltrate a revival. As a Japanese wrestler uses his opponent's own motion to bring about his defeat, so Satan capitalizes on human defects and frailties. If he cannot stop a revival, he will pervert it with false doctrine, chaotic disorder, extremism, and the like.

Third, Satan will attempt to inspire a false revival to deceive the saints and confuse the world. For example, the Mormons

---

[67]William B. Sprague, *Lectures on Revivals of Religion* (London: The Banner of Truth Trust, 1959 reprint) 13–23.

[68]Ibid., 18.

[69]Lovelace, *Dynamics of Spiritual Life,* 257–61.

and Shakers were counterfeits of the Second Great Awakening, mimicking the phenomena, but through a different spirit and with a different gospel.

In summary, the past has taught us that even the greatest revivals were not exempt from the attacks and deception of the Enemy. In every great move of God, Satan is sure to manifest. I hope that ministers in the current renewal detect the Enemy's schemes, lest they fall into deception as have many others in the past.

# REVIVAL: DISCERNMENT AND PROSPECTUS

Sandra is a vibrant Christian. She is balanced, discerning, and has read some negative material on the current renewal. Her friend Molly believes that the Toronto Blessing is of God. Molly has seen the change in her own life after she experienced Holy Laughter. Sandra is convinced, however, that Molly is following a counterfeit move of the Spirit. Their disagreement is so strong that they decide to break off their friendship.

Was this even necessary? Having worked in discernment ministry a number of years, I have seen relationships, engagements, and families disturbed, divided, and destroyed when a loved one becomes involved in a cultic group. The price people pay for the truth can be a high one. But I have also seen relationships break up over nonessential doctrines and issues, in situations in which the parties could have learned to disagree agreeably. Such incidents are sometimes as tragic as losing a loved one to the cults, and they are even more pathetic, because they should never have happened.

At the crux of the Holy Laughter issue lies this all-important question: Is Holy Laughter so misleading that it causes people to stray away from the Christian faith? If personal experience consistently takes precedence over God's word in this movement, then it *could* lead some from the faith. If this kind of reversal of priorities is caused by an outbreak of Holy

Laughter in a particular congregation, the minister should be notified immediately. If it persists with the support of the minister, then those who are uncomfortable should leave that fellowship. I am trusting, however, that this would be the exception rather than the rule.

Relational matters involving loved ones are another matter. Generally speaking, I do not think this issue is worth dividing over. Rodney Howard-Browne is not a cultist, and the Vineyard is still an orthodox church. Now obviously if a loved one starts manifesting demonic voices after he or she has attended a "renewal" meeting, this is a different story. Once again, however, such an incident would be a rare exception to the rule. Since the renewal is not monolithic—rather, displaying an assortment of mixed fruits—one must discern the behavior of loved ones on a case-by-case basis. I have listed five guidelines for discernment that can be applied to a church, a loved one, or oneself.

*Check the fruit (self-examination)*

Am I drawing closer to God through prayer, the word, and godly character? Am I emotionally up one week and down the next until I get my Holy Laughter "fix"? Am I living a consistent Christian walk? Have there been any negative results from my experiencing the phenomena? Is my experience drawing me outside myself, to witness and help those around me, or more inside myself, to satisfy my own needs and wants?

*Check the personality*

Does the person involved in Holy Laughter have an unstable emotional or mental history? Are they easily susceptible to peer pressure or suggestion? Does the person have a romantic "quick fix" outlook on Christianity? Are they undiscerning new converts? Are they immature? Are they grounded in the word of God? Are they a regular member of a good church? Where do they draw the line regarding disorderly conduct? What would constitute disorder from their perspective? Do they think the Holy Spirit would be offended if they critically tested their experiences (cf. 1 Thess 5:19–21; Acts 17:11; 1 John 4:1)?

*Check the church*

Are the renewal manifestations superseding the word of God? Are members getting properly fed with the word of God?

Are the sermons incoherent, digressive, unprepared, or simply geared to "prime the pump" for renewal? Is false doctrine being taught? Are new doctrines based on visions or revelation being taught? Are scriptures being taken out of context? Have there been any false prophecies in the church, and if so, are false prophecies left uncorrected?

*Check the worship*

Is there order in the church or virtual chaos? Is the minister encouraging or justifying the disorder? Are the disorderly ones new converts, unbelievers, members of other churches, or members of the church who should know better? Are they trying to attract attention to themselves—do they seem to be overcome by the same manifestation in every service?

*Check for unity and division*

Is there a spirit of elitism, which holds up those who have experienced the phenomena as "first-class citizens," while those who have not are considered as less spiritual "second-class citizens"? Do the ministers mock or condemn those who have not experienced the renewal? Are the ministers humble and open to correction? How do they respond when being corrected through Scripture? Are those who are leaving the church uncommitted carnal Christians or mature discerning ones?

## SATAN'S STRATEGY: DIVISION AND PRIDE

In the twilight years of the Second Great Awakening, William Sprague wrote that divisions and censorship were a lamentable evil arising out of revivals. He admonished ministers to correct those in error: "But this is something quite different from that censorious, denouncing spirit, to which I here refer; which, though it be exercised in reference to religion, is nothing better than the spirit of the world."[1] He continues:

> It is not uncommon to find this spirit marking the conduct of private Christians toward each other. There are some who will condemn their brethren as cold Christians, or perhaps even no

[1]Sprague, *Lectures on Revivals of Religion*, 230.

Christians at all, because with less constitutional ardor than themselves, and possibly more prudence, they are not prepared to concur at once in every measure that may be suggested for the advancement of a revival; or because they talk less of their own feelings than some others; or because they attend fewer public religious exercises than could be desired; or because from extreme constitutional diffidence they may, either properly or improperly, decline taking part in such exercises. . . . On the other hand, it is not to be questioned that men of a cautious habit, who are constitutionally afraid of excitement, sometimes unjustly accuse their more zealous brethren of rashness, and impute to spiritual pride what really ought to be set to the account of an honest devotedness to Christ. Especially, if real and great abuses actually exist, they may be so much afraid of coming within the confines of disorder, that they may rush to the opposite extreme of formality; and from that cold region they may look off upon the Christian who evinces nothing more than a consistent and enlightened zeal, and hail him as if he were burning to death in the very torrid zone of enthusiasm.[2]

Little excites the devil more than to see divisions among Christians. Hyper-critical Christians are as prime a target as undiscerning ones. The critical Christian condemns the undiscerning Christian instead of lovingly attempting to stir him or her in more discerning ways. The undiscerning Christian mocks and takes an air of elitism over the "dead" critical Christian— and the devil loves it so. This affects not just individuals, but churches and denominations as well. Sprague adds:

The same spirit which discovers itself in private Christians toward each other, is also frequently manifest in respect to different churches. . . . where a church differs from another in its views of the economy of revivals, it may denounce that other as chilled with the frost of apathy on the one hand, or scorched with the fires of fanaticism on the other . . . Any church, whether it be distinguished by its zeal or its want of zeal, that takes the responsibility of dealing out violent censures upon its sister churches, especially if they are walking in the faith and order of the gospel, certainly assumes a degree of responsibility which it can ill afford to bear; and it will have no just ground for surprise, if it should meet a painful retribution, not only in bringing back upon itself the censures of men, but in bringing down upon itself the displeasure of God.[3]

Just as Jonathan Edwards affirmed, pride is perhaps the greatest atrocity of all. Sometimes we think we have God all

---

[2]Ibid., 232–33.
[3]Ibid., 233–34.

figured out—the Holy Spirit can move only in ways we approve of. For the Holy Laughter advocate, in order for the Spirit to be considered as moving in a powerful way, there must be phenomena such as laughter and falling down. For the opponent of Holy Laughter, the Spirit cannot really be present in the midst of laughter or falling down. Thus the sovereignty of the Spirit is surrendered to the sovereignty of individuals, in service of our prejudices and packaged preconceptions of what the Spirit should or should not do in our church services.

When our relationship with God distills to a mere science of phenomena, the spiritually dynamic reduces to the spiritually static. We cast anathemas on anything that violates our God-in-a-box mentality, forgetting that Christ's miracles didn't "fit" the religious leaders' agenda. The religious leaders of the Gospels preferred blaspheming the Holy Spirit to reexamining their preconceptions of how the Messiah should act. I think a good dose of humility will help break our pride. Those on both sides of this debate need to repent of their divisiveness and humble themselves before those they have wronged. Until this happens, the devil may be the one who gets the last laugh.

## BIBLICAL REVIVAL

Biblical revival involves a religious awakening and zeal for the things of God. Just as the church of Ephesus did not love Christ as they once did (Rev 2:4–5), or as the church at Sardis needed to "wake up" (Rev 3:1–3), or as the Laodicean church had become "lukewarm" (Rev 3:15–16), so Christians can lose their spiritual enjoyment, interest in religious matters, desire for prayer and Scripture, and compassion for the lost. Fervency marks a dedicated life (Rev 3:19; Rom 12:11; Acts 18:25). In 2 Chron 7:14, humility, prayer, and repentance are God's conditions for restoration.

### NEHEMIAH 8–9

Nehemiah 8–9 gives us some sound biblical principles to follow on the subject of revival. After the Jews returned from the Babylonian captivity (c. 586–539 B.C.), Nehemiah, the Persian king's cup-bearer, felt burdened to rebuild the walls of Jerusalem. After he finished rebuilding the walls, the Israelites held a celebration beginning the first day of the seventh month, during the Feasts of Trumpets and Tabernacles. Here are some characteristics of that worship-celebration:

1. *Extensive Bible reading* (Neh 8:1–3a): Ezra the scribe read the law of Moses before the assembly. He read it from "daybreak till noon." This went on "day after day" (8:18).

2. *Attentive listening* (Neh 8:3b): The people listened to Ezra's reading. The word of God was the center of attention.

3. *Worship* (Neh 8:5–6): Ezra praised God as the people "lifted their hands" and "bowed down," worshipping the Lord.

4. *Sound teaching* (Neh 8:7–8; cf. 8:12): The Levites instructed the people in the word of God, "making it clear and giving the meaning so that the people could understand what was being read."

5. *Permitting emotional response, with guidance* (Neh 8:9–12a; cf. 8:17): The people wept, apparently convicted of their sins. But since this was a time of celebration, Nehemiah thought it inappropriate. Thus he encouraged them to rejoice instead, for the "joy of the Lord is your strength."

6. *Almsgiving* (Neh 8:12 cf. 8:10): Nehemiah directed the people to share their blessings of food and drink with those who were less fortunate.

7. *Proclaiming the word of God to others* (Neh 8:13–16): The heads of the Jewish families were encouraged to share the message of God's word regarding the Feast of Tabernacles throughout their towns.

8. *Repentance* (Neh 9:1–3): The Jews fasted, humbled themselves with sackcloth and ashes, separated themselves unto the Lord, and "confessed their sins and the wickedness of their fathers." A quarter of the day was spent in the word of God and another quarter in confession and worship.

## ACTS 2

We also discover some revival themes in the account of the day of Pentecost in Acts 2:

### PRAYER (ACTS 1:14; 2:1; 2:42)

First, we find the disciples praying together and waiting to be endued with power from on high. Great revivals break forth when the believers earnestly pray and expect God to move. According to one leading demographer, about 170 million Christians pray every day for revival and world evangelism (20 million of these believe this is their primary calling in Christ).[4] With such a vast number of interceders, why are so many quick to attribute contemporary moves of God to Satan? David Bryant, chairman of America's National Prayer Committee, gives us seven encouraging reasons why we can pray expectantly and prepare for a coming great revival:[5]

- God intends to restore Christ's rightful position as Redeemer King of the universe, and every revival is meant to accelerate this process.

- If God has been faithful in blessing past generations with revival, we can believe that he is willing and ready to do it for this generation also.

- God knows that the world suffers crises and needs deliverance from the forces of darkness. He understands that the nations rest on his sovereignty to deliver them.

- God loves the church and does not desire it to be spiritually powerless. He will not leave the body of Christ in an unrevived state.

- As the church is working toward the Great Commission, God is setting the stage for that Commission to be fulfilled through a revival that will result in new advancements of the kingdom of God.

- God is stirring up the church to pray for worldwide revival. He will not let us pray in vain.

---

[4]David Bryant, *The Hope at Hand: National and World Revival for the 21st Century* (Grand Rapids: Baker Book House, 1995) 31.
[5]Ibid., 69–156.

- God is increasing the number of those who earnestly desire revival, which they believe is the only hope for the church and the nations. They will pay any price to see it happen.

## THE OUTPOURING OF THE SPIRIT
(ACTS 2:1–13; 2:43)

The early believers experienced the outpouring of the Holy Spirit when they were filled with the Spirit and spoke in tongues, and signs and wonders followed. This does not mean, however, that every outpouring of the Spirit must manifest the same signs any more than we should expect to see tongues of fire hovering over our heads. What this passage does indicate is that when the faithful earnestly pray, the Spirit sovereignly moves in extraordinary ways. God is in charge of the moving of his Spirit; humans are in charge of maintaining order in their church services. Sadly, these roles are sometimes reversed in the current renewal, with God getting the blame for the disorder at renewal meetings.

## EVANGELISM (ACTS 2:14–41)

On the day of Pentecost, Peter preached the gospel of Jesus Christ. As Peter urged them to repent, the hearts of the unbelievers were convicted, and 3,000 repented. The message was the central focus of Acts 2, not the tongues or the miracles. It was through the message that conviction came upon the listeners. Peter pulled no punches as he claimed that his listeners were the ones who crucified Christ and needed to repent. In any outpouring of the Spirit, we often see the work of God accelerated as great multitudes are reached in little time.

## FAITHFULNESS TO BIBLICAL DOCTRINE (ACTS 2:42A)

The new believers did not stray from the apostolic truths of the gospel which they received. In contrast, the aberrant and heretical groups that arise out of the backwash of revivalism transgress or completely fail to keep the orthodox teachings of Christianity. Essential doctrines such as salvation by grace through faith, the nature of God, the deity of Christ, and Christ's sacrificial death and bodily resurrection should never be denied or compromised.

Groups such as the Shakers, Oneness or "Jesus Only" Pentecostalism, and the Latter Rain movement strayed into new revelations, false doctrines and/or false prophecies. Part of the problem is that revivals give us an exquisite taste of the future kingdom of God. Many often mistake this taste for a sign that the coming kingdom has arrived or is just about to.

### FELLOWSHIP (ACTS 2:42–47)

The early church continued meeting together daily with one accord. The unity was so contagious that many sold their possessions to give to those less fortunate, and shared what remained among themselves. They continued in prayer and worship, and they experienced great joy. The Lord added to their numbers daily. Here we see that in a revival atmosphere, worship services may occur every day. Apparently, the joy of the early Christians did not result in ecstatic phenomena, for the general public was not offended by them. Instead they gained "the favor of all the people." The Spirit's power was evident through the miracles and wondrous signs done through the apostles.

## PROSPECTUS

We should hope that the leaders of the renewal will clean up the disorder and stress more of the revival principles outlined in this and the previous chapters. We should all long for genuine revival and not be offended if it comes in ways and through vessels that we deem inappropriate due to our own short-sightedness.

Also, let us not think that Holy Laughter has cornered the market on revival. Other movements such as the Promise Keepers—a Christian men's movement started by Bill McCartney, former football coach for the University of Colorado—have been accelerating in growth and touching the lives of many men.

Other groups rarely get recognized, even though their evangelistic efforts have reached revivalistic proportions. One of these is La Puente-based Victory Outreach ministries,

founded by Sonny Arguinzoni, a former heroin addict delivered at David Wilkerson's Teen Challenge Center in New York.
For almost thirty years, this ministry has reached into the
inner cities of America and overseas delivering gang members,
drug addicts, and other hard to reach peoples for Christ by the
thousands.

Revival, or at least renewal, has also arisen recently on
many of the college campuses across America. At Wheaton
College, Gordon College, Trinity College, Taylor University, and
other campuses, Christian students cry and openly confess
their sins.[6] The "Youth Revival," however, is not completely
separated from Holy Laughter. Baltimore-based B.A.S.I.C.
(Brothers And Sisters In Christ), which equips students with
missionary training at retreats and conferences so they can
reach their respective campuses for Christ, is one example of
the influence of Holy Laughter on student ministry. One testimony in their newsletter reads: "The retreat was the high
point of my semester. I was equipped! I laughed with joy for
over 2 hours. What liberty! God delivered me!"[7] I hope the
campus movement starts reaching into the secular colleges. If
the heretical Boston Church of Christ succeeds in reaching
many secular students, how much more should evangelical
Christians?

---

# EPILOGUE

---

It was the summer of 1992. I spent many of my Saturdays
playing bass guitar in a street band from our church. We would
minister in parks located in ghettos and barrios, sharing our
faith through song and sermon. One day, as we ministered in a
drug-infested neighborhood in Los Angeles County, an agitated woman who was a known drug addict started cursing at
us. Seeing that this woman simply wanted to argue, our street
evangelism coordinator asked if members of our church could
pray for her. She grudgingly consented, so a number of us laid

---

[6]J. Lee Grady. "Revival Fervor Sweeps Campuses," *Charisma*, June
1995, 64–65.

[7]*The Impala (A Memorial Newsletter Dedicated to the "Falcon's"
Faithful Years of Service)* 2 no. 12, Dec. 1994.

hands on her and started praying. Several moments later, her knees buckled and she fell down on the hot summer pavement. I know we didn't push her down. She lay where she had fallen, dazed and weeping. It turned out she was a backslidden Christian. As soon as she stood back on her feet, she recommitted her life to Christ. She then took out of her trench coat a bag of crack and threw it away. That very evening she checked into our church's rehabilitation home.

Was this woman slain in the Spirit? I don't know if you would call it that, but whatever you want to call it, I believe God touched her in a special way that day. I say it was biblical, balanced, and in the right setting. When you read the book of Acts, the signs and wonders the Spirit worked through the apostles often occurred out in the streets as they evangelized the lost.

If this current renewal wishes to become a genuine revival, I believe it must make a stronger impact on the lost. As described in Keith Green's classic song "Asleep in the Light," many a renewal practitioner is crying out "bless me Lord, bless me Lord" but "no one aches, no one hurts, no one even sheds one tear" for the lost. If the renewal advocate is convinced this move is of God, why not let the signs and wonders he or she experiences touch the lost? Why not bring church to them through evangelism? It always amazes me how those who claim to have a gift of healing often fail to go to the place where it is most needed—the hospitals, the mental institutions, the slums, and skid row. Bringing healing to the lost is the biblical pattern set in the book of Acts.

Let's see multitudes of unbelievers touched by this renewal. Let's see an unprecedented number of new Christians coming into the kingdom. Let's see the church cry for the lost as hard as they cry for a refreshing. Let's see the church become nothing less than what Jesus intended it to be—the salt of the earth and the light of the world.

Ironically, as the twentieth century comes to a close, it seems that the world is influencing the church more than the church is influencing the world. It took the Los Angeles riots in 1992 to influence many communities to turn over a new leaf in racial understanding and fairness. But why was this tragedy necessary? Why hasn't the evangelical church influenced the world regarding racial equality? Was it that many of the churches were themselves racially and socially biased? As long as there are white churches, black churches, Hispanic churches, Asian churches, or any ethnic churches at all which are segregated for reasons other than language or geographic barriers, how *can* the church influence the world? Only now do we see these walls coming down. Tragically, they may be coming down primarily because bringing them down is the politically correct thing to do.

If the evangelical church is serious about breaking down racial and social barriers, where is its evangelistic effort to reach the inner cities? Why is it that only a handful of ministries seem to heed this call? Instead of being light in the dark streets of the inner cities, evangelicals often hide in the plush churches of well-lit suburban neighborhoods. While someone is experiencing Holy Laughter for the umpteenth time at a Vineyard church, another gang member in South Central L.A., who never heard a clear presentation of the gospel, is being gunned down.

Evangelicals are pouring time and resources into Christian night-clubs, Christian TV, Christian radio, and the Christian schools that have now replaced many of their secular counterparts. In their fanatical fear of worldliness and end-time conspiracies, many conservative Christians are isolating themselves from the very world they were called to reach. In essence, they are saying "Retreat!" while a bleeding world is crying "Help me!"

All of this perpetuates the evangelical church's problem. How can it influence a world it is afraid of? So it settles with others of its own kind, points out the legitimate faults of other Christians to ease its conscience for not being a better witness, and selfishly hoards up the Spirit's blessings to relieve its boredom. The church has to Christianize the world's inventions, technology, methods, fashions and gimmicks because it is too afraid of the real thing and too intellectually handicapped to create original things. The evangelical church at the end of the twentieth century has thus been reduced to second-class status, reveling in the world's hand-me-downs.

Revival? Until the church once again takes the driver's seat and makes the social-political impacts it did through people like Edwards and Finney—until the church once again produces evangelists like Wesley, reformers like Luther, artists like Bach, scientists like Mendel, inventors like Bell, thinkers like Pascal, and writers like Bunyan—don't make me laugh!

# INDEX OF ANCIENT SOURCES